T0000799

PASSIONATE SAGE

ALSO BY JOSEPH J. ELLIS

*The Cause: The American Revolution and Its Discontents,
1773–1783*

American Dialogue: The Founders and Us

*The Quartet: Orchestrating the Second American Revolution,
1783–1789*

Revolutionary Summer: The Birth of American Independence

First Family: Abigail and John Adams

*American Creation: Triumphs and Tragedies
at the Founding of the Republic*

His Excellency: George Washington

Founding Brothers: The Revolutionary Generation

American Sphinx: The Character of Thomas Jefferson

After the Revolution: Profiles of Early American Culture

School for Soldiers: West Point and the Profession of Arms
(with Robert Moore)

The New England Mind in Transition

PASSIONATE SAGE

*The Character and Legacy
of John Adams*

❧≈≈❧

JOSEPH J. ELLIS

W. W. NORTON & COMPANY
Celebrating a Century of Independent Publishing

FRONTISPIECE: This Benjamin West portrait of the men who negotiated the Treaty of Paris remains unfinished because the British diplomatic team refused to pose. Left to right, they are John Jay, John Adams, Benjamin Franklin, Henry Laurens, and William Temple Franklin, Ben's grandson.

Copyright © 2023, 2001, 1993 by Joseph J. Ellis

All rights reserved
Printed in the United States of America
First published as a Norton paperback 1994; reissued with a new preface 2001 and 2023

For information about permission to reproduce selections from this book, write to Permissions, W. W. Norton & Company, Inc., 500 Fifth Avenue, New York, NY 10110

For information about special discounts for bulk purchases, please contact W. W. Norton Special Sales at specialsales@wwnorton.com or 800-233-4830

Manufacturing by Lakeside Book Company
Production manager: Erin Reilly

ISBN 978-1-324-03615-9 (pbk.)

W. W. Norton & Company, Inc., 500 Fifth Avenue, New York, N.Y. 10110
www.wwnorton.com

W. W. Norton & Company Ltd., 15 Carlisle Street, London W1D 3BS

1 2 3 4 5 6 7 8 9 0

To Ellen and the boys—
Peter, Scott, and Alexander

PREFACE TO THE REISSUE

THIS REISSUE OF *PASSIONATE SAGE* prompts a look back from retirement that is eerily similar to the same kind of retrospective that occupied John Adams during his twilight years at Quincy.

Bear with me, as I try to remember why I decided to write about Adams, what I now wish I had done differently, and how our current condition as a deeply divided people should only enhance our admiration for his prophetic prowess.

On the first score, in 1990 I was just finishing a ten-year tour as dean of faculty at Mount Holyoke College, casting about to decide how to resume my career as a historian. The profession had moved decisively toward social history, more specifically the recovery of African Americans, Native Americans, and women as previously ignored players in the American narrative.

Meanwhile the modern editions of the papers generated by the most prominent members of the founding generation were rolling off the presses, creating the fullest record of any political elite ever assembled. Like Adams, my contrarian instincts dictated my

decision to go against the current trend and, using the unprecedented collection of primary sources now available, to write the
history of what I called the American Founding.

Why John Adams? That was easy. Because the *Adams Papers*
were the richest body of letters and documents from the founding
generation. The *Family Correspondence* between John and Abigail
first caught my eye for its prevailing eloquence, unprecedented
candor, and relentless quotability. George Washington's diaries
are mostly about the weather. Adams's diaries are about the winds
gusting through his soul.

As for second thoughts, I wish I had concluded the legacies
chapter with a section on Adams's distinctive role at the founding as the political philosopher of the emotions, perhaps contrasting him with Jefferson as the advocate for human reason.
While one can trace Adams's interest in the emotional side of
the human story to David Hume, Adam Smith, and the Scot-
tish Enlightenment in general, his primal source was his own
Vesuvian personality and his constant efforts to control it. He
anticipated Sigmund Freud, Henry Adams (his grandson), and
Hannah Arendt. I should have made more of his originality as a
political thinker.

Finally, Adams was the outspoken prophet on two fronts that
threaten us now. First, he warned that the free market would generate unprecedented economic inequality and that the elite would
use its wealth to control the government. He foresaw the first
Gilded Age and now our own.

Second, he was the loudest voice at the founding for viewing
our republican framework as an inherently fragile experiment that

would always be vulnerable to demagogues and swoonish swings in popular opinion. In his own day he regarded Aaron Burr as a major threat. If he was looking down from heaven at post-Trump America, he would have whispered, "I told you so."

Plymouth, Vermont
January 2022

CONTENTS

CONTENTS

ILLUSTRATIONS

PREFACE

W HEN JOHN ADAMS ARRIVED as an American diplomat to France in 1778, one of the first questions he encountered proved awkward and a good test of his personal diplomatic skills. Everyone asked him if he was "the famous Adams, Le fameux Adams?—Ah, le fameux Adams?" It seems he was the victim of a double dose of mistaken identity. On the one hand, he was being confused with his cousin Samuel Adams, the fiery propagandist of the American Revolution and organizer of the Boston Tea Party, who currently headed the British lists of American traitors most wanted for hanging. On the other hand, the French mistakenly believed that a "Monsieur Adams" was also the author of Tom Paine's celebrated pamphlet *Common Sense*, which had electrified readers in Europe as well as America with its seductive argument that fomenting a revolution was a natural and sensible act.

Despite his best efforts to persuade the French that he was neither Sam Adams nor the author of *Common Sense*, John Adams discovered that no one believed him. "All that I could say or do," he reported to his diary, "would not convince any Body, but that

I was the fameux Adams." For weeks the French attributed his denials to excessive modesty, thereby demonstrating conclusively that they were completely misinformed. When they eventually came to believe his protestations, however, and acknowledged that he was not "the famous Adams," the question then became: who was he? Adams himself observed rather grudgingly that no one knew. He was quickly transformed from an American celebrity to an American obscurity. He had suddenly become, as he put it, "a Man of whom Nobody had ever heard before, a perfect Cypher, a Man who did not understand a Word of French—awkward in his Figure—awkward in his Dress—no Abilities—a perfect Bigot—and fanatic." At dinner parties he came to be known simply as "the other Adams." Who *was* he?

The pages that follow could be construed as an explanation to his French hosts. If so, it is a somewhat ill-timed explanation, not only because it is more than two centuries too late to do them much good, but also because it focuses on Adams as an older man, long after he had suffered their slights, even after his active political career was over. But while concentrating on Adams in retirement, my intention has been broader and more ambitious than a chronicle of his twilight years at Quincy. It is true that previous studies of Adams have paid less attention to the last quarter century of his life, so that there is more fresh material available here that has never before found its way into the books. But my motives for focusing on old man Adams reach beyond the desire to bring previously unpublished letters into print. For reasons that I try to explore, John Adams remains the most misconstrued and unappreciated "great man" in American history. Not only does he deserve better; we will be better for knowing him. Adams used his retirement to engage in a long and often bittersweet retrospective on his public career and personal life. That is also my purpose—to use his latter years as a perch from which to meditate on his thought and character, to assess his proper place within the revolutionary generation, to appraise his legacy for us, to offer an answer to the question his French hosts posed long ago.

꙾

NOT THAT HISTORIANS and biographers have been wholly negligent in seeking an answer to that question, especially during the past forty years. During that time there has been a veritable Adams industry dedicated to the goal of recovering his reputation.

I acknowledge my debt to the staff of *The Adams Papers* and the Massachusetts Historical Society, where the papers of the Adams family have been housed since 1902. The real breakthrough for Adams scholars came in the 1950s, however, when the enormous collection was put on microfilm. (Stretched in a straight line, the 608 reels would extend about five miles.) All students of Adams also owe an incalculable debt to Lyman Butterfield, who supervised the modern letterpress edition of *The Adams Papers* with a combination of wit and wisdom that remains unmatched in modern editorial scholarship. Butterfield effectively rescued the passionate and pungent parts of the Adams character from the massive probity of Charles Francis Adams, who had published the initial edition of the papers in the 1850s according to standards that were exemplary for their day, but which also served as a singular example of those cloistered qualities that have given the Victorian era a bad name ever since. (Humorless, self-restraining to the point of parody, Charles Francis earned a reputation within the family and without as "the greatest Iceberg in the Western Hemisphere.") Thanks to Butterfield, John Adams was allowed to "come out," to become a man of endearing eccentricities, the most lovable and fully human member of his remarkable generation of American statesmen.

Additional thanks are also owed to that generation of Adams biographers who first exploited the uncensored papers that Butterfield and his staff made available: Catherine Drinker Bowen, who recovered Adams's prominent role in the American Revolution in her best-selling novel; Zoltán Haraszti, whose perky and persuasive study of the Adams library enhanced Adams's status as a thinker; Manning Dauer and Stephen Kurtz, whose respective books on the Adams presidency refurbished his image as the principled political leader of the Federalists; Lester J. Cappon, whose unabridged edition of the correspondence with Thomas Jefferson returned Adams to his old position as Jefferson's intellectual alter ego; Page Smith, whose authoritative two-volume biography captured the passionate friendship with Abigail; Peter Shaw, who probed the complex character of the Adams personality more deftly and deeply than had ever been done before; the writers and actors who created *The Adams Chronicles* for public television, who brought Adams to life before a huge national audience as the founding father of America's most prominent and intellectually distinguished family. They have all been my predecessors, guides, and teachers as I tried to conjure up my own picture of "the famous Adams."

At Mount Holyoke my fellow conjurers, who read parts of

different chapters of my work-in-progress, included Christopher
Benfey, Daniel Czitrom, Rebecca Faery, John Faragher, Amy
Kaplan, Anthony Lake, Carole Straw and Donald Weber. Two
old friends, William Henry and David Maytnier, read early drafts
and offered encouraging responses from outside the scholarly circle. Students who helped with the ordering of microfilm, checking
of notes, and clarity of the prose included Catherine Allgor, Julie
Seibert, and Caroline Wood.

The staffs of the University of Massachusetts Library at
Amherst and the Williston Memorial Library at Mount Holyoke,
especially Marilyn Dunn, always came through when it counted.
A generous grant from the John Simon Guggenheim Foundation
freed me from my deanly duties for the year 1988–89, when the
bulk of the research was done. I am also grateful to the Trustees
of Mount Holyoke College, especially William Smethurst, who
awarded me the Ford Foundation Chair in American History,
which carried an annual allowance that subsidized research trips.
The faculty at Mount Holyoke presented me with a hefty sum of
money for use on my scholarship when I stepped down from my
position as Dean of Faculty in 1990. I hope they will conclude that
I have made appropriate use of their remarkable largesse.

I was especially fortunate in the calibre of criticism I received
on the manuscript as a whole. John Patrick Diggins and Gordon
Wood, each of whom has made seminal contributions of his own
to the intellectual and historical issues at stake here, gave the pen-
ultimate draft a careful and close reading. So did Mary Jo Salter,
who asked the kind of innocent questions every scholar needs to
hear and every writer cherishes. Eric McKitrick, whose upcoming
book on the Federalist era (done with Stanley Elkins) will almost

certainly establish itself as the authoritative account of the political history of the 1790s, read all the chapters as the drafts poured— or rather seeped—out. He also arranged for me to present my work before the faculty seminar in American history at Columbia University and scheduled a series of now-legendary lunches where the main course was always Adams. Finally, Edmund Morgan also read the entire thing as it emerged in chapter-size pieces. He has been my mentor and my friend for longer than either of us cares to remember and has shaped my sense of the craft more than anyone else.

All the customary caveats apply, which is to say that I have often resisted excellent advice with the kind of contrarian's instinct that I attribute here to Adams. My insistence that Adams's political vision speaks directly to us and our troubled times, for example, will strike some readers as ahistorical. All I can say in my defense is that I have tried to remain true to the historical sources, while also listening for wisdom that speaks across the ages. The errors of fact and interpretation that result from these tendencies must, then, be my own burden.

My typists, Helen Canney and Ellen Ortyl, rescued me from many minor errors. The entire manuscript was handwritten, though not (as some of my colleagues claimed) with a quill pen. Given the slant of my scrawl, typists actually became translators whose competence transcended mere transcription. They never failed me.

My agent, Gerald McCauley, kept the faith from beginning to end. My editor, James Mairs, still owes me a lunch, but I owe him much more.

My family has borne the burden of living with a preoccupied

author for several years. My wife has listened to readings of the day's work with patience and a good editorial ear. My sons learned to leave me alone when the writing was not going well and developed the habit of asking, "How's the book, dad?" when they thought the answer was good news. They deserve more than the dedication offered at the start.

PASSIONATE SAGE

MEMORIES

◆◆◆

A Prologue

Not denying to Mr. ADAMS patriotism and integrity, and
even talents of a certain kind, I should be deficient in candor,
were I to conceal the conviction, that he does not possess
the talents adapted to the *Administration* of Government,
and that there are great and intrinsic defects in his character,
which unfit him for the office of Chief Magistrate.

—Alexander Hamilton, *Letter . . . Concerning the Conduct and
Character of John Adams, Esq., President of the United States* (1800)

He [Adams] is liable to gusts of passion little short of
frenzy, which drive him beyond the control of any rational
reflection. I speak of what I have seen. At such moments the
interests of those who support him, or the interests of the
nation, would be outweighed by a single impulse or rage.

—James Bayard to Alexander Hamilton, August 18, 1800

L EGEND HAS IT that John Adams spent his last night in the presidential mansion eventually known as the White House furiously signing appointment letters for Federalist friends and cronies, thereby defying the will of the electorate and the wishes of Thomas Jefferson, his former friend and successor to the presidency. By appointing those "midnight judges" Adams sustained the legacy of Federalism well beyond the time of its time, at least so the story goes, bedevilling Jefferson and subsequent Republican presidents with the judicial opinions of John Marshall and a Federalist-dominated court.

One can easily conjure up the image of a defiant President Adams, hunched over his huge desk in the Oval Office, scratching his signature onto commissions as various aides and clerks put the papers before him, somber and cynical and perhaps a bit grumpy as he gestures for the next appointment letter, still bitter about his failure to win a second term, full of petulance and a craving for political revenge. We know that his bags were already packed and that he planned to take the four o'clock stage out of town the next morning, making him the first and one of a very few sitting presidents in American history to refuse attendance at the inauguration of his successor.

This unflattering picture of Adams contains some accurate features, but like all legendary renderings, and more especially like all attempts to fit the boisterously unorthodox character of Adams into the conventional categories of democratic politics and popular psychology, it misses the essential truths.

Even at the mundane level of factual accuracy, it distorts more than it describes. On the evening of Tuesday, March 3, 1801, the outgoing president actually appointed only two minor officials in Pennsylvania and three lower court judges in the District of Columbia. That was all the official business he did. Soon after the passage of the Judiciary Act in February of 1801, Adams had made the key appointments to the circuit courts and the Supreme Court, including John Marshall as Chief Justice. There was no last-minute, spasmodic act of political defiance. The important business had been completed weeks earlier.[1]

Moreover, the atmosphere in the room that evening was neither as magisterial nor as melodramatic as the legend suggests. Because the national government had only recently moved from Philadelphia to Washington, D.C., neither the city nor the presidential mansion was really ready for occupancy. The streets were unpaved, muddy cesspools, waiting for the summer heat to become mosquito-infested swamps. The presidential residence itself remained unfinished and unfurnished, still damp and cold in early March, requiring fires in thirteen fireplaces to offset the weather. There was, as yet, no Oval Office. Instead of mahogany desks, plush carpets, and obsequious aides, Adams spent his last night as president surrounded by barren walls, packing crates, moving trunks, and clotheslines which his wife, Abigail, had strung across the main conference room for drying the wash. These were the kind of domestic sacrifices one made for being the first president to occupy a capital city that, as Washington himself had predicted, would be ready for greatness "in about a century."[2]

It is, of course, much easier to know the physical context surrounding Adams that final evening in the White House than it is to recover what was in his mind and heart. We do know that, throughout his personal correspondence over the preceding weeks, Adams had claimed to feel more a sense of resignation than revenge, more relief than distress. "My little bark has been oversett in a squall of thunder & lightning & hail attended with a strong smell of sulphur," he told his son Tommy, declaring that "I feel my shoulders relieved from a burden" and that "the short remainder of my days will be the happiest of my life." This was the same message of stoic acceptance he went out of his way to convey to friends: "The remainder of my days will probably be spent in the labors of agriculture and the amusements of literature," a typical letter put it, "on both of which I have always taken more delight, than in any public office of whatever rank." Whether this was a brave pose, or perhaps a sincere expression of one facet of his many-faceted personality, is impossible to know for sure. Adams himself probably would have had a difficult time sorting out the different layers of conflicting emotions brewing inside him at the time.[3]

We do know one aspect of his thinking that evening with reasonable certainty: he did not harbor any deep resentments toward Jefferson. Over the preceding months his fellow Federalists had expressed amazement at his tendency "to speak of him [Jefferson] with much regard . . . adding that he is a good patriot, citizen and father." Fisher Ames, the arch Federalist from Adams's own state of Massachusetts, noted that "the good Lady his wife has been often talkative in a similar strain, and she is as complete a politician as any Lady in the old French Court." Ames observed with incredulity that Adams "acts as if he did not hate or dread Jefferson, and *it is clear that his friends pursue a course in conversations and in the papers which can help nobody's cause but Jefferson's.*" If there was any doubt that the friendship between Adams and Jefferson was still intact, it was removed when Adams made a point of inviting Jefferson for dinner at the presidential quarters a few days before the inauguration; Jefferson for his part made a point of visiting again to see Abigail off when she departed for Quincy. Whatever reservations Adams harbored toward Jefferson's political convictions and his followers in the Republican Party—and there certainly were some—he still respected the man who was to succeed him.[4]

In fact, if there was one person whom Adams spent his last hours as president cursing under his breath, it was not Jefferson but Alexander Hamilton, who was one of the leading lights in the same Federalist Party that Adams officially headed. Adams's hatred for Hamilton—and hatred is not too strong a term—had many causes, but the most immediate and culminating cause was a public letter, eventually published in pamphlet form a few weeks before the presidential election of 1800, entitled *Letter from Alexander Hamilton, Concerning the Public Conduct and Character of John Adams, Esq. President of the United States.* "Not denying to Mr. ADAMS patriotism and integrity, and even talents of a certain kind," the letter began, ". . . he does not possess the talents adapted to the *Administration* of Government. . . ." Hamilton then went on to claim that, in lieu of talent, Adams possessed a deeply flawed character, which rendered him "unfit for the office of Chief Magistrate." And Hamilton's description of the Adams character minced no words: "he is a man of an imagination sublimated and eccentric; propitious neither to the regular display of sound judgment, nor to steady perseverence in a systematic plan of conduct . . . that to this defect are added the unfortunate foibles of a vanity without bounds, and a jealousy capable of discoloring every subject."[5]

Hamilton's diatribe purported to review Adams's entire public career, from his role in the making of the American Revolution in the 1770s, through his diplomatic efforts in France and England in the 1780s, then culminating in his actions as vice president and president in the 1790s. The underlying pattern Hamilton discerned, the key to explaining much if not all of his conduct, could be traced to what he called "the ungovernable temper of Mr. ADAMS." Americans had already begun to think of the leaders of the founding generation—and no one could deny that Adams was one of those leaders—as paragons of virtue and models of magisterial self-control. Hamilton felt compelled to make public what, so he claimed, the entire political leadership of the new nation had known but been concealing for many years; namely, that Adams did not belong in their distinguished company, that he was a vain, volatile, and dangerous man: "It is a fact that he is often liable to paroxisms of anger, which deprive him of self command, and produce very outrageous behaviour to those who approach him." Virtually all the Federalists who had served with him in government had witnessed his tantrums, so Hamilton claimed, and "been humiliated by the effects of these gusts of passion." They could all testify to "the disgusting egotism, the distempered jealousy, and the ungovernable indiscretion of Mr. ADAMS' temper. . . ." They could all verify that Adams's successful decisions "were not the effects of any regular plan, but the fortuitous emanations of momentary impulses." In short, Adams was precisely the kind of unstable, imprudent, and capricious character that a new nation with a fragile republican government did not need; and might not be able to survive.[6]

Hamilton was not only arguing against the election of Adams to a second term; he was also arguing that the long-standing weaknesses of Adams's character should disqualify him from admission into the pantheon reserved for America's founding heroes. "I was one of that numerous class who had conceived a high veneration for Mr. ADAMS," Hamilton acknowledged, "on account of the part he acted in the first stages of the revolution . . . as a man of patriotic, bold, profound and comprehensive mind." But subsequent events had demonstrated that this reputation was undeserved, that "the gentleman [was] infected with some visionary notions, and that he was far less able in the practice, than in the theory, of politics."[7]

It seems plausible, indeed probable, that Adams spent at least a portion of those last few hours in office muttering epithets at Hamilton, brooding about the political motives that underlay the criticism of his character. But even though Adams was the most candid and self-revealed member of the revolutionary generation, there are some private moments that even he preferred to keep to himself. And this was one of them. We know for a fact that in his letters to friends, Adams claimed to pity Hamilton more than resent him. "This pamphlet I regret more on account of its author, than on my own," he claimed, "because I am confident, it will do him more harm than me." Hamilton had made himself into a pathetic creature, who ought not be answered or punished, Adams insisted, since "the public indignation he has excited is punishment enough."[8]

Adams's political judgment proved correct. Even Hamilton's staunchest Federalist friends and followers concurred that the publication of such a scandalous document on the eve of the presidential election seemed to cast Hamilton in just the role of wild-eyed eccentric that he had tried to impose on Adams. As it turned out,

Hamilton's vendetta against Adams proved to be an act of political suicide, fully as fatal to Hamilton's career as his decision two years later to face Aaron Burr in a duel proved to his life.[9]

But Adams's claim that he felt more pity than anger does not ring true. Even though Adams's analysis of public reaction proved correct, there is good reason to believe that his own personal reaction more resembled a volcanic eruption than a graceful bow to Hamilton's self-destruction. We know that the suppressed rage against Hamilton exploded in the Adams autobiography and in a series of nearly endless diatribes in the *Boston Patriot* a few years later. It was characteristic of Adams to deny the existence of a seething anger that virtually vibrated inside his soul, not because he habitually lied to others or himself, but because the emotions he felt were too ferocious to allow for controlled expression or modulated articulation. The last thing he wanted to do was to confirm, by the very vehemence of his reaction, the essential truth of Hamilton's charges against him.[10]

In the end, then, it is impossible to know with any clinching certainty what the stout, balding, toothless, ever proud John Adams was thinking as he sat in the semi-darkness of the presidential mansion amidst the packing crates, clotheslines, and memories, waiting for the dawn stage to carry him out of public life and into retirement. We can be reasonably sure that the legend has it wrong—he was not thinking about ways to prolong Federalist policies against the will of Jefferson and his followers. We can speculate that Hamilton's accusations occupied a portion of his conscious mind during those final hours as president. It seems safe to conclude that his unconscious mind, which is usually less accessible, was brimming over with angry recriminations and rebuttals.

The advantages afforded by hindsight and relative detachment allow us to see that Hamilton's indictment of the Adams character, much like the mythical account of the "midnight judges," mixed together painful truths and outright falsifications. But despite Hamilton's political prejudices and ulterior motives, he effectively framed the question that has haunted Adams's reputation ever since: how was it that one of the leading lights in the founding generation seemed to exhibit such massive lapses in personal stability? how could the man who, next to George Washington, did most to assure and then secure the independence of the United States, strike so many of his contemporaries, friends and enemies alike, as a wild man, "liable to gusts of passion little short of frenzy, which drive him beyond the control of any rational reflection"? If Adams did try to provide answers to those questions that final night as president, it is virtually certain that his answers were inadequate. After almost two hundred years, during which time the deeper patterns of the Adams story have become available for our balanced consideration, we should be able to do better.[11]

CHAPTER ONE

The Education of John Adams

I am not about to write lamentations or jeremiades
over my fate nor panegyricks upon my life and
conduct. You may think me disappointed [in losing the
presidency]. I am not. All my life I expected it. . . .

—Adams to William Tudor, January 20, 1801

If Virtue was to be rewarded with Wealth, it would not
be Virtue. If Virtue was to be rewarded with Fame,
it would not be Virtue of the sublimest Kind.

—Adams to Abigail Adams, December 2, 1778

THE EDUCATION OF John Adams was effectively complete by
the time he reached the presidency, but his conduct during
his four-year term served to exhibit the dominant features of the
Adams personality in all their full-blown splendor. It was quite
likely, in short, that he would succeed in the area of policy but fail
politically. Which is to say that he could do what was right for his
country, but arrange events so that his personal fate suffered as

a consequence. This was the established Adams pattern: to sense where history was headed, make decisions that positioned America to be carried forward on those currents, but to do so in a way that assured his own alienation from success.[1]

Although there were, as we shall see, elements of deep-rooted perversity that dictated this pattern, events conspired to place Adams in a historical situation that virtually assured personal and political failure regardless of his affinity for psychological mischief. First and foremost was the elemental fact that he succeeded George Washington. Whatever frustrations Washington had experienced as president, his impeccable credentials and bottomless reputation assured a national consensus that any successor would be hard-pressed to sustain. Jefferson, who had been defeated by Adams in the election of 1796 by a mere three electoral votes, had an uncanny appreciation of his own good fortune in losing. As he explained to James Madison—while mixing his metaphors uncharacteristically—Washington was "fortunate to get off just as the bubble is bursting, leaving others to hold the bag." Washington's departure from office "will mark the moment when the difficulties begin to work," Jefferson shrewdly predicted, and even though serious political and foreign policy problems were inherited from Washington, "they will be ascribed to the new administration. . . ." Most historians of this period like to notice Jefferson's gracious deferral to Adams after the close election, when Jefferson acknowledged Adams's seniority and prior claim on the honor of the office. But when Jefferson said that he was "sincerely pleased at having escaped the late draught for the helm, and have not a wish which he [Adams] stands in the way of," his motives were more calculating than charitable. He knew whoever followed Washington was in for trouble.[2]

Meanwhile, it was characteristic of Adams to recognize the danger presented by what might be called the problem of Washington's shadow, but to regard all thoughts of political self-interest as violations of virtue. Adams was one of the most astute political analysts of the era, whose understanding of the shifting configurations of power that shaped the national interest had few if any equals. But when it came to political thinking of the self-protective sort, he was worse than naive; he was congenitally committed to the active suppression of all such impulses. He wrote wryly to Abigail on the eve of his inauguration that, while aware of the problems he inherited from Washington, he preferred to ignore them and press on: "I think a man had better wear than rust."[3]

If succeeding a national hero posed one set of difficulties, divisions within the Federalist camp presented even worse ones. At the top of the list was Alexander Hamilton, who, while not occupying any official position within the government, continued to exercise considerable influence over the members of the president's cabinet, most of whom regarded him as the real leader of the High Federalists, who in turn saw themselves as the very soul of the national government. During the election of 1796 Hamilton had concocted an elaborate scheme to deprive Adams of the presidency by manipulating the electoral votes in South Carolina so that Thomas Pinckney would emerge with a majority, thereby knocking Jefferson out altogether and relegating Adams to another term as vice president. James Madison wrote Jefferson that what he called Hamilton's "jockeyship" was rooted in an intense dislike for Adams, "and by an apprehension that he

[Adams] is too head-strong to be a fit puppet for the intrigues behind the screen." After Hamilton's plot failed and Adams was elected, Jefferson warned him to watch out for "the tricks of your arch-friend of New York . . . who most probably will be disappointed as to you." And Jefferson was right, since Hamilton had begun a whispering campaign within the High Federalist network even before the inauguration, describing Adams as "a man of great vanity . . . and of far less real abilities than he believes he possesses." The scandalous pamphlet of 1800 was merely the published version of innuendo against Adams that Hamilton had been spreading throughout Federalist circles before Adams had made a single decision or uttered one word as president.[4]

Finally, the Adams presidency was destined to be dominated by a single question of American policy to an extent seldom if ever encountered by any succeeding occupant of the office. Simply put, that question was whether the United States should declare war against France or find a way to resolve differences diplomatically. The country was already on the verge of what historians have called a "quasi-war" against French privateers in the Atlantic and Caribbean when Adams took office. Over the course of the next four years there were several startling twists and turns in diplomatic relations between the two countries, a bewildering cascade of reports, speeches, commissions, posturings, and gestures on both sides, as well as schemings within the different political factions inside each country. But amidst this massive body of ever-shifting detail and particularity, one simple and unattractive truth remained constant until the last months of Adams's presidency; namely, that the conditions necessary for a peaceful settlement were not present. Successful negotiations required a French government with the desire and the authority to end the hostilities, and an American government united on a peaceful course of action and backed by public opinion that could accept such terms. Since these conditions simply did not exist before 1800, and since there was very little that anyone could have done to bring them into being any earlier, the central policy problem of the Adams administration was inherently insoluble. And this would have remained true even if Adams had not inherited a weak and ultimately disloyal cabinet, if the shadow of Washington had somehow disappeared, if Hamilton had not behaved so treacherously, and if Adams himself had possessed the political finesse of a Talleyrand.[5]

If these were the realistic contours within which it is now clear that the Adams presidency took shape, they nevertheless allowed for some latitude of movement, for key decisions and choices that put the stamp of Adams's personality on an important moment in the early history of the American republic. In the weeks before his inauguration he let it be known that he was willing to have Jefferson play a major role in his administration, perhaps giving the vice president a prominent place in cabinet meetings and a role in the looming negotiations with France. "My letters inform me that Mr. Adams speaks of me with great friendship," Jefferson reported to Madison; he noted that Adams had even hinted at "the prospect of administering the government in concurrence with me." For his part Adams apprised friends that he felt "no apprehension from Mr. Jefferson," and that "the cause of the irritation upon his Nerves, which broke out in some disagreeable Appearances a few years ago, is now removed as I believe." Adams's original intention was to seek a peaceful resolution of the conflict with France, enlisting the support of Jefferson and his considerable political following to create a bipartisan administration and a foreign policy that remained true to what Adams called "my system," which entailed a commitment to American neutrality at almost any cost and the creation of a naval force of sufficient size to fight a defensive war if either France or England left America no choice.[6]

Much could be said for this vision. In his autobiography, Benjamin Rush, Adams's dearest friend save for Abigail, claimed that it was the consensus of his contemporaries that Adams possessed "more learning probably, both ancient and modern, than any man who subscribed the Declaration of Independence." And in the next century the prominent Unitarian minister Theodore Parker recalled that as a boy he had been taught that "with the exception of Dr. Franklin . . . no American politician of the eighteenth century was Adams' intellectual superior." Adams possessed a mind that grasped intuitively and comprehensively the essential ingredients of a strategic decision. He was a veritable genius at recognizing what was central and what was peripheral, what the national interest required and what history would allow. In the spring of 1797 he recognized that the Hamiltonians who would tilt the country toward England and the Jeffersonians who would lean toward France were both wrong. He understood that neither misplaced patriotism nor party spirit at home, nor for that matter the imperialistic maneuverings of the English ministry nor the hopelessly erratic policies of the French Directory, should be allowed to seduce America into a foreign war that diverted national energies from the main task of the next century, which was to develop stable domestic institutions and to expand across the continent. He realized that the creation of an American navy, what he called "wooden walls," was vastly preferable to an army, for a navy allowed the new nation to defend its coastline and protect its shipping without running the risks of a large land force, which conjured up all the historical dangers posed by a standing army and would serve as an irresistible temptation for would-be American Napoleons like Hamilton.[7]

Finally, he sensed that effective national leadership meant bridging the widening gap between the High Federalists and the Jeffersonians. Neither Adams nor Jefferson, nor any other member of the revolutionary generation for that matter, thought about political parties in anything like our modern sense of the term. So Adams did not consider his conciliatory behavior toward Jefferson as the gracious gesture of a Federalist president welcoming the leader of a Republican opposition into the councils of power. Instead, he saw it as an effort to carve out a centrist political position from which he might better implement policies that served the long-term national interest. His vision here was prescient, but it quickly ran afoul of the party spirit it was designed to transcend, as well as the quirks of his own personality.[8]

The party spirit struck from both sides. Before sending off his own accommodating response to Adams's conciliatory letter in January of 1797, Jefferson showed it to Madison, who immediately warned his mentor and fellow Virginian that working alongside Adams, inside the administration, would deprive him of the freedom to lead the opposition to Federalist policies. (Jefferson probably needed little persuading.) Over dinner two days after the inauguration Jefferson apprised Adams that he did not wish to be included in cabinet deliberations and that neither he nor Madison was willing to serve in the proposed peace delegation to France.

"We parted as good friends, as we had always lived," Adams recalled later, "but we consulted very little together, afterwards."[9]

By the summer of 1797 even the long-standing mutual respect was at risk. As Adams saw it, Jefferson had chosen "the future of his party [over] the future of his friendship." When word reached Adams that Jefferson had written a critical account of a presidential speech to Congress, Adams exploded: "It is evidence of a mind, soured, yet seeking for popularity, and eaten to a honeycomb with ambition," he complained, "yet weak, confused, uninformed and ignorant." Meanwhile, on the other side of the political equation, his cabinet had balked at the suggestion of welcoming Jefferson or involving the Republican opposition in the negotiations with France. Adams later recalled that, when he proposed the idea, the entire cabinet threatened to resign. Not only was the hope for a bipartisan coalition dead, but the centrist position Adams had chosen to occupy was now a no-man's-land, raked by a crossfire from what had now become two distinct political parties.[10]

There was a sense in which Adams, or at least an important part of him, preferred it that way. He certainly could not be blamed for the drift of the Jeffersonian Republicans toward becoming the first opposition party. Nor was he responsible for the tendency of the High Federalists to rally around Hamilton. But whether it was a function of unconscious design, pure accident, or sheer fate, the isolated position in which he found himself as president replicated a familiar Adams pattern in which personal independence usually transformed itself into alienation. Commitment to principle somehow necessitated unpopularity for John Adams, and the fullest expression of his best energies occurred in singular acts of passionate defiance. Whether they knew it or not, his opponents inside and outside the Federalist Party had created precisely the political conditions in which Adams could act out his preferred role as virtuous statesman, above all claims of party.

Over the course of the first two years as president, another familiar piece of the Adams personality gradually emerged. As he clung tenaciously to his policy of American neutrality and naval preparation—and this despite outrageous acts of duplicity by the French Directory in demanding payment of bribes from the American peace delegation—Adams began to focus his mounting frustrations on a single person who became, for him, the embodiment of evil. That person, of course, was Hamilton. Most members of the cabinet and many key Federalists in Congress were convinced that a war with France and a commercial alliance with England would best serve America's longterm interests, and Hamilton's advocacy of a large army was a central feature of that policy. Against Adams's wishes, the High Federalists introduced legislation for the creation of an army of ten thousand regular troops, with provisions for an even larger force once hostilities broke out.

Adams's first reaction was incredulity and confusion. Even if his strenuous efforts to avoid war with France failed, what was the point of an American army? "Where is it possible for her [France] to get ships to send thirty thousand men here?" he asked. Armies were costly items; they would require heavy taxes and, most importantly, "at present there is no more prospect of seeing a French army here, than there is in Heaven." When he recalled this moment long after his retirement, he remembered thinking that "this man [Hamilton] is stark mad or I am."[11]

Then it dawned on him that Hamilton intended to have himself appointed head of the army. Or rather that Hamilton was maneuvering to be appointed second-in-command to Washington, who would presumably remain at Mount Vernon and leave the actual command of the army to his former aide-de-camp. The whole horrid picture now came into focus for Adams. "If I should consent to the appointment of Hamilton," he wrote to a member of his cabinet, "I should consider it as the most [ir]responsible action in my life." Hamilton had talents, to be sure, but Adams claimed they were like the dangerous talents of John Calvin, recalling the old ditty: "Some think on Calvin, heaven's own spirit fell; While others deem him instrument of hell." Whatever his peculiar talents, Hamilton's true designs were now clear. He obviously intended "to get an army on foot to give himself the command of it & then to proclaim a Regal Government, place Hamilton at the Head of it & prepare for a Province of Great Britain." (If he had been able to read Hamilton's private correspondence, Adams would have discovered that Hamilton's plans were even more grandiose: he hoped to march his conquering army through the Louisiana Territory, then down to Mexico and Peru, liberating all the inhabitants from French and Spanish domination in the name of the United States.) By midway through his term Adams began to lash out in cabinet meetings against the man who had become the epitome of treachery. "His [Adams's] language is bitter even to outrage and Swearing . . . ," Fisher Ames reported to his Federalist colleagues, and "he is implacable against a certain great little man [Hamilton] whom we mutually respect." In addition to a well-thought-out policy and a position of principled isolation, Adams now possessed the final prerequisite for the release of his enormous moral energies—a personal focal point for his suppressed anger.[12]

Adams acted decisively on February 19, 1799, when he

forwarded to the Senate the nomination of William Vans Murray to serve as minister plenipotentiary to France, which was, in effect, his unilateral decision to send a new peace mission despite the failure of all previous efforts. Theodore Sedgwick, a Federalist leader in the Congress, claimed to be "thunderstruck" and summed up the reaction of all the High Federalists: "Had the foulest heart and the ablest head in the world, been permitted to select the most embarrassing and ruinous measure, perhaps it would have been precisely the one which had been adopted." For by his action Adams simultaneously reopened prospects for diplomatic relations with France, ended all speculation about an alliance with England, and called into question the need for an American army. And if there were no need for an army, there would be no military command for Hamilton.[13]

The British ambassador reported that "The federal party were thunderstuck with this step," for it was taken "without the advice, indeed without the knowledge of the Secretary of State or the other members of the Administration, and without consultation with any of his own friends." Abigail reported that in the bedrock Federalist enclaves of Massachusetts, "the whole community were like a flock of frightened pigions; nobody had their story ready; Some called it a hasty measure; others condemned it as an inconsistent one; some swore, some curs'd." Timothy Pickering, the disloyal Secretary of State whom Adams had come to despise, also admitted to being "*thunderstruck*"—this was apparently the operative word of the day—and offered the most perceptive comment on Adams's motives: "it was done without any *consultation with any member of the government* and for a reason *truly remarkable—because he knew we should all be opposed to the measure!*"[14]

In retrospect, of course, there was nothing misguided or crazy about Adams's decision. In fact, avoiding war with France proved a wise and statesmanlike course of action, the first substantive implementation of Washington's message in the Farewell Address, a precedent for American isolation from Europe that would influence American foreign policy for over a century. Yet if the decision itself has survived historical scrutiny, the manner in which it was made still appears as abrupt and bizarre to historians as it did to the High Federalists of the day. Adams apparently consulted not a single member of his cabinet or party, made no effort to persuade or prepare the political leadership in Congress and, most incredibly, proceeded to absent himself from the seat of government for the next seven months, remaining ensconced in Quincy while reading the collected works of Frederick the Great. During this extended interlude the delegation to France was not dispatched and the High Federalists continued to bemoan what Theodore Sedgwick called "the misfortunes to which we are subjected by the wild and irregular starts of a vain, jealous, and half-frantic mind." Letters began to circulate among Federalist leaders, wondering how "the best friends of government" might find a way to "get rid of Mr. Adams. . . ." Eventually Hamilton went so far as to admit that he preferred Jefferson to Adams in the looming election: "If we must have an enemy at the head of the government," he told Sedgwick, "let it be one whom we can oppose, and for whom we are not responsible." Benjamin Stoddert, his newly appointed and completely loyal Secretary of Navy, pleaded with Adams to come out of hibernation at Quincy, reporting that "artful and designing men" were plotting to scuttle the mission to France as well as Adams's reelection prospects. "I have only one favor to beg," Adams replied to Stoddert, "and that is that a certain election may be wholly laid out of this question and all others." Merely to notice the linkage between important matters of national policy and presidential politics was not permissible in the Adams scheme of things.[15]

Eventually Adams pried himself loose from his books and thoughts at Quincy. In October of 1799 he travelled down to Trenton, New Jersey, to meet with the members of the peace commission. In a dramatic encounter with Hamilton, who tried vainly to persuade him to change his mind, Adams remained serenely defiant. "Never in my life," he recalled nearly a decade later, "did I hear a man talk more like a fool." The peace mission eventually proved successful, negotiating a treaty with France that ended hostilities and restored diplomatic relations between the two countries. News of this success, however, did not arrive in time to affect the presidential election of 1800.[16]

Whether it would have made any difference to the outcome remains, nearly two centuries later, a matter of lively historical debate. Historians of the Adams presidency also disagree over how to interpret his eccentric version of personal independence during the last half of his term, most especially his seclusion in Quincy during those critical months in 1799. Abigail was ill, probably with rheumatic fever, much of this time. Perhaps his concern for her explains the Quincy hibernation, an explanation he himself offered whenever prodded by friends to return to Philadelphia. Or perhaps Adams was deliberately delaying the dispatch of the peace mission until he was assured that political conditions within France made success more likely, all the while allowing more time for the infant American navy then being assembled by Stoddert to

Abigail Adams (1801), at the time of John's retirement.
Gilbert Stuart oil on canvas. *GRANGER Historical Picture Archive*

grow in size and strength. Or perhaps he was truly torn between the anti-French, pro-army position of the High Federalists and his desire for a peaceful settlement. All are plausible explanations; there is some semblance of historical evidence to support each view, although the latter interpretation would require us to accept a version of the Adams temperament completely at odds with the characteristic patterns of his personality.[17]

Adams never doubted the essential wisdom of his French policy, which was rooted in convictions about American foreign policy that he had developed during a quarter century of public service. Nor did he have any second thoughts about breaking with the High Federalists, especially Hamilton. By doing so he placed himself in the most attractive position imaginable, at least for a man of his disposition: a leader without a party, whose independence is unalloyed and whose virtuous motives cannot be attributed to a crass craving for popularity. His reasons for remaining away from the government for so long at such a crucial time are more difficult to fathom with equivalent assurance. But it seems most likely that he sequestered himself in Quincy because, for good reason, he had come to distrust most members of his cabinet and, for reasons rooted in his own combustible temperament, he feared that regular exposure to them would produce the infamous Adams explosions, which were incompatible with the model of virtuous, self-possessed leader he wished to convey to the world as well as to himself. And once he finally did return to the capital, it did not take long for the fireworks to start. "He every where denounces the men . . . in whom he confided at the beginning of his administration, as an oligarchish faction," Theodore Sedgwick reported, shouting out loud in cabinet meetings that "they cannot govern him" and that "this faction and particularly Hamilton its head . . . intends to drive the country into a war with France and a more intimate . . . union with great Britain. . . ." Fisher Ames concurred with this image of the president, claiming that "he inveighs against the British faction and the Essex Junto like one possessed."[18]

During his last year as president, in short, Adams frequently behaved in the tempestuous, wild-eyed way that Hamilton was soon to describe in his open letter of 1800. Whether Adams's avowed honesty allowed him to acknowledge the accuracy of

Hamilton's description during that last evening in Washington, we can never know. If so, Adams could certainly have justified his behavior, much in the way of a man accused of paranoia who is able to demonstrate conclusively that, in fact, his friends *were* attempting to do him in. As for the deeper sources of his virtuous ideal and his passionate disposition, we might try looking back to an earlier time, when he made his first appearance on the national stage.

THE HABITS OF MIND and heart that exhibited themselves in mature form during Adams's presidency were still in the process of congealing in the 1770s, when he made his major contribution to American independence. Between 1774, when he became a delegate to the Continental Congress, and 1778, when he sailed for France to become part of the American delegation in Paris, a great deal of history happened. Not only was the American Revolution launched and set on a successful course, but Adams himself first came into focus as a national leader. He began the period as a moderately successful thirty-eight-year-old lawyer and dabbler in provincial Massachusetts politics. He ended it as one of the two or three most prominent men in the country. The four years between his arrival on the national stage and his emergence as a major figure, while brimming with important events and historical decisions, is also one of the best documented chapters of Adams's long life, replete with personal letters, official correspondence, an extensive diary, and a colorful, if not always trustworthy, autobiography. We know more about John Adams during this propitious moment in American history than about any other member of the revolutionary generation. For all these reasons, it is the optimum moment to catch an extended glimpse of Adams-in-the-making.[19]

The man who travelled on horseback from Boston to Philadelphia in August of 1774 was an intense mixture of political commitment, palpable ambition, and painful insecurity. At thirty-eight he was already old enough to worry that life was leaving him behind. In July he had written Abigail that he was "full of Fears" about his professional prospects, especially since he had associated himself with opposition to British policy. "I will not see Blockheads, whom I have a Right to despise, elevated above me," he proclaimed. But if his chief problem was an excessive passion for what he called "the Cause and Friends of Liberty," Adams realized that there was little he could do to suppress it. "I have a Zeal in my Heart, for my Country and her Friends, which I cannot smother or conceal," he admitted to Abigail, noting that "it will burn out at times and in Companies where it ought to be latent in my Breast." He was capable of excess when the issue at stake ignited his internal fires.[20]

Part of him was not at all sure how to think about the Continental Congress. "I view the Assembly that is to be there, as I do . . . I know not what," he confessed, wondering why he had been elected as a delegate from Massachusetts and feeling a personal "insufficiency for this important Business." But another part of him was already beginning to dream grandly. "It is to be a School of Political Prophets, I suppose," he wrote James Warren, then his closest friend, "a Nursery of American Statesmen." As one of the erstwhile prophets, he even wondered out loud to Warren "What Plans would be adopted at the Congress, if a Sully, a Cecil, a Pitt . . . a Demosthenes or a Cicero were there—or all of them together." He was clearly conscious of the Continental Congress as a personal opportunity to join his own career with a potentially historic enterprise, to be, as it were, present at the creation.[21]

If the official business of this first session of the Continental Congress was to draft a Declaration of Rights and Grievances against Parliament's authority over the colonies, the main business for Adams was to gauge his talents against those of the other delegates. "Fifty Gentlemen meeting together, all Strangers," he wrote to Abigail, "are therefore jealous, of each other—fearful, timid, skittish. . . ." Because most of the delegates were leaders in their respective colonies, accustomed to dominating the debate, the deliberations of the Continental Congress initially struck Adams as an endless exercise in preening and conspicuous eloquence: "I believe if it was moved and seconded . . . that Three and Two make five, We should be entertained with Logick and Rhetorick, Law, History, Politicks and Mathematicks. . . for two whole Days, and then we should pass the Resolution unanimously in the Affirmative."[22]

Mostly, however, he was trying to assess where he stood in this procession of aspiring statesmen. His diary entries contained brutally clinical portraits of his fellow delegates. Edward Rutledge of South Carolina, he decided, was "sprightly but not deep," and had the unfortunate habit of speaking through his nose. Benjamin Rush of Pennsylvania, who eventually became a dear friend, was initially dismissed as "too much of a Talker to be a deep Thinker. Elegant but not deep." Roger Sherman of Connecticut, on the other hand, was properly grave, but otherwise a model of gracelessness:

There cannot be a more striking contrast to beautiful Action, than the Motions of his Hands. Generally, he stands upright with his Hands before him. The fingers of his left Hand clenched into a Fist, and the Wrist of it, grasped with his right. . . . But when he moves a Hand, in any thing like Action, Hogarth's Genius could not have invented a Motion more opposite to grace. It is Stiffness, and Awkwardness itself. Rigid as Starched Linen or Buchram. Awkward as a junior Batchelor, or a Sophomore.[23]

After a few weeks of silent watching and calculated comparing of his own gifts with those of the other delegates, his initial insecurity and sense of inferiority began to dissipate. He began to make friends with members of the Virginia delegation. He decided to explore Philadelphia, even attending a Catholic service. "The scenery and Musick [of the Mass] is so callculated to take in Mankind," he noted in his diary, "that I wonder, the Reformation ever succeeded." And eventually he began to speak out in the public debates. Before he was finished, he had earned a reputation as "the Atlas of American independence."[24]

Adams possessed one great advantage over most of the other delegates to the Continental Congress. He had already developed a keen sense that reconciliation with England was highly unlikely, that war was probably unavoidable, and that, if war should come, American military victory was virtually inevitable. While most of the other delegates were trying to find a way to avoid the American Revolution, Adams believed it had already begun. Just before departing for Philadelphia he wrote Abigail about what he called "Moody's Doctrine," a cautious piece of wisdom attributed to Samuel Moody, an eccentric New England minister. The essence of "Moody's Doctrine" was "that when Men knew not what to do, they ought not to do they knew not what." Adams acknowl-edged that this "oracular Jingle of Words . . . contained some good sense," but it did not apply to him or to the situation America confronted in the summer of 1774. Just as he began his presidency with a clear vision of the foreign policy interests of the United States and the conviction that war must be avoided, he arrived at the Continental Congress with an equally clear vision of where his-tory was headed, which in this case meant that war with England could *not* be avoided. His autobiographical recollections of this moment exaggerated his prescience only slightly. From the very start his biggest fear was "that we shall oscilate like a Pendelum and fluctuate like the Ocean and . . . be trimming" rather than "bring the Question to a compleat Decision." In part because he was from Massachusetts, which was the first colony to bear the brunt of British commercial restrictions and martial law, and in part because of his accurate reading of British intentions, he had little faith in compromise. As he put it in 1775, "I am as fond of Reconciliation . . . as any Man . . . [but] the Cancer is too deeply rooted, and too far spread to be cured by any thing short of cutting it out entirely . . ."[25]

This meant that, as events unfolded over the ensuing three years, Adams came to seem more and more like the radical prophet whose predictions kept coming true. "We are waiting. . . for a Mes-siah that will never come," he lamented to Abigail just before the outbreak of hostilities at Bunker Hill. The persistent hope that rec-onciliation was still possible would prove futile, Adams insisted: "as Arrant an Illusion as ever was hatched in the Brain of an Enthusiast, a Politician, or a Maniac. I have laugh'd at it—scolded at it—griev'd at it—and I dont know but I may at an unguarded

Moment have rip'd [ripped] at it—but it is vain to Reason against such Delusions." In the current political situation, he told Horatio Gates, just appointed a major general in the Continental Army, "the Middle Way is none at all," adding that "if We finally fail in this great and glorious Contest, it will be by bewildering ourselves in groping after this middle Way. . . ." To those fellow delegates who argued that war with the mightiest military power on earth was suicidal, he replied with an aphorism: during the Reformation, he said, the Catholics had the Pope, as well as kings and emperors, on their side, and "those poor Devils the Protestants, they had nothing on their side but God Almighty."[26]

Each time the crisis escalated to a new level of intensity, Adams already occupied the ground most of the other delegates were still scrambling to reach. He had thought through the relevant constitutional arguments and political strategies and was poised to draft the official resolution. Thus in October of 1774 he became the author of the Declaration of Rights and Grievances, the main business of the First Continental Congress. The following winter and spring he published the *Novanglus* essays, a self-conscious display of learning and legalistic reasoning in support of the constitutional position taken by the Congress and effectively denying Parliament's authority over the colonies. *Novanglus* not only served to make the radical repudiation of Parliament seem respectable and in keeping with the deepest traditions of English common law, it also gave national exposure to Adams's emerging leadership role in the Congress.[27]

During the spring and summer of 1775, in the aftermath of Lexington and Concord, he became the major proponent for the creation of new governments and constitutions for each colony.

In his autobiography he recalled that "almost every day, I had something to say about Advizing the States to institute Governments . . . ," claiming that he had "in my head and at my Tongues End, as many Projects of Government as Mr. Burke says the Abby Seieyes [Sieyès] had in his Pidgeon holes." By then he was also serving on over thirty committees in the Congress and was besieged with requests from fellow members for advice about the drafting of their respective state constitutions. In response to these requests he published *Thoughts on Government* in the spring of 1776, which advocated republican governments for all the states, along with a plea for a bicameral legislature and an independent judiciary. His reputation as the leading advocate of independence and the premier political thinker in the Congress had become so widespread that several delegates mistakenly presumed he was the author of Thomas Paine's *Common Sense*.[28]

It was therefore natural that he was chosen to chair the committee charged with drafting the Declaration of Independence and that he delivered the major speech in behalf of its passage. "You have all the Topicks so ready," he remembered the delegates telling him, even though he claimed to prefer that "someone less obnoxious than myself . . . [who] was . . . believed to be the Author of all the Mischief" should have the honor. He was also the obvious choice to draft the Plan of Treaties in July 1776, the document which established the framework for a treaty with France—Adams had been arguing for over a year that such a treaty was essential for American success in the war with England—and which, almost incidentally, laid down the strategic priorities that would shape American foreign policy for over a century.[29]

Finally, he was the unanimous choice to head the newly

established Board of War and Ordnance, which made him, in effect, a one-man war department responsible for raising, equipping, and assuring civilian control over the entire American military. In this capacity he worked eighteen-hour days for over a year. His mastery of detail was awesome, insisting on grooved muskets because of their superior accuracy, badgering the Harvard faculty to find new ways to produce gunpowder, demanding that the entire army be inoculated, warning recalcitrant generals that he favored "Shooting all [officers] who will not [lead] and getting a new set," and (or so he claimed later) reading "as much on the military Art and much more on the History of War than any other American officer... General [Richard] Lee excepted." Along the way he predicted, to the year, how long the war would last, held tenaciously to the strategic assumption that the British army could win battles but could not win the war, and promoted the creation of the infant American navy. Little wonder, as one of the delegates put it in 1777, that it was "the opinion of every man in the house ... that he [Adams] possesses the clearest head and firmest heart of any man in the Congress." His own reputation and the American Revolution had erupted onto the world simultaneously.[30]

As with most eruptions, however, there was a significant amount of collateral damage. It was inevitable that Adams would make enemies. He was surging onto the national scene with strong political opinions; he must have proved infuriating to the more moderate delegates, especially when his views so often proved correct. In later years Adams liked to recall these political collisions, attributing them to personal jealousy and sometimes making far-fetched connections with his subsequent political enemies. The High Federalists who opposed him during his presidency, for example, he claimed were the same men, or the successors of the same men, whom he had dragged, kicking and screaming, into the American Revolution and who had never forgiven him for such treatment.[31]

But the human wreckage Adams created went far beyond what one might expect from the inevitable petty jealousies. And his latter-day version of a long-lingering vendetta against him is itself a symptom of the deeper problem. Put simply, Adams showed himself in the Continental Congress to be an intensely sensitive and thin-skinned public figure. On the one hand, that meant that he often took criticism as a personal affront. His diary and letters are full of speculations on the jealousy he aroused in other delegates, even elevating his own hostile reaction to the level of a philosophical principle: "Resentment is a Passion, implanted by Nature for the Preservation of the Individual. Injury is the Object which excites it. . . . A Man may have the Faculty of concealing his Resentment, or Suppressing it, but he must and ought to feel it. Nay he ought to indulge it, and to cultivate it. It is a Duty." He seemed to believe not only that it was unnecessary to suffer fools gladly, but also to tell them to their faces that they were fools. It was not the kind of personal philosophy calculated to win over the faint of heart.[32]

On the other hand, his personal intensity also meant that he frequently accused those who disagreed with him of being motivated by selfish, personal prejudices. A typical entry in the Adams diary contrasted his own disinterested aims with those motivated by "private Friendships and Enmities, and Provincial Views and Prejudices," which he regarded as "degrees of Corruption" and "Deviations from the public Interest, and from Rectitude." The most celebrated scandal in the Continental Congress occurred when several of Adams's private letters were intercepted by the British, including a letter that described John Dickinson, the leading moderate and advocate of reconciliation, as a man of "great Fortune and piddling Genius whose Fame has been trumpeted so loudly, [but who] has given a silly Cast to our whole doings." The immediate consequence was an icy relationship between Adams and Dickinson, whose opposition to the radical Adams agenda was clearly based on honest political differences. Adams later claimed that the exposure of his correspondence had the more lasting consequence of publicizing the presence of an independence faction in the Continental Congress and stimulating public discussion of that radical possibility as early as 1775. Perhaps so, but the most obvious effect of the Dickinson episode, at least for our purposes, was to illustrate the Adams penchant for personal animosity.[33]

Some of the more unattractive traits identified by Hamilton in the infamous open letter of 1800—Adams's alleged irritability and reputation for being difficult—seem to have a basis in the record during the Continental Congress. Adams as much as admitted the existence of a problem in two private letters written at the moment of his triumph during the summer of 1776: "Besides if I were to tell you all that I think of all Characters [in Congress], I should appear so illnatured and censorious that I should detest myself," he wrote to Samuel Chase. "By my Soul, I think very heinously, I can't think of a better Word, of some People. They think as badly of me, I suppose, and neither of us care a farthing for that." Similarly, he wrote to James Warren, vowing that he would "not write Strictures upon Characters. I set all Mankind a Swearing, if I do. . . . I make the Faces of my best Friends a mile long, if I do." He seemed as dedicated to the task of making enemies as he was to promoting American independence.[34]

The primal source of this syndrome lay buried deep in the folds of the Adams psyche, beyond the reach or view of orthodox historical analysis. What is accessible and readily discernible is a clear pattern of behavior. During his service in the Continental Congress, as during his presidency, Adams began with a clear sense of the direction in which the country needed to go, clung to it tenaciously, and had his vision vindicated by events. In both instances he alienated a large number of his peers; in the 1790s much of the blame for his isolation can be attributed to the disloyalty of his own cabinet, the behind-the-scenes plotting of Hamilton and the High Federalists, and the unforeseen emergence of two distinct political parties; in the 1770s some of the blame for the deep animosities that developed can be attributed to the radical implications of the political doctrines he was urging, the understandable reluctance of moderate delegates to move as far or as fast toward American independence, the unavoidable conflict, if you will, between the requirements of his leadership role and the customary civilities. Yet it was all so *personal*. Although his hostility toward Hamilton exceeded his ill-will toward Dickinson, in both cases he focused his fire on one person who symbolized the opposition. And finally, as a member of the Continental Congress and as president, he embraced a version of virtue that went beyond any mere ideological conviction based on reading in classical or modern texts; for Adams, virtue demanded a level of disinterestedness and a purity of public spiritedness that derived its compulsion from psychological imperative which seemed to *require* isolation and unpopularity as evidence of its authenticity.

The ultimate source of this syndrome is unclear, but it seems to have been triggered by Adams's fear of success. In 1777, while complaining to Abigail about the in-fighting between military officers who were, as he put it, "Scrambling for Rank and Pay like Apes for Nuts," Adams for the first time articulated in full form what was to become a central tenet of his mature political thought:

> I believe there is no one Principle, which predominates in human Nature so much in every Stage of Life, from the Cradle to the Grave, in Males and females, old and young, black and white, rich and poor, high and low, as this Passion for Superiority. . . . Every human Being compares itself in its own Imagination, with every other round about it, and will find some Superiority over every other . . . or it will die of Grief and Vexation.[35]

His own compulsion to excel in the Continental Congress, and to be acknowledged as having done so by the other delegates who were also vying for recognition, was, in this view, an inherent, irresistible human urge. Adams was uncomfortably aware of his ambition, and claimed that to deny its presence and power was to engage in self-delusion. Here was one source of his public relations problem: what others so often saw as arrogance and vanity was, in Adams's view, simply a case of candor; or, to put it somewhat differently, Adams could not imagine how he appeared to others who did not share his own realistic estimate of human nature or his own habit of honest introspection. Why should he not speak to *them* with the same kind of brutal honesty that he practiced on *himself*?

But if he could acknowledge ambition, he could not quite tolerate success. In the spring of 1776, as his own reputation and American independence ascended together, he confessed to Abigail the pride he felt in influencing "the great Events which are passed, and those greater which are rapidly advancing. . . ." Three weeks later he announced to his wife that he had "purchased a Folio Book . . . and intend to write all my Letters to you in it from this Time forward." He would copy his private correspondence in what amounted to a personal declaration of his own historical significance.[36]

Whatever satisfaction and sense of fulfillment Adams derived from his success, however, was more than offset by his self-doubt; not about his contribution to the American cause—he was supremely confident about that—but about his capacity to survive success. Men, like nations, advanced toward greatness, reached the apogee of their ascent, then spiralled downwards into decadence and sloth, corrupted by the very affluence and pride that was the reward for their success. England was the prime example of this familiar cycle among nations. And his diagnosis of corruption within English society and politics was central to Adams's advocacy of American independence. He was profoundly conscious of repeating on a microscopic scale the same pattern England had traced at the macroscopic level. He distrusted his own popularity for much the same reason he recommended that governments establish checks against the unrestrained democratic impulses of a single-house legislature; namely, there were powerful passions deep in the individual soul and in the people-at-large that required restraint. What struck some of his colleagues as irritability was actually a by-product of the internal struggle with his own vanity and ambition, the nervous energy generated by the incessant operation of his own internal checks and balances.

All of which helps to illuminate the sources for Adams's personal intensity as they developed with full force in the 1770s: he thought about politics and the entire world "out there" in terms of forces he felt throbbing inside himself. Virtually all of his political convictions, especially his most piercing political insights, derived from introspection, or what we would call psychology. Just as James Madison established a reputation as "Father of the Constitution" because of his leading role in the Constitutional Convention in 1787, Adams established his reputation as the premier political theorist of the American Revolution because of his leadership in the Continental Congress. But if Madison is the master sociologist of American political theory, Adams is the master psychologist. Virtue was not an abstract concept he learned about simply by reading Montesquieu, David Hume, or the writers of the English Commonwealth tradition. It was a principle of self-denial he harbored in his heart and kept preaching to himself in his diary. A state constitution was not just an agreed-upon framework of social customs and laws. It was a public replica of one's internal order or constitution. The very idea of government itself was the act of implementing in the world the lessons learned in dealing with one's own internal demons.

The reason why Adams seemed to take the making of American policy in the 1770s super-seriously is obvious: he realized before most others that the future of a nation was at stake. Even that realization, however, was at least partially indebted to the overlap between America's fate and his own ascent. And the reason he seemed to take public decisions so personally emerged out of the same overlapping habit: his political commitments were, quite literally, projections onto the world of his own layered and paradoxical personality. He was the kind of man, as his critics put it, who could unfailingly mistake a prejudice for a conviction, but it was all part of a larger confusion in the Adams mind between private and public affairs, which kept intersecting and interacting in patterns that defied neat separation.

IF HIS BEHAVIOR in the Continental Congress affords the best glimpse at Adams as he emerged as a national figure, he was less fully formed twenty years earlier. The pieces of the Adams puzzle had yet to align themselves in any discernible pattern in the fall of 1755, when he was still a young man grappling with his purpose in life. He had just graduated from Harvard the previous summer, was unsure whether he should pursue a career in the ministry or the law, and needed time to mull over his prospects. An offer from the minister at Worcester, about forty miles west of Boston, promised to provide a small salary and a large space in which to ruminate in return for his services as a schoolmaster. During the three years he remained in Worcester Adams read much, brooded even more and, most importantly for our purposes, began to keep a diary in which he recorded a good deal more than the weather. In that rather remarkable diary, one can already discern if only dimly the paunchy, balding, toothless patriarch and president sitting in the semi-darkness of the presidential mansion nearly a half century later. If the origins and sources of his complex character left any traces in the historical record, this is surely the place to look for them.[37]

The Adams diary begins, quite literally, with a jolt: "We had a severe Shock of an Earthquake," he noted, describing the considerable damage done to New England houses and chimneys by the seismic movements that, unbeknown to the young Adams, had virtually levelled the city of Lisbon on the other side of the Atlantic. The seismic shiftings occurring inside Adams himself at the time were less visible but just as disconcerting. A half century earlier the question over which he was anguishing would have had a decidedly religious cast: Am I saved or damned? By the middle of the eighteenth century the form of the question had changed, although the underlying psychological forces set in motion in the rite of passage to adulthood were still saturated with moral and religious meanings that had not lost their power. For Adams, the questions he was posing to himself were more recognizably modern: what should I do with my life? what is my proper calling? who am I? But his way of answering them remained indebted to Puritan traditions as old as New England and as compelling for young Adams as an earthquake.[38]

In one sense, the essential Adams qualities were already visible in 1755, eminently discernible once one knows what to look for. The eerily accurate sense of what was in store for America, which gave Adams such a headstart over his colleagues in the Continental Congress and then shaped his policy toward France as president, had already assumed articulate form. In a letter to Nathan Webb, a longtime friend and distant relative, Adams first sketched out his vision of an expanding American empire. "If we look into History we shall find some nations rising from contemptible beginnings, and spreading their influence, 'till the whole Globe is subjected to their sway," he wrote in October of 1755. Rome was obviously the illustrative example for the ancient world. And England was clearly the heir to Rome's greatness in the modern world. But history demonstrated that whenever great nations reach "the summit of Grandeur, some minute and unsuspected Cause commonly effects their Ruin, and the Empire of the world is transferr'd to some other place." Just what the "unsuspected Cause" that would unseat England might be, Adams could not say for sure. The growing population of North America, however, which "in another century [will] become more numerous than England itself," suggested the time would eventually be ripe for transferring "the great seat of Empire into America," a development, Adams predicted, that "looks likely to me." Much later, during his retirement years, when Adams was given a copy of this youthful letter, he showed it to friends and made it available for publication, joking that he had forgotten how prophetic he had once been. Strictly speaking, his early prediction of an independent America did *not* foresee a violent rupture with England, but rather a gradual evolution (*à la* Canada) rather than a revolution. But the young man did have an instinct for the flow of history.[39]

The famous, or perhaps infamous, Adams ambition was also fully present. The job of schoolmaster, he needed to assure his friends, was a mere way station; he was not about to romanticize the life of the classroom, which struck him as "a school of affliction, [with] a large number of little runtlings, just capable of lisping A.B.C. and troubling the Master." Uplifting talk to his diary about "Cultivating and pruning these tender Plants in the garden of Worcester" never lasted long. The realistic truth was that "keeping this school any length of Time would make a base weed and ignoble shrub of me." If the ultimate destination of his already quite palpable ambitions was not yet clear, it surely lay beyond the provincial world of Worcester, perhaps along the ascending slope that America seemed fated to travel.[40]

What proved to be a life-long internal dialogue with those ambitions had also begun by this time. Which is to say that he was already painfully aware of the passions that were to bedevil him throughout his long life. "Vanity I am sensible, is my cardinal Vice and cardinal Folly," he lectured himself, "and I am in continual Danger, when in Company, of being led an ignis fatuus Chase by it, without the strictest Caution and watchfulness over my self." He must be more careful and restrained in groups, he kept reminding himself, so that his conversation did not betray his sense of superiority. "A puffy, vain, conceited Conversation, never fails to bring a Man into Contempt," he told his diary, "altho his natural Endowments be ever so great, and his Application and Industry ever so intense." He must rein in his congenital pugnacity, his urge "to shew my own Importance or Superiority, by remarking the Foibles, Vices, or Inferiority of others," which only alienated the very people he wished to impress. In general, he must lash down his passions: "Untamed they are lawless Bulls," he wrote to himself, "they roar and bluster, defy all Controul, and some times murder their proper owner." Too often, however, his imagination would form an alliance with his ambition, easily snapping all ties and overwhelming all injunctions. For example, in March of 1756, he recorded this daydream about his little schoolroom as a model "of the great World in miniature":

I have severall renowned Generalls but 3 feet high, and several deep-projecting Politicians in peticoats. I have others . . . accumulating remarkable pebbles, cockle shells &c.,

with as ardent Curiousity as any Virtuouso in the royal society. Some rattle and Thunder out A, B, C, with as much Fire and impetuosity, as Alexander fought. . . . At one Table sits Mr. Insipid foppling and fluttering, spinning his whirligig, or playing with his fingers as gaily and wittily as any frenchified coxcomb brandishes his Cane or rattles his snuff box. At another sits the polemical Divine, plodding and wrangling in his mind about Adams fall in which we sinned all as his primer has it. In short my little school like the great World, is made up of Kings, Politicians, Divines, L.D. [LL.D's?], Fops, Buffoons, Fidlers, Sychophants, Fools, Coxcombs, chimney sweepers, and every other Character drawn in History or seen in the World.

Over this human menagerie, Adams confessed in mocking tones that "in my sprightly moments, [I] consider myself, in my great Chair at School, as some Dictator at the head of a commonwealth," a sort of Cromwell of the kindergarten.[41]

Finally, it was evident very early during his time at Worcester, long before he made the decision explicit, that Adams was destined to reject a career in the ministry in favor of the law. His earliest diary entries reflect his distaste for the endless, and to him futile, theological disputations, his impatience with what he called "the whole Cartloads of other trumpery, that we find Religion incumbered with in these Days." He confided to himself that the deepest design of Christianity "was not to make men good Riddle Solvers or good mystery mongers"; but that was what the clergy of the day seemed to prefer, with their "Ecclesiastical Synods, Convocations, Councils, Decrees, Creeds, Confessions, Oaths, [and]

Subscriptions. . . ." Some of his own private opinions, scribbled into the margins of his new diary booklet, suggested an impatience with religious wrangling that verged on sacrilege. After listening to an argument in behalf of the divinity of Jesus Christ that concluded with the unknowability of it all, Adams jotted down his own conclusion: "Thus Mystery is made a convenient Cover for absurdity." These were not the kind of private thoughts likely to lead toward a flourishing clerical career.[42]

Despite the deeper disinclinations, Adams felt an obligation to keep open the possibility of a ministerial calling, in part because his parents seemed to prefer that course, in part because the ministry represented, in its clearest and purest form, a commitment to the virtuous life. "The Man who lives wholly to himself is of less worth than the Cattle in his Barn," he wrote to Charles Cushing, a college friend who was also facing the same questions about career. The right choice, he told Cushing and himself, would reveal itself through incessant introspection and would probably defy popular opinion: "But upon the Stage of Life, while Conscience Clapps, let the World hiss! On the contrary if Conscience disapproves, the loudest applauses of the World are of little Value." Even at this early age, Adams was predisposed to cast his choices into categories that juxtaposed what was popular with what was right. The distinguishing mark of the proper calling, he assured Cushing, was its social utility, its tendency to require "service to our fellow men, as well as to ourselves." All callings have their advantages and disadvantages, but the chief problem with the lawyer was that "he often foments more quarrells than he composes, and inriches himself at the expense of impoverishing others more honest and deserving than himself."[43]

Less than six months later, however, Adams declared in his diary, albeit a bit defensively, his decision to study the law. "Necessity drove me to this Determination," he explained, claiming that the ministry might have been his preference, but that his "Opinion concerning some disputed Points" of theology essentially disqualified him. Nevertheless, he would make himself the *right* kind of lawyer: "I set out with firm Resolutions I think never to commit any meanness or injustice in the Practice of Law." In fact, he resolved to bring to his legal career the same other-worldly qualities that were associated with the ministry: "The study and Practice of Law," he reminded himself, "I am sure does not dissolve the obligations of morality or of Religion."[44]

Here, at last, we begin to catch a central feature in the Adams character just as it was congealing. Put most simply and succinctly, he carried with him into the secular calling of lawyer and later public official the moral obligations and self-imposed expectations of the New England ministry. And his conscious self-doubt—probably too his less conscious guilt—about the path he had chosen encouraged him to make any conflict between personal and public interests into a test of his moral sincerity. Indeed, he sought out such tests, actively pursuing opportunities to demonstrate to himself the purity of his own motives and the depth of his own virtue. He was driven by insecurity and self-doubt, not in the sense of doubting his talent or intelligence, but in the sense of requiring incessant assurance that what he knew to be his considerable gifts would be given to a cause larger than himself. Those powerful passions for worldly success and fame were, in the end, fuelled by a compulsion to serve an otherworldly ideal that truly dominated his soul.

Once he departed Worcester in 1758, then, he was like a cannon ball streaking toward the center of American history, aimed at the enemies to his own and America's advancement and destined to destroy his own prospects for popularity upon impact. Which is to say that his behavior in the Continental Congress and the presidency followed naturally, if not inevitably, from his internalization of spiritual standards of conduct that defied worldly measures of success. "If Virtue was to be rewarded with Wealth, it would not be Virtue," he would later explain to Abigail, and if "Virtue was to be rewarded with Fame, it would not be Virtue of the sublimest Kind." Such was the impossible standard he imposed on himself as a young man, and later, in ways he came to regret, imposed on his son John Quincy.[45]

Finally, the process by which Adams reached a decision about his calling reveals more about the primal dynamics of his character than does the decision itself. More than any other prominent American of the revolutionary generation, Adams brought the private energies generated by a truly searching self-scrutiny into the public arena. Unlike Benjamin Franklin's similar-sounding injunctions—work hard, conquer pride, rise early, resist temptations—Adams's introspections remained true to the original intent of reformed Christianity. That is, Adams was obsessed with interior integrity, not with the external rewards that the mastery of appearances could bring. Humility, piety, self-denial, and other habits of the heart were not just means to an end for him, but the ends themselves. The Worcester phase of his development was the New England equivalent to the early Christian retreat to the desert, where worldly ways could be purged and the soul forged into the kind of hard and sharp implement required to do God's

work. Within the Puritan tradition of New England, the process
was similar, though the language to describe it spoke of a "time of
atonement" and the "doctrine of preparation." Like the Puritans
of old, Adams was obliged to confront his own sinfulness—his
vanities, ambitions, jealousies—and to acknowledge at the deepest
level that these powerful forces could never be destroyed or conquered; at best they could be controlled; they were profane drives
that might be harnessed to sacred causes in the world. And like the
devout Puritan who could never be sure he was saved, lest his very
assurance reveal a sense of pride that sabotaged the whole effort at
saintliness, Adams's compulsions were inherently insatiable.[46]

He could never rest until he found a worthy cause in which
to spend himself; preferably a cause sufficiently large to allow the
ferocity of his ambition and the fury of his nearly limitless reservoir
of pent-up energy to work in the world. It would also be helpful
if the cause made some contribution to the providential advancement of America toward its destiny; the cause would be even more
attractive if it had enemies whose vanity and self-aggrandizement
allowed him to eviscerate in public those very qualities that he
battled inside himself. And the picture would be complete if the
cause required leadership that defied conventional methods and
popular opinion, thereby demanding independence of style as well
as judgment, disdain for worldly measures of success, an attraction
to adversity, an urge, indeed a determination, to stand alone.

ALONE HE WAS on the early morning of March 4, 1801, preparing to leave the presidential mansion. He had travelled a course
that fit his youthful prescriptions more or less perfectly and arrived

at the destination he claimed to foresee. If his thoughts did wander back over that long course from Worcester to Washington before the stage arrived at four o'clock, no trace has remained in the surviving record. We do know that Theodore Sedgwick, the former Speaker of the House and High Federalist leader—he regarded Adams as deranged—was also on the stage. But what they said, or refrained from saying, to each other has also been lost to posterity.

We do know that it took Adams two weeks to reach Quincy, as he put it, "having trotted the bogs five hundred miles." His first recorded observation after settling in was characteristically indiscreet: "I found about a hundred loads of sea weed in my barnyard," he noted. "I thought I had made a good exchange . . . of honors and virtues for manure." (This was not necessarily a sign of bitterness. As the most knowledgeable scholar of the Adams correspondence reminds us, throughout his life "John Adams had an irrepressible habit of comparing his own manure piles with others' and boasting of the superiority of his own.") On the day of his arrival "a violent equinoctial gale of wind" struck Quincy, which prompted the first cosmic speculation from the retired statesman: "This is so old fashioned a storm," he reported, "that I begin to hope that nature is returning to her old good-nature and good-humor, and is substituting fermentations in the elements for revolutions in the moral, intellectual and political world." The calm after the storm inspired him to write a supportive note to Jefferson, perhaps as a way of indicating that the turbulence inside his own soul had also subsided: "This part of the union is in a state of perfect tranquility," he assured his successor, "and I see nothing to obscure your prospect of a quiet & prosperous administration, which I heartily wish you."[47]

Typically, he had been telling friends contradictory stories about his retirement plans, both of which were undoubtedly honest expressions of his different moods. The dominant line fit the classical model of the serene patriarch who divided his time between work in the fields and reading. "Far removed from all the intrigues," he explained, "and now out of reach of all the great and little passions that agitate the world . . . I hope to enjoy more tranquillity than has ever before been my lot." On the other hand, as he confessed to other friends, there was such a thing as too much peace and quiet. For so many years he had kept up a fast pace: "When such long continued and violent exercise, such frequent agitations of the body, are succeeded by stillness, it may shake an old frame." With physical as with political constitutions, gradual change was best: "Rapid motion ought not to be succeeded by sudden rest."[48]

Barely a month after his declaration of pastoral serenity he was wondering if he might resume his long-interrupted career as a lawyer. "There I should forget in a moment that I was ever member of Congress, or foreign minister, or President of the United States." What stood in his way, however, was not a lack of energy or a distaste for the active life, but a lack of teeth. When he rose to address the judge or jury, he worried that he would mumble and slur his words. A toothless mouth meant that "I cannot speak." Law was out.[49]

That left his fields and books to occupy him for what the sixty-six-year-old ex-president presumed was the little time that remained. Abigail spied him working with the haymakers one day in July, talking to himself as he swung the scythe. She mused about the vagaries of nature: "I regret that a fortnight of sharp draught has shorn away many of the beauties we had in rich luxuriance. The verdure of the grass has become a brown, the flowers hang their heads, droop, and fade . . . yet we still have a pure air." And John Adams still had a full quarter century of life before him.[50]

A view of Peacefield, or Montezillo, the Adams family homestead at Quincy.
Artist unknown. *Library of Congress*

CHAPTER TWO

History and Heroes

> Mausoleums, statues, monuments will never be
> erected to me. I wish them not. Panegyrical romances
> will never be written, nor flattering orations spoken,
> to transmit me to posterity in brilliant colors. No,
> nor in true colors. All but the last I loathe.
> —Adams to Benjamin Rush, March 23, 1809

> When I was running the gauntlet [as a public figure] I
> refused to suffer in silence. I sighed, sobbed, & groaned,
> and sometimes screeched and screamed. And I must
> confess to my shame and sorrow, that I sometimes swore.
> —Adams to Harrison Gray Otis, March 29, 1823

FOR THE FIRST TWELVE YEARS of his long retirement, Adams twitched in and out of his preferred posture of pastoral serenity. But when he allowed the old urges to escape, they took the form of an outright obsession with the vicissitudes of recent American history and a private crusade over his proper place in it. "How is it," he asked Benjamin Rush, now his closest confidant outside the family, "that I, poor, ignorant I, must stand before Posterity as differing from all the other great Men of the Age?" He then went on to list his gallery of "greats"—Joseph Priestley, Benjamin Franklin, Edmund Burke, Thomas Jefferson, James Madison— and concluded that, even when his own name was admitted onto the list, it was often accompanied by the judgment that Adams was "the most vain, conceited, impudent, arrogant Creature in the World."[1]

In Virginia, where, as Adams observed, "all Geese are Swans," the great heroes of the Revolution all had magnificent estates. Jefferson had Monticello; Washington had Mount Vernon; Madison had Montpelier. "Every one of these gentlemen had noble sentiments," he acknowledged; and the nobility of their sentiments were nicely embodied in the splendor of their surroundings. But then there was John Adams, who harbored, as he put it, "the childish vanity to think that in some lucid intervals in my life, I have had some generous sentiments." Yet he had retired to Peacefield, his modest country home in Quincy that seemed to symbolize his impoverished reputation, a dwelling that one French visitor described as "a small house which a sixth-rate Paris lawyer would disdain to choose for his summer home."[2]

Typically, Adams turned the painful realization that his comfortable but humble home was an accurate reflection of his tattered reputation into a joke. "You may call me," he told his younger son, "the monarch of Stoney Field, Count of Gull Island, Earl of Mount Arrarat, Marquis of Candlewood Hill, and Baron of Rocky Run." As the letters began to pour out from Quincy, he soon listed his location with a variety of comical and cynical titles, beginning with "Mount Wollaston" and fastening at last on

"Montezillo" as his favorite. "Montezillo," he explained, "is a little Hill." Jefferson's reputation required a grander title: "Monticello is a lofty Mountain."[3]

He could also joke when he thought that sycophants and fawning admirers were stroking his vanity without really understanding what he had accomplished during his public career. "It is become fashionable to call me 'The Venerable,'" he observed disapprovingly. "It makes me think of the venerable Bede . . . or the venerable Savannarola. . . ." The title smacked of excessive reverence and religiosity to Adams. He knew it was applied to such patriots as Washington, Jefferson, or Franklin. But he did not wish it applied to John Adams. He also, again part in jest and part in pain, swore solemn repudiation of any effort to coat him with a veneer of sanctity: "Don't call me 'Godlike Adams,' 'The Father of His Country,' 'The Founder of the American Republic,' or 'The Founder of the American Empire.' These titles belong to no man, but to the American people in general."[4]

But if laughter and mockery provided his best defense, he could not deny that his abiding preoccupation, indeed obsession, was with the judgment of posterity. Both the laughter and the preoccupation were on display in a story he liked to tell about the American artist John Singleton Copley. It seemed that Copley was painting the portrait of Lord Mansfield in London when Mansfield told him that he was not as famous as his talent justified because he had no "puffers." To his beloved Rush, Adams confided, semi-seriously, that "these puffers, Rush, are the only killers of Scandal. Washington and Franklin killed off scandal by Puffers. You and I never employed them and therefore scandal has prevailed against us."

This was a typical exchange with Rush, who became Adams's chief outlet outside the family. When they first met in 1774, Adams had thought the Philadelphia physician and political gadfly was a bit too talkative and eccentric in his opinions. But in the ensuing years, Rush's gregariousness had become beguiling and his mad-hatter approach to letterwriting had made him into Adams's alter ego at the writing desk, an intimate who could be trusted to respond in kind to Adams's most idiosyncratic and lovably outrageous notions. While the correspondence he eventually established with Jefferson is more stately and justifiably famous, the letters to Rush are the most revealing, the most relaxed and candid he ever wrote. Like two poker players who kept calling and raising each other in a game of high-stakes honesty, Adams and Rush turned the painful episodes that tortured Adams's memory into self-deprecating jokes about the lunacy of all political life.[5]

His eldest son, John Quincy, sensing the wounded pride that festered beneath the jokes, recommended a more direct approach: he suggested that his father write an autobiography in order to set the record straight and deal directly with his personal demons; that is, John Quincy was encouraging his father to write an autobiography as a form of what we would call therapy. "You have recommended to me, a Work, which instead of increasing my indifference to public affairs, would engage my feelings and enflame my passions," complained father to son: "I wish not to be reminded of my Mortifications, Disappointments or Resentments. As to my good deeds . . . I shall never be rewarded, nor will they ever be acknowledged upon Earth." But, in typical Adams self-contradiction, when he wrote these words in 1804, he had already been working for two years on the very autobiography that his son suggested and that he honestly claimed to disdain.[6]

Lurking in the recesses of Adams's mind was a sophisticated understanding of how the American Revolution had happened and why the new nation, unlike France after its revolution, had been able to consolidate its revolutionary energies by means of stable political institutions and constitutions. It was a story he was eminently qualified to tell. In fact, Adams's understanding of the revolutionary era foreshadowed many of the major scholarly interpretations proposed by modern historians in the twentieth century. But lurking in his heart was a frantic and uncontrollable craving for personal vindication, a lust for fame that was so obsessive, and so poisoned by his accurate awareness that history would not do him justice, that he often appeared less like a worthy member of the American gallery of greats than a beleaguered and pathetic madman.

For twelve years, from his retirement at the Adams homestead in 1801 to the resumption of his friendship with Jefferson in 1812, Adams's heart and his obsession with personal vindication were in ascendance. "If I were to go over my Life again," he declared in this moody phase, "I would be a Shoemaker rather than an American Statesman." The autobiography, begun in October of 1802 and then composed in fits and starts until he stopped, literally in mid-sentence, in 1807, was a series of vituperative salvos at his enemies. But the barrage of invective never really lifted, because in the summer of 1807 he began an extensive correspondence with Mercy Otis Warren concerning her three-volume *History of the American Revolution*. No sooner had this embarrassing exhibition of wounded pride run its course than

Adams launched an apparently interminable attack in defense of his actions as diplomat and president in the pages of the *Boston Patriot*. This series ran for three years and several hundred thousand words. Adams admitted that, in deciding to publish his views in the newspapers, he had committed himself to a war of attrition in a losing cause: "I shall be so tedious," he wrote Rush, "that I shall have neither Readers nor Printers. I dare say that as much as you love me you have not read, and it would be impossible you should read all that I have published, much less all that I shall publish. . . ."[7]

All these angry words and embattled arguments about American history and his role in its making—the fragmented autobiographical essay, the petulant exchange with Mercy Otis Warren, and the pedantic series of articles in the *Boston Patriot*—showed Adams at his worst. If he had chosen to suffer in silence, to imitate what he called "the eternal Taciturnity of Washington and Franklin," his reputation would surely have recovered some semblance of its one-time lustre.[8] But silence was not in him. He needed to exorcise demons, do just the kind of painfully difficult therapy that John Quincy had misguidedly recommended. He needed to settle scores, expend himself in a worthy, if hopeless, cause.

ADAMS'S AUTOBIOGRAPHY BEGAN on a typically self-defeating note: "As the lives of Phylosophers, Statesmen or Historians written by themselves have generally been suspected of vanity, and therefore few People have been able to read them without disgust; there is no reason to expect that any sketches I may leave of my own Times would be received by the Public with any favour, or read by individuals with much interest." He claimed to be writing, not for the public but for posterity, and "for my Children."[9]

He was really writing for himself. As Peter Shaw, Adams's most insightful biographer, has so nicely observed, the Adams effort at autobiography contrasts almost perfectly with Benjamin Franklin's classical account of his own life. Both men began their careers as poor New England colonists. By dint of hard work and personal investment in a successful revolutionary cause, they rose to national and even international prominence. But Franklin managed his autobiography with the same cunning, guile, and self-control that he managed his life. The result was an artfully conceived success story in which both the subject and the author conceal from the reader the deepest sources of motivation. The emotional seams, cracks, fissures, and failures are hidden beneath a façade of psychological artifices, which are in turn hidden beneath a variety of effectively playful literary masks.[10]

Adams's autobiography, on the other hand, was less like a well-crafted work of literature than an open wound, a text that requires no "deconstructing" because it was never "constructed" in the first place. Like Adams's life, it was impulsive, exuberant, and candid. And its theme, as well as its form, was the exact opposite of Franklin's. It was about self-doubt and failure rather than self-fulfillment and success, about the ironic ravages of history rather than the triumph of the individual. When Adams eventually read Franklin's autobiography in 1818, he admitted defeat: "My own appears, upon retrospection, a dull dreary unfruitful Waste." But then defeat and failure in the face of American popular opinion had always been his dominant message. In that sense, Adams's autobiography was a clumsy model for his great-grandson's masterpiece, *The Education of Henry Adams,* as well as an anguished expression of the dark and hidden underside of Franklin's beguilingly happy narrative.[11]

Villains and intrigues had always played a crucial role in Adams's thinking about the American Revolution, although it was usually British leaders like Lord North or American Loyalists like Thomas Hutchinson who bore the brunt of Adams's accusations of conspiracy in the 1760s and 1770s. (As Adams once put it, "Mr. Hutchinson never drank a Cup of Tea in his life without Contemplating the Connection between that Tea, and his Promotion.")[12] Now, in the autobiography, after an opening section that described his early years as a student, grammar school teacher, and country lawyer, he got down to the serious business of eviscerating his enemies on the American side.

Alexander Hamilton—no surprise here—was the chief villain. The fact that Hamilton had only recently died in a duel with Aaron Burr, Adams declared, was no cause for mercy. Adams claimed to feel no obligation "to suffer my Character to lie under infamous Calumnies, because the Author of them, with a Pistol Bullet through his Spinal Marrow, died a Penitent." During the final year of his presidency Adams had periodically terrified the High Federalists and startled the members of his cabinet with outbursts against Hamilton. But he had not seen fit to record his personal feelings toward the unofficial leader of the Federalist faithful. And he had adopted a stately pose in the wake of Hamilton's slanderous and scandalous *Letter . . . Concerning the Public Conduct and Character of John Adams. . . .* All the while, however, the suppressed anger had been throbbing away inside him. Now the invective poured out. Hamilton was a "Creole Bolingbroke . . .

Born on a Speck more obscure than Corsica . . . as ambitious as Bonaparte, though less courageous, and, save for me, would have involved us in a foreign war with France & a civil war with ourselves." Writing to his good friend Judge Francis Vanderkemp at the same time, he amplified his accusations: Hamilton was "a bastard brat of a Scotch pedlar," who lived constantly "in a delirium of Ambition" and who "had fixed his Eye on the highest Station in America and . . . hated every man young or old who Stood in his Way." To Rush, he acknowledged that such diatribes against the man regarded as "the Sovereign Pontiff of Federalism" would probably cause "all his Cardinals . . . to excite the whole Church to excommunicate and Anathematize me." But Adams claimed to be unfazed, adding: "It was time for a Protestant Separation." It was the closest he ever came to a direct assertion of what was his de facto desertion of the Federalist Party. If Hamilton was, as his worshippers claimed, the guiding light of Federalism, it was a light that deserved to go out.[13]

Tom Paine ranked second only to Hamilton in Adams's version of the American rogues gallery. Paine, wrote Adams, was "a Disastrous Meteor," "a disgrace to the moral Character and Understanding of the Age." Everyone knew that Benjamin Rush had given him the title for his wildly popular pamphlet, *Common Sense,* and that the arguments about the inevitability of American independence that Paine advanced had, in fact, been circulating throughout the colonies since 1760. In the midst of the accelerating events of early 1776, when *Common Sense* first appeared, Adams's initial reaction had been more generous, though even then he was somewhat wary. Paine's pamphlet, he noted then, contained "a great deal of good sense, delivered in a clear, simple, concise and nervous Style." In fact, it was the electricity and accessibility of the prose that caught his attention, causing Adams to recognize that Paine's message was identical to his own—the American Revolution was both inevitable and natural—but that he himself "could not have written any thing in so manly and striking a style. . . ." What worried him then was Paine's endorsement of a single-house legislature as the prescribed form of government for the new states, a prescription that revealed that "this Writer has a better Hand at pulling down than building." What worried him in his autobiography was the credit Paine had received for his elegant statement of the obvious. Paine was a mere cypher, a nonentity in the Continental Congress. Worse, Paine was "the Satyr of the Age . . . a mongrel between Pigg and Puppy, begotten by a wild Boar on a Butch Wolf." Only if one wished to call the eighteenth century "the Age of Frivolity" could one call it "the Age of Paine."[14]

The verdict on what he called "the American untouchables"—Jefferson, Franklin, and Washington—was decidedly less vitriolic, but sufficiently equivocal to sense Adams's ego throbbing just beneath the surface. All three American greats served as an illustration of the principle "that Eloquence in public Assemblies is not the surest road, to Fame and Preferment, at least unless it be used with great caution, very rarely, and with great Reserve." This was the lesson of "eternal taciturnity" that Adams preached to John Quincy and anyone else who would listen, and it derived from Adams's sure but somewhat neurotic sense that, as "the Atlas of Independence" who made the fierce and ferocious speeches that were needed to assure separation from England in the Continental Congress, he inevitably made lifelong enemies. The rule seemed to be that men who played leading roles in controversies became controversial. Jefferson, on the other hand, "had attended his duty in the House [the Second Continental Congress] but a very small part of the time and when there had never spoken in public." Adams recalled, with a mingled sense of admiration and accusation, that "during the whole Time I sat with him in Congress, I never heard him utter three sentences together."[15]

He acknowledged that Jefferson was a masterful stylist; Adams claimed to have "a great opinion of the Elegance of his pen and none at all of my own." It was for this reason, along with the awareness, as Adams put it, that he himself "had been so obnoxious for my early and constant Zeal in promoting the Measure, and that any draught of mine, would undergo a more severe Scrutiny and Criticism in Congress," that, as chairman of the committee encharged with the task, he chose Jefferson to write the Declaration of Independence. Jefferson, according to this version of history, was no more than an important ornament. Like Paine, he put into words the sentiments and ideas that others—like Adams—had hammered out in combat with lukewarm Whigs and surreptitious Tories in the real but unrecorded conversations within the corridors and subcommittees of Philadelphia. "I admire Bonaparte's expression The Scenery of the Business,'" he wrote Rush. "The scenery has often . . . at least in Public Life, more effect, than the Character." Then he added, more explicitly, "Was there ever a Coup de Theatre, that had so great an effect as Jefferson's Penmanship of the Declaration of Independence?" Adams implied that the real business of fomenting a revolution happened behind closed doors, that propagandistic documents like Paine's *Common Sense* and Jefferson's Declaration of Independence were "a theatrical side show . . . Jefferson ran away with the stage effect . . . and all the glory of it." Even when writing to Jefferson himself years later, he belittled "the importance of these compositions," claiming that they were "like children's play at marbles or push pin. . . . Dress and ornament rather than Body, Soul and Substance."[16]

His jealousy of Jefferson was palpable. It wrankled Adams that his own massive efforts on behalf of American independence were blotted out by a piece of parchment that was conclusive only in the sense that it was culminating. Alongside the not-so-hidden jealousy, however, rested an important matter of substance about the true moment when the American Revolution began and about the relationship between propaganda and political events. In brief, Adams consistently argued that the decisive step toward independence occurred on May 15, 1776, when the Continental Congress adopted his resolution calling for new constitutions in each of the states. In his diary and in letters written at the time, he described this decision as "the Last Step, a compleat Separation from her [England], a total absolute Independence. . . ." This was crucial to Adams's view of what the American Revolution was about, not just because he was the author of the resolution, but also because it meant that American independence was a positive and constructive act, a voluntary choice of self-government and not just a repudiation of British tyranny. In his autobiography he repeated this interpretation of the hallowed events, along the way adding yet another related argument of considerable weight, that the resolution to form state governments had specifically stipulated that each state call a convention to draft the new constitution. "These were new, Strange and terrible Doctrines, for the greatest Part of the Members," he recalled, because the requirement of a constitutional convention both symbolized and actually implemented the principle of popular sovereignty, the doctrine that "the People were the Source of all Authority and [the] Original of all Power." This had all been decided six weeks before Jefferson's lyrical prose declared the same political doctrine to be the basis for an independent America. Like the thunder in an electrical storm, Jefferson's Declaration made much noise, but it was the lightning that did the work. And it had already flashed.[17]

Benjamin Franklin provoked the most quotable (and subsequently quoted) anecdotes in the entire autobiography. Franklin seemed to inspire folksy stories in Adams, to bring out the Franklin in his own personality, if you will. Perhaps the best of the lot, and the most revealing of Adams's envious admiration of the man already regarded as the prototypical American, was the story of Adams and Franklin sleeping together in the same bed.

It was September of 1776, and the two men were travelling through New Jersey for a futile, last-gasp conference with Lord Howe, then commander of the British army in North America. Forced to take accommodations for the night in a small room with a single bed, they broke into amiable argument over the question of whether the window should be open or closed. Franklin favored an open window. "The Doctor then began an harangue, upon Air and Cold and Respiration and Perspiration," Adams recalled, "with which I was so much amused that I soon fell asleep, and left him and his Philosophy together." The story effectively reversed the roles of the two great men, with Franklin the garrulous enthusiast and Adams the self-possessed pragmatist. Adams ended the story with the observation that, according to his sources, Franklin eventually died "a Sacrifice at last . . . to his own Theory; having caught the violent cold, which finally choked him, by sitting hours at a Window, with the cool Air blowing upon him."

At least in the pages of his autobiography, if not in life, Adams emerged triumphant over the most infuriatingly likable figure of the age, a man who seemed to be put on earth to embody the deficiencies in Adams's personality. But vindication was only possible for Adams by exchanging identities with Franklin, clothing himself in Franklin's temperament of controlled self-confidence while making Franklin play out the role of stubborn John Adams, clinging tenaciously to wrongheaded theories that eventually did him in.

Adams's more explicit major message about Franklin, like his rendering of Jefferson, was qualified praise, tinged with a warning to his countrymen against making mere mortals into demigods. Franklin was "a great Genius, a great Wit, a great Humourist and a great Satyrist, and a great Politician. . . ." Throughout his life, Adams professed admiration for Franklin's way with words, acknowledging that "there is Scarce a Scratch of his Pen that is not worth preserving." But the widespread belief that Franklin was also "a great Phylosopher, a great Moralist and a great Statesman," Adams pointedly concluded, "is questionable."[18]

The ultimate "great," of course, transcending mortal appreciation or analysis, was George Washington. In his autobiography, even Adams regarded the reputation of Washington as off-limits. Indeed, there were two subjects—the preservation of slavery in the South and the symbolic significance of Washington—that Adams considered too elemental and too fraught with danger to explore candidly in any writings that might find their way into the public press. Still, in private letters to trusted friends like Rush and Vanderkemp, Adams expressed his unease with the emerging mythology about cherry trees and godlike wisdom. Whenever the celebration of Washington's birthday was reported in the Boston newspapers, Adams cringed, and usually fired off a letter of protest. "The feasts and funerals in honor of Washington," he wrote Rush, "is as corrupt a system as that by which saints were canonized and cardinals, popes, and whole hierarchical systems created."[19]

The Federalists were especially guilty of idolatry, and "have done themselves and their country invaluable injury by making Washington their military, political, religious and even moral Pope, and ascribing everything to him." The Federalists should have known better, for by identifying their party so totally with one person, who now was gone, they had committed political suicide. But the nation suffered too from such single-minded patriotism, because the Revolution should be remembered as a broad-based popular movement with many leaders who played different roles at different moments of the crisis. "It is to offend against eternal justice," Adams complained, "to give to one, as the People do, the Merits of so many." When an aspiring historian asked Adams if Washington's decision to repudiate the offer of king or dictator-for-life after the war did not deserve admiration, Adams replied stiffly that, had Washington accepted the offer, "he would have become the contempt and abhorrence of two thirds of the People of the United Colonies." No individual deserved the lion's share of credit for the American Revolution. It was successful precisely because it had been a collective enterprise.[20]

Adams consistently bemoaned "the pilgramages to Mount Vernon as the new Mecca or Jerusalem." When John Marshall's mammoth biography of Washington appeared in 1807, Adams described it as "a Mausoleum, 100 feet square at the base and 200 feet high," and "as durable as the Washington benevolent Societies." And when a Philadelphia artisan sent him a miniature statue of the great man, Adams claimed that, because of his poor eyesight, he could not "distinguish the features of the figure clearly enough to know, whether it is a fair representation of the hero, not even with the help of a solar microscope." Then he added: "I am always pleased to correct representations of that great man . . . but I totally despise the miserable catch-penny tricks by which he is represented in situations where he never stood & as the author of measures in which he had nothing to do."[21]

And of course Washington was the supreme example of "eternal taciturnity" and enigmatic wisdom couched in stoic silence. He knew how to stand and how to affect an appearance of profundity, especially in public. At times, especially in letters to Rush, Adams came close to suggesting that Washington was primarily an actor, playing a role he never fully understood: "We [in the Washington administration] all agreed to believe him and make the world believe him." Adams described a conversation he had with Timothy Pickering in 1791, in which Pickering claimed that Washington often dozed in cabinet meetings, never read dispatches, wrote few if any of his own speeches, needed chalk marks on the floor to know where to stand at receptions and levees, and was, in general, an illiterate, intellectually incompetent cipher who was propped up in public by his staff.

But Adams was careful to put these scandalous (and to our contemporary ears, familiar) accusations in Pickering's mouth, then to note that, as everyone knew, Pickering was a third-rater whose mediocrity was only surpassed by his duplicity. Adams hinted at his own sense of intellectual superiority to Washington, suggesting that, as far as he could tell, all of Washington's philosophy was derived from a cursory reading of Rollins's *Ancient History*. Beyond that level of glancing criticism, Adams was unwilling to go, preferring to "take my deepest secrets to the grave." Washington should be esteemed but not adored. He was an object lesson in the efficacy of enigma. But he was also the one American leader whom even Adams grudgingly acknowledged as an overall superior in terms of virtuous public service.[22]

ADAMS PUT DOWN his autobiography in 1807, never again to pick it up, and ever after resisted requests for a published version of his life with eloquent protestations of inadequacy: "I have been importuned by many persons both Europeans and Americans to write my own life," he explained, "but if I could once prevail upon myself to travil [sic] over such a Series of Egotisms, it is now become as impossible as to cast the Blue Hills . . . into the Sea." The more excruciating truth was that, even though his formal efforts at autobiography were over, he was still haunted by his eventual place in posterity and still unable to conceal his wounded pride or to control his emotional outbursts when the question of his role in history was raised publicly.[23]

And in 1805 it was raised, when Mercy Otis Warren published her *History of the American Revolution* in three volumes. Warren was a friend of John and Abigail Adams of nearly fifty years standing. The younger sister of James Otis, whom Adams considered the true instigator of the movement for independence and his first political hero, she was the wife of James Warren, one of Adams's

closest confidants during the war, who could outdo even Adams
in acts of virtuous eccentricity. Mercy Otis Warren was herself a
complex blend of apparent opposites: devoted wife, mother, and
staunch republican propagandist during the war; a charming and
elegant lady, but one who also wrote polemical poems, plays, and
histories for public consumption. In Copley's portrait she appears
the epitome of cultured New England gentility, but friends and
enemies alike knew from her writings that "Mrs. Warren," whom
the Adamses knew as "Marcia," had one of the sharpest minds in
New England. She was, without much doubt, the most intellectually accomplished woman in revolutionary America.[24]

Adams genuinely enjoyed the company of intelligent and spirited women. He had married a woman of just that sort. And over
a long friendship with Mercy Otis Warren he had shown himself
capable of establishing a relationship of both intimacy and intellectual equity with a woman whose unconventional abilities would
have terrified most men into postures of stiff-backed supremacy
or gallant silence. For example, when Warren had written him for
information about his role as American commissioner in Holland,
Adams confessed that he lacked the important diplomatic virtue of
patience: "I had rather you should immortalize my Imprudence,"
he wrote her half-jokingly, "for I rather think it was this quality,
than the other, which produced the Effect in Holland." Adams felt
a special kinship with Warren that often allowed him to be as candid with her as with Abigail or Rush. "The Times, Madam, have
made a Strange Being of me," he admitted in 1783, "an irritable
fiery Mortal . . . as profuse as a Prodigal and as proud as a Caesar.
But an honest Man in all and to the Death."[25]

None of this history of mutual trust and respect, however,

could rescue Adams from the demons that were still eating away at his soul. In July of 1807, after reading Warren's *History of the American Revolution*, Adams wrote the first of ten lengthy letters to his old friend that, in effect, continued the therapy begun with the autobiography. "I shall observe no order in selecting the passages," he began, "but take them up as they occur by accident." For any seasoned Adams-watcher this was a bad sign, an indication that the sage was in mid-explosion. No sensible or systematic rebuttal of Warren's version of the American Revolution was possible when Adams felt the furies, like waves, rising inside himself.[26]

"A man never looks so silly as when he is talking or writing concerning himself," Adams admitted, "but Mrs. Warren's severity has reduced me to the necessity of pouring out all myself." And pour he did. Adams charged that Warren had willfully reduced his role in the making and securing of the Revolution. Warren, he claimed, had taken no notice of his contribution to the debate over Parliament's authority to tax the colonies in the 1760s. "I ought to have been considered in your History as a figure on the stage from 1761 to 1774," he complained, "call it the figure of a doorkeeper, a livery servant, a dancer, a singer, or a harlequin, if you will." He was one of the earliest advocates of independence. He had not been one of those Johnny-come-latelies to the American cause. Adams reminded Warren that James Otis, her famous brother, had called attention to his contribution and had predicted that "John Adams would one day be the greatest man in America."[27]

The claims became more extreme and exaggerated. He was not only one of the earliest revolutionary zealots, he was the real author of the decisive motion in the Continental Congress that produced independence. He singlehandedly negotiated the treaty that ended the war—"For the whole time I was in the commission with Franklin and Lee, I did the whole business of it." His political writings provided the constitutional model which all the framers acknowledged was the basis for the federal Constitution. Among the entire revolutionary generation, he claimed to "have done more labor, run through more and greater dangers, and made greater sacrifices than any man among my contemporaries living or dead, in the service of my country. . . ." On and on he went, effectively belittling his very real achievements by serving as his own public relations spokesman.[28]

Warren responded with a combination of incredulity and mockery. Her *History* was deficient in Adams's eyes because, as Warren put it, it was an inadequate "panegyric on your life and character," and because it failed to demonstrate that "nothing had been done, that nothing could be done, neither in Europe nor America, without [your] sketching and drafting the business, from the first opposition to British measures in the year 1764 to signing the treaty of peace with England in the year 1783." Warren refused to be the butt of such bombast: "I am so much at a loss for the meaning of your paragraphs, and the rambling manner in which your angry and undigested letters are written, that I scarcely know where to begin my remarks." She chose to begin candidly. "What is Mrs. Warren to think of your comments?" she asked: "I readily tell you she thinks them the most captious, malignant, irrelevant compositions that have ever been seen."[29]

Adams was engaging less in an argument than a tantrum, and Warren had the courage of her long-term friendship to draw upon in apprising him how much of an embarrassment he was making of himself. "Had not Mr. Adams been suffering suspicions that

Mercy Otis Warren (1763). John Singleton Copley oil on canvas.   *Bequest of Winslow Warren. Courtesy, Museum of Fine Arts, Boston*

his fame had not been sufficiently attended to," she suggested, "he would not have put such a perverse construction on [my] every passage. . . ." As one of "your warmest friends and acquaintances," she advised him to remember one of his wisest maxims; namely, that "Passions are sometimes the heavenly gales that waft us safely to port, at others the ungovernable gusts that blow us down the stream of absurdity." Clearly, Adams was currently moving toward the latter location. "The truth I have witnessed from my first acquaintance with you," Warren recalled, that "your nerves have not always been wound up by the same key." But the criticisms of her *History*, she concluded, "cap the climax of rancor, indecency, and vulgarism," and appear less like the musings of a retired states-man than "like the ravings of a maniac." He had said that he was "in a blushing mood." Well, she countered, you can if you wish "blush for Mrs. Warren" and "blush for your country," but most of all, you should "blush for yourself."[30]

Adams found one particular assertion in Warren's *History* even more painful than her failure to make him the central figure of the revolutionary era. In the midst of what any detached reader would have regarded as a very favorable assessment of Adams's contribution, Warren charged that he went through an import-ant change in the 1780s, that "by living long near the splendor of courts and courtiers" during his eight-year stay in Europe, he became "beclouded by a partiality for monarchy" and suffered "a lapse from [his] former republican principles." Warren reiterated the charge in a letter to Adams, claiming that "the pure principles of republicanism were contaminated in your breast."[31]

It was the same accusation that the Jeffersonian Republicans had made in the 1790s, this time enshrined in a full-fledged his-tory, where it would function as a tin can tied to the Adams name, rattling through the ages and the pages of subsequent histories. Adams regarded it as the ultimate charge of corruption, "a charge," he wrote to Warren, "that I cannot and will not bear." He chal-lenged her, as well as "the whole human race, and angels and devils too, to produce an instance of it from my cradle to this hour." But given the hyperbolic character of Adams's other complaints to Warren, and the frantic tone of his entire response to her *His-tory*, Warren felt justified in lumping this particular lamentation with the rest of Adams's invective. "I am yet at a loss to conjecture," she wrote defiantly, "what you have left in your storehouse of thunderbolts. . . ."[32]

In fact, Adams was correct in his claim and in the substance, if not the style, of this particular dispute with Warren. Adams had never favored the establishment of a European-styled monarchy or nobility in America. He consistently opposed all inherited titles and privileges. He favored a stronger executive than the Constitution provided, though an executive that derived its power from the consent of the governed offered in frequent elections. Warren's charge merely repeated the libelous attacks of the Antifederalists in the late 1780s and Jeffersonians in the 1790s, enhancing their credibility while ignoring their inaccuracy. Since being accused of crypto-monarchism was synonymous with being accused of betraying the republican principles of the Revolution, Adams had a legitimate reason to protest.

And thanks in large part to the impressive body of historical scholarship on the ideology of the revolutionary era that has appeared over the past twenty years, it is possible to recover the quite different definitions of "republicanism" that Adams and Warren harbored in their respective heads. For both of them, the phrase "republican principles" resonated with more meaning than any mere description of a representative form of government, without kings or lords or divine right presumptions, could convey.[33]

Adams sensed the source of disagreement, without being able to clarify the specific differences. "There is not a more unintelligible word in the English language than republicanism," he warned Warren, adding that "the word republican is so loose and indefinite that successive predominant factions will put glosses and constructions on it as different as light and darkness. . . ." (Twentieth-century historians would prove him right here.) He accused Warren of imposing in her *History*, and then upon him, a particularly naive and misleading use of the term: "The only effect of it [Warren's use] that I could ever see is to deceive the people," something Adams himself claimed he would never countenance since he, unlike his critics, was "no Pharisee, Jesuit, or Machiavellian."[34]

Again, Adams was historically correct, even though he stated his disagreement with Warren in the belligerent style of a wronged defendant rather than in the spirit of accommodation. For Warren clung tenaciously to a radical version of republicanism that had flourished only briefly in the heady wartime years of the 1770s, a version that then was used by many of the Jeffersonians as the basis for their ideological opposition to the Federalists in the 1790s. It presumed that the American Revolution had effected a clean break not only from English rule, but also a complete separation from the historic corruptions of European society. Warren and her *History* embodied "pure republicanism," the conviction that the very character of American society, once purged of European contaminations, was forever changed. Much like the radical theorists of the French Revolution, and later revolutionaries in Russia and China, Warren believed that America had experienced a fundamental break with the past, that American citizens were now capable of truly disinterested and virtuous behavior, that powerful political institutions were unnecessary impediments to the inherently civic-minded instincts and habits of the populace.[35]

This was why she regarded the suppression of Shays' Rebellion as the repudiation of the very ideals on which the Revolution rested. This was why she interpreted the Constitution and the Federalist political leadership as embodiments of the very arbitrary power the Revolution was intended to eliminate. And this was why John Adams, who held with equal tenacity to fundamentally different notions of republicanism and the meaning of the American Revolution, served Warren's interpretive purpose perfectly in the *History*, as the example of the betrayal and corruption of an austere classical ideal.

All of which helps to explain, if not excuse, Adams's fanatical reaction in the summer of 1807; for he believed, quite correctly, that his own reputation was being stigmatized in order to manipulate the meaning of the Revolution to suit one historian's idiosyncratic interpretation. This was not the occasion for him to spell out fully his own interpretation of the Revolution or his own definition of the deeper meanings of republicanism. He was too enraged to make much sense anyway.

But he did offer Warren one anecdotal clue. He repeated the story of a trip he once made to Antwerp, where he was able to view the masterpieces of Rubens, Rembrandt, and Van Dyck. One of the paintings depicted Jesus "in the midst of the twelve apostles, leaning familiarly on the shoulder of the beloved disciple [John], and distinguishing him from all the other eleven by some peculiar marks of attention and kindness." The truly revealing feature in the painting, however, was the reaction of the other apostles, "the jealousy painted on every countenance," especially the face of Peter, which was "transported with rage," his eyes bulging out of the sockets, lips seeming to quiver and teeth clenched so that "you are apt to fancy you hear them grit against each other." This was human nature as it really existed in the world, in America as well as Europe, among divinely sanctioned disciples as well as secular political leaders and followers. No revolution, not even the successful one he had helped promote, could ever change that intractable fact.[36]

THE FINAL INSTALLMENT in Adams's long effort to exorcise his personal demons, all undertaken in the guise of "setting the record straight," took three years. From 1809 to 1812 he submitted regular essays to the newly founded *Boston Patriot*. "Let the jackasses bray or laugh at all this, as they did at the finger of God," he wrote to his sometime friend William Cunningham when the series began. "I am in a fair way to give my cricks and enemies food enough to glut their appetites," he announced defiantly: "I take no notice of their billingsgate." The *Patriot* series proved to be his final spasm of unbridled self-vindication, Adams's last futile effort at overwhelming his real and imagined enemies with the sheer energy of his rage. He expected immediate responses and recriminations and was surprised, at first, that a "most profound silence is observed relative to my scribbles. . . . The Newspapers are still as midnight." But, on second thought, he suspected his enemies were gathering silently in the darkness. "I suppose the sulphureous combustibles are preparing under ground," he wrote Cunningham, "and the electrical fire collecting in the clouds. . . . If I am neither drowned in the rain, nor pierced with the bolts, nor blown into the atmosphere by the eruptions, I must be invulnerable." Only the muted self-mockery of his characterization saved him from the charge of being close to crazy.[37]

The central theme of the nearly interminable series in the

Patriot was Adams's accomplishments as a diplomat and maker of American foreign policy. While he covered his career in Europe and England in the 1780s, the major episode on which he focused his obsessions, predictably, was his decision as president to negotiate with the French government in 1799–1800 rather than declare war. Adams declared, over and over again, that he was prepared to "defend my missions to France, as long as I have an eye to direct my hand, or a finger to hold my pen. They were the most disinterested and meritorious actions of my life." He even went so far to request that his tombstone contain only one inscription: "Here lies John Adams, who took upon himself the responsibility of peace with France in the year 1800."[38]

As we have seen, what has come to be called the "quasi-war" with France was the dominant event of Adams's presidency. And as we have also seen, the detailed history of this early chapter in American foreign policy is enormously complex—it took Adams the rough equivalent of one thousand pages to tell his version of the story in the *Patriot*—for it involved such formidable characters as Hamilton, Jefferson, and Talleyrand, the split of the Federalists, the emergence of the Jeffersonian Republicans as the majority party, the bribery of American ministers to France, negotiations with a constantly changing French government still in the trauma of revolution and headed for dictatorship under Napoleon, systematic piracy by both French and English naval vessels, and all the vacillations and misunderstandings rendered inevitable by the communication problems of an era ignorant of the telephone or telegraph. That said, the elemental political and strategic issues at stake in the crisis were straightforward. And Adams did a decent job of accurately identifying them later in his retirement:

two Parties . . . existed in this Country headed by Men
of the most determined Ambition, the one [Jeffersonian]
inclined to France the other [Federalist] to England. One
was for closer connection to France and going to War with
England . . . the other was for an Alliance Offensive and
Defensive with Great Britain. It was my destiny to run
the Gauntlet between these two factions, in support of a
Neutrality. . . .[39]

Most, in fact virtually all, modern-day historians concur that
Adams made the correct decision to avoid war, and that it took
considerable courage, as well as principled resistance to popular
opinion and party pressure, to assert the long-term interests of the
nation in the face of overheated patriotic and party zeal. In that
sense, history has vindicated both Adams's most crucial presidential decision and his frequently expressed judgment that "it was
the most splendid diamond in my crown; or, if anyone thinks this
expression too monarchical, I will say the most brilliant feather in
my cap."[40]

But that was not the considered opinion in 1809 when Adams
began to write for the *Patriot*. Nor was Adams's confidence that
posterity would vindicate him sufficient to allay his throbbing
sense of having been wronged. Years later he could write a friend,
Nicholas Boylston: "Voltaire boasted that he made four presses
groan for Sixty Years—but I have to repent that I made the Patriot
groan for Three Years," admitting that he was on a fool's errand "in
vindicating my Conduct . . . against the charges and insinuations
of conceited Blockheads." He conveyed a clear notion of his tortured personal anguish in one of the first *Patriot* pieces. There he

compared himself to "an animal I have seen take hold of the end of a cord with his teeth, and be drawn slowly up by pulleys, through a storm of squils, crackers, and rockets, flashing and blazing around him every moment." And although the "scorching flames made him groan, and mourn, and roar, he would not let go. . . ."[41]

So much was at stake for Adams because his handling of this crisis epitomized his self-image as the man who could stand above party in behalf of national interests. It was his defining moment in American history, at least in retrospect. Small wonder, then, that Hamilton was the chief villain in the story Adams told, or rather the chief defendant in Adams's lengthy case, which often read like a legal brief written by a slightly deranged polemicist. Only "the disturbed imagination of Alexander Hamilton," Adams argued, could find fault with his handling of the foreign crisis, "though Hamilton was pleased to wield it as a poisoned weapon with the express purpose of destroying me." He backhandedly thanked Hamilton for his treachery, claiming petulantly, "it has given me eight years, incomparably the happiest of my life, whereas, had I been chosen President again, I am certain I could not have lived another year." Hamilton was determined to make himself head of the army in a war with France, Adams charged, then launch a military expedition to conquer the continent and liberate South America. This turned out to be factually accurate, as we now know from the modern edition of Hamilton's private correspondence. But in Adams's hands the account smacked of self-serving slander, or worse, a paranoid pomposity. He claimed that not even Cicero—the comparison was plausible but, again, self-defeating— was "sacrificed to the vengeance of Anthony more egregiously than John Adams was to the unbridled and unbounded ambition of

Alexander Hamilton and the American triumvirate." In opposition to "all their diabolical intrigues," Adams boasted, he "hardily pursued my own System in 1799 and 1800, made Peace with France at the expense of all my consequence in the World, and their unanimous and immortal hatred."[42]

The accuracies and inaccuracies of Adams's account cannot easily be sorted out. In a historical episode as complex as Adams's handling of the French question, and as dependent for its complexity on the collision of mutually exclusive perceptions by all participants, the very notion that there is a single true or objective version of the story probably requires scrutiny. But the crucial historical question raised by the *Boston Patriot* series is not, What is the true story?, so much as Why did Adams feel compelled to put his version before the public? What cries out for an explanation is his persistence for three years in a cause that was so obviously beyond his capacity to affect. It bears repeating: the pieces in the *Patriot* were interminable; and Adams acknowledged to Rush and other close friends that he realized his efforts were futile; in some perverse sense, and again he acknowledged this too, he was motivated by the very futility of it all. He was churning out page after page on the details of a decade-old chapter in American relations with France at just the time when public attention was focused on the looming War of 1812 with England. Finally, the vendetta-like tone of his prose, the accusatory style of his argument, the sheer massiveness of his self-defense, all robbed his writing of any semblance of credibility or persuasiveness. And it hardly bears mentioning that, even if his tales of corruption and betrayal by his cabinet were essentially accurate, he was the last person to set the record straight. Much like Hamilton's notorious *Letter . . . Concerning the*

Public Conduct and Character of John Adams . . ., which it was intended to refute, the series in the *Boston Patriot* was a misguided and self-defeating performance explicable only in terms of compulsive urges that defy logic.

There are, however, at least two ways of making Adams's compulsions comprehensible. First, Adams needed to purge himself of all the accumulated animosity toward the High Federalists—especially Hamilton—that had built up inside him. Seen in conjunction with his autobiography and then his exchange with Mercy Otis Warren, the *Boston Patriot* writings constituted his final spasm of vindicative energy, the last extended eruption of the Adams volcano. Unlike Jefferson, who suffered similar wounds in his public career, Adams could not lick his wounds in private and allow them to heal silently over time. In Adams's case, wounds did not heal; they festered; he kept reopening them. The sheer massiveness and often inchoate character of the *Patriot* pieces accurately indicated how much anger Adams had been suppressing. Only after it had all poured out was he capable of authentic tranquility. In this sense his monumental vituperations in the public press were not so much efforts to rewrite history as they were culminations of his personal catharsis.

Secondly, and somewhat contradictorily, the energy he gave to the rebuttal of Warren and the revision of his actions as president also accurately reflect how much Adams cared about his place in history. Despite his incessant denials, and what became an almost formulaic denunciation of history's capacity to comprehend the way it *really* was, he desperately wanted to be appreciated in the annals of history. And this desperation, illustrated in the singular ferocity with which he defended his reputation during the first twelve years of his retirement, possessed a special poignance for him precisely because of his habitual aversion to conventional forms of popularity and worldly success. If traditional success must be avoided because it inevitably carried with it the seeds of a great man's destruction—Caesar, Napoleon, and Hamilton were his favorite examples—it then followed that posterity was the only safe place left for him to achieve heroic stature. It was the only place because he had personally destroyed his prospects for popularity in his own lifetime. And it was the only safe place because popularity beyond the grave presented no temptation to his vaunted vanity. Only posthumous fame avoided the risk of self-corruption. Only in the minds and memories of subsequent generations could a virtuous public figure rest easy with acclaim. Here was the one necessary condition that all true heroes had to satisfy in the Adams schema: they had to be dead.

THE MAJOR PROBLEM with posthumous fame, what in fact made it such an effective antidote to vanity, of course, was that one was not around to enjoy it. With the completion of the *Boston Patriot* series, Adams began to accept the implications of that incontrovertible fact. Perhaps, after the enormous expenditure of energy in the *Patriot*, he was simply played out. Or perhaps the lengthy therapy that had begun with the autobiography reached the kind of conclusion commonly achieved: not brilliant new insights or discoveries, but a steadier and more balanced perspective on his life and the intractable ingredients of his personality. Whatever the reason, Adams mellowed discernibly. "I have prattled and scribbled two [sic] much and too freely," he wrote the publisher

Mathew Carey, adding the old refrain that "the unsearchable reserve and eternal taciturnity of Franklin and Washington are the only sure passports to Fame and immortality in the Poets and Politicians Creed." At last, however, he seemed capable of heeding his own advice.[43]

Through the good offices of their old friend Elbridge Gerry, a reconciliation was arranged with Mercy Otis Warren before her death in 1814. And Benjamin Rush's genial intercessions recovered the long-latent friendship with Jefferson. Letters between Monticello and Montezillo started flowing in 1812. The news, incorrect as it turned out, that Jefferson kept a huge scrapbook filled with the most scurrilous libels against his own reputation, led Adams to scold his grandchildren, who "ought to have done the same thing for me." Such a valuable volume "would have been the most splendid of all," for he would have had it "bound in Moroccan leather with gold gilt." Critics, he claimed, for some strange reason just did not seem to bother him as much. "What shall we do with the Insects that buzz about us?" he wrote to John Quincy, who was soon to assume the office of Secretary of State. "Their bite in former times tingled," he confessed, "but I am grown almost as insensible, as a Boston Dray Horse in September."[44]

Embracing one's former enemies and errors proved exhilarating and rekindled the old playfulness. He fended off requests for a published version of his life with dismissive caricatures: any true account must be "a bundle of weakness and error & petulance"; or, perhaps recalling Warren's language, "I should blush to see it committed to writing"; or, instead of writing his own life, he would write a history of all the major errors of the founding generation, in which the volume on John Adams would be "the only folio Volume," twice as large as the others, and would begin with his original sin, "birth on the Eastern Side of the Hudson River." When Harrison Gray Otis, the prominent Massachusetts Federalist, chided him that a commissioned biography was owed the public because his character was the property of the public, Adams protested: "So it is, but in what money scales it will be weighed by posterity, I know not. If it is to be estimated by the newspapers . . . it will be found to be of less value, than the meanest drug in an apothecary shop."[45]

The fact that the great volcano of American statesmanship was in apparent remission did not mean that the fires had gone out. Nor that hope in the judgment of posterity had cooled. "The inquiring mind in future times will find reasons to diminish the glories of some and to increase the esteem of others," he noted without mentioning names. "Some characters now obscured under a cloud of unpopularity"—no names necessary here—"will come out with more lustre."[46]

But counting on posterity was not quite the same thing as trusting in historians. Written history, Adams was more convinced than ever, "seems like Romance. It shows Mankind in such a light I can hardly believe any of it. Though I cannot keep my Eyes off it." He bet Rush one hundred dollars that there would never be a true history of the Whiskey Rebellion and offered another "hundred thousand eagles for a true history of the American Revolution." When Jedidiah Morse petitioned him for information to be included in his history of Revolution, Adams said it was futile: "I know not whether to laugh or cry. I have little faith in history. I read it as I do romance. . . ." Hezekiah Niles, another aspiring historian making the same request, got the same treatment: "In plain

English, and in few words Mr. Niles, I consider the true history of the American Revolution & the establishing of our present Constitution as lost forever. And nothing but misrepresentation or partial account of it, ever will be recovered."[47]

Part of the problem, as Adams saw it, was the inevitably incomplete historical record—the lost documents and the crucial decisions and conversations that never were recorded in the first place. In addition, the contemporary urge to mythologize and romanticize messy realities would undoubtably contaminate future accounts. So the concept of "true history" was an oxymoron. It never existed and never would exist. "It is a common observation in Europe that nothing is so false as modern history," he told one friend; "I should say nothing is so false as modern history except ancient history and I would add nothing is so false as ancient or modern history in Europe except modern American history."[48]

It was perfectly natural for Adams to diagnose a situation as impossible and then proceed to try to do something about it. "Tell Mr. A," he wrote in 1818 to Louisa Catherine, John Quincy's wife, "that I am assiduously and sedulously employed in Exertions to save him trouble, by collecting all my Papers. What a Mass!" The public and private papers he had saved over the years were, in truth, the largest such collection, by far, preserved by any member of the revolutionary generation. When he composed his autobiography, Adams had begun the habit of inserting original documents and letters into the record. That trickle had become a flood by the time he got to the *Boston Patriot* articles, where readers were bludgeoned to death with stacks of documentary evidence to clinch even minor points, as Adams himself withdrew as narrator and let the primary sources do the talking. The growing tendency to consult his collection of papers reached its logical culmination in the decision to let them, and them alone, speak to posterity.

He described himself to John Quincy as "deeply immersed in researches, not astro[no]mical or mineralogical or metaphysical; but after old Papers. Trunks, Boxes, Desks, Drawers, locked up for thirty years have been broken open because the Keys are lost. Nothing stands in my Way." The same impulsive energy that had gone into the earlier efforts at self-vindication had at last found the proper outlet and the proper motive. "Every Scrap shall be found and preserved for your Affliction [or] for your good," he wrote lecturingly to his son: "I shall leave you an inheritance sufficiently tormenting [that it will make you] Alternately laugh and cry, fret and fume, stamp and scold as they do me." In one of his last letters to Rush, in 1812, he cried out: "Have mercy on me Posterity, if you should ever see any of my Letters." But his deepest and most abiding hope was that those letters, uncontaminated by the prejudices of historians, full of the human weaknesses that went with real life, would prove his eventual ticket into the American pantheon.[49]

———— ·+·+· ————

CHAPTER THREE

Irreverencies and Oppositions

My nerves were so vibrated, that I seem to hear the
Dongle at this moment. "Dongle!" there is no such
Word in Johnson. What then? I have as good a right to
make a Word, as that Pedant Bigot Cynic and Monk.
—Adams to Catherine Rush, February 23, 1815

Five and forty years ago, when any terrible News arrived
from England of their hostile designs against our
Liberties, when the people, gaping and staring, pale and
trembling, asked me, "What I thought of the News,"
my invariable Answer was, "The worse, the better."
—Adams to Elbridge Gerry, July 14, 1814

WHEN ADAMS'S GRANDSON, Charles Francis Adams, sat
down in 1850 to write the introduction to his ten-volume
edition of the papers and letters that the family patriarch had so
meticulously preserved, he too asked, however subtly, for a measure of mercy. "At no time in his life was John Adams a man of
many concealments," he warned readers accustomed to a Victorian

code of etiquette and self-restraint. But there was "no hypocrisy in him whilst alive," he noted correctly, "and it would scarcely be doing him justice to invest him with a share of it after his death." Then the grandson repeated a refrain that his famous grandfather had shouted to friends and muttered to himself throughout his retirement. "We are beginning to forget that the patriots of former days were men like ourselves," wrote Charles Francis, "acting and acted upon like the present race, and we are almost irresistibly led to ascribe to them in our imaginations certain gigantic proportions and superhuman qualities, without reflecting that this at once robs their character of consistency and their virtues of all merit."[1]

John Adams often made the same point, usually as part of a critical assessment of such heroic patriots as Washington and Franklin, whom Adams considered competitors for a prominent placement in the American pantheon. His argument therefore smacked of jealousy and self-vindication. And especially during the earliest years of his retirement, when his pugnacious energies flowed so fully into the campaign in behalf of his own reputation, the argument had a defensive tone, as if lowering the standards used to measure historic greatness would assist the elevation of his own cause. Or, to put the same point somewhat differently, Adams was complaining that he was being penalized for his candor, that he said out loud what others only whispered, or wrote down what others shrewdly kept to themselves.

There was unquestionably some truth to the notion that Adams felt compelled to reveal himself more fully than any prominent leader of the revolutionary generation. He claimed that his impulsive candor was a life-long habit, that two boyhood friends "used to tell me I had a little capillary vein of satire, meandering about in my soul, and it broke out so strangely, suddenly, and irregularly that it was impossible ever to foresee when it would come or how it would appear." Certain feelings seemed to move instantaneously from his soul to his mouth or pen, without passing through any filter in his head. Once, when Abigail saw a letter he was writing to Rush in which he was comparing the scientific writers of the day to a group of lunatics who should be confined to an asylum, she told her husband, as Adams reported, "that he 'thinks my head, too, a little crack[ed].'" (Adams, ever playful with Rush, admitted, "I am half of that mind myself.") Adams was aware of his reputation for indiscretion, but counted it an intractable part of his personality, beyond redemption. "The astonishment of your Family at my vivacity is very just," he told Rush, adding: "Nothing is indeed more ridiculous than an old man more than three quarters of a hundred rattling like a boy of fifteen at School or at College. I am ashamed of it yet ten to one I shall fall into it again before I finish this letter."[2]

And he invariably did, rattling on with colorful irreverencies that endeared him to friends and often embarrassed the unsuspecting. When, for example, Jefferson mentioned several new theories proposed by European writers on the origin of Native Americans, Adams responded in his typically pungent style. "I should as soon suppose," he wrote, "that the Prodigal Son, in a frolic with one of his Girls made a trip to America in one of Mother Carey's Eggshells, and left the fruits of their Amours here, as believe any of the grave hypotheses and solemn reasonings of Philosophers or Divines upon the Subject of the Peopling of America."

The same irreverence applied to great philosophers. When asked his opinion of Plato, he claimed to have learned "Two things only," even though he had struggled through the original Greek version of *The Republic* with the help of a Latin translation: first, that Franklin's wild idea that farmers and seamen should be exempted from the horrors of war was borrowed, which is to say stolen, from Plato; and second, "that sneezing is a cure for the Hiccups." Devout Christians got the same treatment when invited to speculate on the possibility that there was no God; he announced that, if it could "be revealed or demonstrated that there is no future state, my advice to every man, woman, and child would be, as our existence would be in our own power, to take opium."[3]

Presidential decorum was fair game. Jefferson once bemoaned the self-proclaimed prophets and mystics who took up so much of his time as president. Adams replied that visitors who claimed to be seers had posed no problem for him: "They all assumed the Character of Ambassadors extraordinary from the Almighty; but as I required miracles in proof of their credentials, and they did not perform any, I never gave public Audience to any of them." Or when, during his final months as president, the Secretary of State asked his reaction to a request from the German authorities for a group of writers and artists to emigrate to America, Adams wrote back from Quincy that "The German letter . . . will require no answer. . . ." Since the aspiring immigrants were just the kind of dreamers to be seduced by Tom Paine's doctrines, Adams preferred they remain in Europe. "I had rather countenance the introduction of Ariel and Caliban," he claimed colorfully, "with a troop of spirits the most mischievous from fairy land."[4]

His own style was itself mischievous, as well as being a finely crafted expression of the contradictory impulses within his personality: colorful and tart in its choice of language; willing to run risks in its allusions, metaphors, and verbal juxtapositions; prone to irreverent conclusions designed to surprise or startle; capable of remarkable incisiveness and almost photographic specificity when the issue at stake did not arouse his ire; but when it did, given to litanies of abstract nouns brought to the end of their frenzied march across the page by insulting verbs, which went off like a series of exploding skyrockets.

Conventional wisdom, as Adams saw it, seldom got very close to the truth, which was always paradoxical and, like history itself, maddeningly resistant to any all-encompassing perspective. His style in letters—appropriately unorthodox and sufficiently flexible to convey different moods and meanings simultaneously—was an excellent vehicle for his personal complexity, an instrument shaped over the years to express his layered disposition. And the most discernible shape that the style and disposition consistently took was what we might call "oppositional." In his old age as well as his youth, Adams instinctively mobilized his enormous verbal and intellectual energies in opposition to established conventions, personal enemies, or fashionable ideas. He was only comfortable in dialogue and he was most invigorated when the dialogue took the form of an argument. What many commentators on his life diagnosed as sheer irascibility was less a mood than a habit of mind. It was related to his urge toward alienation and an isolated version of independence—the kind of tendency best illustrated in his behavior as president. But what we might call his dialectical style had a separate set of causes and consequences most closely associated with his almost instinctive need to establish balance in conversations and political arguments. He felt great satisfaction in defending the British troops in the wake of the Boston Massacre in 1770,

for example, not just because their right to a fair trial was a principle of English law he respected, but also because doing so offset the
surging patriotism of the Boston mob. He had been known to rise
in crowded rooms during debates over the Stamp Act to insist that
the rights of suspected collaborators not be trampled in the march
toward colonial independence. Meanwhile, on the other side of the
political spectrum, he loved to correct his Federalist friends whenever they expressed apprehension about the viability of popular
government. Jefferson and his followers got lectures on stability;
Fisher Ames was told about the dangers of a smug, self-appointed
aristocracy. When John Trumbull, the prominent artist, asked for
advice about revolutionary scenes worthy of memoralizing, he was
informed that the fine arts were dangerous weapons almost always
allied with despotism and superstition. Adams seemed to seek out
the illusions and excesses of the age, then press against them all
with his might, as if he equated thinking with performing a set of
mental isometric exercises.

THE CLEAREST EXAMPLE of this tendency is currently housed
in the Boston Public Library. There the bulk of the approximately
three thousand books that Adams accumulated and kept around
himself in the Quincy house have been preserved. Next to Abigail
and their grandchildren, books were his most valued companions
throughout his retirement, and he talked back to them in marginal notes as if their authors were sitting around the fireside in the
library. Zoltán Haraszti, the modern scholar who was responsible
for overseeing the Adams collection and first called attention to the
voluminous marginal commentary contained within their musty

bindings, claimed that the Adams library was "the largest private collection of its day in America." Whether or not this is correct— Jefferson scholars plausibly dispute the claim—Adams had a huge number of books at his disposal throughout his retirement. And Adams did not just collect books; he read them. He was, by the common consensus of his contemporaries, the best-read member of his remarkably literate generation. Even Jefferson acknowledged that he could not match the prodigious Adams pace. After Adams described his reading list for 1816, for example, Jefferson admitted amazement: "Forty-three volumes read in one year," Jefferson exclaimed, "and twelve of them quartos! Dear Sir, how I envy you! Half a dozen 8 vols [octavos] in that space of time are as much as I am allowed."[5]

But Adams did not just read books. He battled them. The casual presumption that there is some kind of rough correlation between the books in the library of any prominent historical figure and the person's cast of mind would encounter catastrophe with Adams, because he tended to buy and read books with which he profoundly disagreed. Then, as he read, he recorded in the margins and at the bottom of pages his usually hostile opinions of the arguments and authors. Rousseau was "a coxcomb and . . . satyr"; Voltaire a "liar" and "complete scoundrel"; Condorcet a "quack," "a fool," and "a mathematical Charlatan"; d'Alembert a "Louse, Flea, Tick, Ant, Wasp, or . . . Vermin. . . ." But beyond such epithets, Adams commented at length on the substance of major works of philosophy, literature, and political theory, sometimes writing as many words in the margins as contained in the original text. Indeed, it is possible to argue—as Haraszti has in fact done—that the Adams marginalia constitute evidence more revealing of his

convictions about political theory than any of his official publications. They also constitute dramatic illustrations of the way he
defined his own elemental ideas in conflict with opposing versions,
the way thought for Adams was synonymous with argument.[6]

One of his favorite authors was Bolingbroke. Henry St. John
Viscount Bolingbroke had been a leader of the opposition against
the ministry of Robert Walpole in England during the middle
third of the eighteenth century. Bolingbroke helped shape the
Whig tradition which American revolutionaries, including Adams,
borrowed from so effectively in fashioning their own arguments
against arbitrary power, political corruption, and British degenera-
tion. Adams first read him soon after his graduation from Harvard,
then reread him five or six times, twice during his retirement.[7]

Even though Bolingbroke's major insights—a belief in the efficacy of "mixed government," the relentless power of self-interest,
and the endorsement of "Country" over "Court" values—were
also bedrock commitments for Adams, the comments he made,
first in 1804 and then again in 1811, suggest a reader relishing
the opportunity to disagree. In his *Dissertation Upon Parties*, for
example, Bolingbroke ridiculed the silly pretense that "the king
never dies," a notion that buttressed the belief in the abiding con-
tinuity of monarchic authority. Adams reacted caustically: "What
is the silliest? That the King never dies or that the King can do no
wrong? Rather too debonair, my Lord." And when in his *Study and
Use of History* Bolingbroke endorsed the ancient Roman custom
of placing images or busts of ancestors in the vestibules of their
houses in order to recall "the glorious actions of the dead," Adams
unleashed his own counter-theory of emulation: "But images of
fools and knaves are as easily made as those of patriots and heroes.

The images of the Gracchi were made as well as those of Scipio, the images of Caesar, Anthony, and Augustus as well as those of Cicero, Pompey, Brutus, and Cassius." He then went on to berate Bolingbroke's limited understanding of art's complex contribution to both the elevation and corruption of human morality. "Statues, paintings, panegyrics, in short all the fine arts," he scribbled in the margin, "promote virtue while virtue is in fashion. After that they promote luxury, effeminacy, corruption, prostitution, and every species of abandoned depravity."

In his *Remarks on the History of England,* which Adams reread in 1804, Bolingbroke celebrated the "patriot king," contending that if "one great, brave, disinterested, active man [should] arise, he will be received, followed, and almost adored, as the guardian genius of these kingdoms." Adams scoffed: "Like Bonaparte, or Hamilton, or Burr." And when Bolingbroke claimed that history almost always punishes villains, or at least that virtuous leaders are invariably acknowledged by posterity, Adams, probably thinking of himself, countered, "Not always," adding that "Tradition and history are radically corrupted." He went on like this, bantering with Bolingbroke paragraph by paragraph, often sentence by sentence, eventually writing about twelve thousand words of his own.[8]

Adams read most of the French *philosophes* several times, too. These were the writers who had promulgated the doctrines on which the ideals of the French Revolution were based. Adams regarded the whole group of them, including Rousseau, Voltaire, Turgot, and Condorcet, as naive romantics. "Not one of them takes human nature as its foundation," he commented after rereading Condorcet's *Progress of the Human Mind* in 1811. "Equality is one of those equivocal words which the philosophy of the 18th

Century has made fraudulent," he continued: "In the last twenty-five years it has cheated millions out of their lives and tens of millions out of their property."[9]

The Abbé de Mably was one of the more popular French philosophers of his day and an ardent advocate of a classless society. Adams had met him in 1782 at a dinner party in Paris and described him then as "polite, good-humored and sensible." But when he read Mably's *De la legislation* in 1806 and encountered Mably's endorsement of community ownership of all property, Adams scribbled "Stark mad" in the margin, then, in a gentler mood: "Abby, thou comprehendest not." As the mounting marginalia eventually made clear, it was not Mably's belief in the power of property that offended Adams, who shared a recognition of the disastrous impact that a grossly unequal distribution of property and wealth had on all hopes for social justice. Adams objected, instead, to the romantic notion that it was possible to achieve economic equality by social engineering, and, more interestingly, to the assumption that the truly primal human emotions were driven solely by material rewards. "The Abby has not seen the true source of the passions," he wrote. "Ambition springs from the desire of esteem and from emulation, not from property." Because of his encounter with Mably's radical version of economic equality, Adams was driven to articulate in stark form what was, in fact, one of his most elemental political principles: that psychological imperatives, "the passions," were more powerful forces than the impulses to accumulate wealth. The human craving for social distinction actually underlay the quest for riches, he thought, so all social engineering that aimed at economic equality was fighting a vain, delusive, and inevitably losing battle with what Adams considered the most basic and dominant forces in the human personality.[10]

If Bolingbroke made him expose his urge to dissent, even with the ultimate English dissenter, if Condorcet drew out his antipathy toward all utopian schemes, if Mably encouraged him to deny the primacy of purely economic motivations, it was Mary Wollstonecraft who called out of his heart and mind Adams's deepest reservations about the assumptions—Adams thought them illusions—that had produced the horror, the devastation, and the seductive pathology of the French Revolution. Wollstonecraft was a brilliant young Englishwoman who had achieved sudden fame in her own day, and is still remembered in ours, for her authorship of *A Vindication of the Rights of Woman* (1792), which presented the first sustained and comprehensive argument for sexual equality in recorded history. But the book that attracted Adams's attention and ire was her *Historical and Moral View of the Origin and Progress of the French Revolution* (1794). He first read it in 1796, just before taking office as president, then reread it in 1812, making notes on virtually every one of its 532 pages, thereby generating a veritable book of his own and what one scholar described as "his own version of the [French] Revolution."[11]

Not that Adams had exactly suppressed his strong opinions on the French Revolution apart from his private criticisms of Wollstonecraft's defense. The French Revolution, in fact, was an event—perhaps the most decisively shaping event of modern history—that Adams frequently used as a kind of backboard for his own political values, a dramatic example of how *not* to effect social change. In his *Discourses on Davila*, composed in the year the French Revolution began, when most American observers were flush with enthusiasm for a revolutionary cause that looked so similar to their own, he had indicated his sense of foreboding at the misguided hope that a whole new chapter in human history was beginning. "Amidst all the exultations," he wrote in 1789, "Americans and Frenchmen should remember that the perfectibility of man is only human and terrestrial perfectibility. Cold will still freeze, and fire will never cease to burn; disease and vice will continue to disorder, and death to terrify mankind." The following year he had written to the English radical Richard Price that "the Revolution in France could not be indifferent to me; but I have learned an awful experience, to rejoice with trembling . . . ; and I own to you, I know not what to make of a republic of thirty million atheists."[12]

As events in France carried the Revolution from exhilaration to subsequent phases of terror, mass violence, and despotism, Adams's initial apprehensions proved prophetic, and the French Revolution became a familiar touchstone that Adams often referred to in letters, combining an "I told you so" bravado with a colorful characterization of the reasons why disaster had been inevitable. "I acknowledge that the most unaccountable phenomenon I ever beheld, in the seventy-seven, almost, years that I lived," he wrote to his old revolutionary colleague Thomas McKean in 1812, "was to see men of the most extensive knowledge and deepest reflection entertain for a moment an opinion that a democratic republic could be erected in a nation of five-and-twenty millions people, four-and-twenty millions and five hundred thousand of whom could neither read nor write." The following year he not-so-tactfully reminded Jefferson of the same lesson: "You was well persuaded in your own mind that the Nation [France] would succeed

in establishing a free Republican Government. I was as well persuaded, in mine, that a project of such a Government . . . was an
unnatural irrational and impractical, as it would be over the Ele-
phants Lions Tigers Panthers and Bears in the Royal Menagerie,
at Versailles."[13]

Jefferson preferred to let the subject drop, but Adams would
not desist. "The French Patriots appeared to me," he wrote in 1813,
"like young Schollars from a Colledge or Sailors flushed with
recent pay or prize money, mounted on wild Horses, lashing and
speering, till they kill the Horses and break their own Necks."
When Jefferson eventually admitted that the French Revolution
had not turned out as he had hoped, Adams told friends, somewhat misleadingly, that "the learned and scientific President Jefferson has, in letters to me, acknowledged that I was right, and
that he was wrong." While he often lamented the carnage and the
countless human tragedies created unwittingly by the French radicals, there was a sense in which the French Revolution became
a providential episode for Adams, an event that God or history
gave to the world in order to illustrate the wisdom of evolutionary
as opposed to revolutionary change. Adams had once confided to
Rush that he saw himself as the Sancho Panza of American politics, destined to tilt at windmills and win his few victories with a
burlesque style that concealed his utter seriousness of purpose: "I
love the people of America," he wrote. "They have been, they may
be and they are deceived. It is the duty of somebody to undeceive
them." Reviewing the lessons of the French Revolution offered him
the ideal occasion to do his duty.[14]

And commenting on Mary Wollstonecraft's *French Revolution*
prompted Adams to spell out more specifically than anywhere else

just why he opposed all modern efforts at radical or revolutionary social change for which the French Revolution was the prototype. As was his custom, Adams spent much of his time and energy hurling epithets without explaining the basis for his disagreement. When Wollstonecraft described a post-revolutionary world where "men will do unto others, what they wish they should do unto them," for example, Adams rolled his eyes and wrote, "Heavenly times!" Or when Wollstonecraft attributed the excesses of the Revolution to the lingering vanities and human weaknesses left over from the *ancien régime* that would eventually be obliterated, he noted simply, "Alas! Poor girl!" But the bulk of his jottings consisted of sustained commentary in which his own political principles took shape against the articulated expectations of Wollstonecraft's revolutionary creed.[15]

First, Adams actually described Wollstonecraft's arguments as a creed, a form of religion, and her belief in the Revolution as most akin to a religious enthusiasm. Her major convictions about human nature and social change were, he thought, "divine objects which her enthusiasm beholds in beatific vision. Alas, how airy and baseless a fabric." Adams had no trouble understanding the seductive attractiveness of such doctrines. In the manner of the modern historian Carl Becker, however, he diagnosed the mentality of revolutionary advocates as reminiscent of Christian belief systems in the Middle Ages, burdened with fanciful superstitions, baseless notions of the possible and the convenient transferral of heaven's rewards to this world "after the Revolution." Although Adams thought that Wollstonecraft's way of thinking was distressingly familiar, he claimed that a new word had been coined to express the concept: "The political and literary world are much

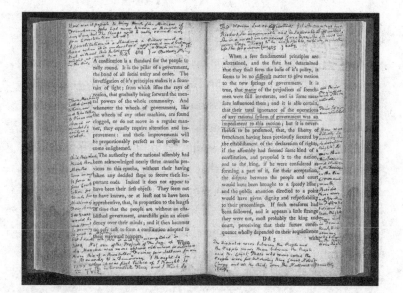

Marginalia of John Adams in his copy of Mary Wollstonecraft's *Historical and Moral View of the Origin and Progress of the French Revolution* (1794).   *Boston Public Library*

indebted to the invention of the word IDEOLOGY," he noted to himself. "Our English words Ideocy, or Ideotism, express not the force of meaning of it. . . . It was taught in the school of folly, but alas, Franklin, Turgot, Rochefoucauld and Condorcet, under Tom Paine, were the great masters of that Academy." In Adams's lexicon, "ideology" was a set of ideals and hopes, like human perfection or social equality, that philosophers mistakenly believed could be implemented on earth merely because they existed in their heads. To imagine was to believe, and to believe was to regard as possible. The revolutionary ideology of Wollstonecraft, he suggested, was a secular version of what Marx would later insist all religion represented, a drug or an opiate that prevented people from thinking clearly or realistically.[16]

Moreover, Adams characterized Wollstonecraft's specific creed as a particularly evangelical brand of religion *cum* ideology, because of the speed with which she assumed lasting social changes could be effected. "Did this lady think three months time enough to form a free constitution for twenty-five millions of Frenchmen?" he asked rhetorically, adding that he suspected "300 years would be well spent in procuring so great a blessing. . . ." Here Adams surreptitiously suggested one of his most elemental convictions: that most enduring political, social, and economic transformations were evolutionary rather than revolutionary, that successful revolutions, like the one he had helped lead in America, were merely the final and most visible stages of what was, in fact, a long process of preparation. When radicals like Wollstonecraft attempted to foment sudden change for which the society was unprepared, the result was political extremism that mirrored the excesses of the regime they intended to overthrow; this then led to an institutionalization of competing pathologies; and this then led inevitably to a permanent despotism. It was therefore "absurd, ridiculous [and] delirious," he concluded, to believe that "a revolution in France, per saltum, from monarchy to democracy" would ever work. "I thought so in 1785 when it was first talked of," he scribbled in the margin, and, "I thought so in all the intermediate time, and I think so in 1812."[17]

Second, Adams disagreed with Wollstonecraft's somewhat hazy assumptions about the relationship between government and society. Her views were not expressed fully, because she considered them such elementary articles of faith that they required minimal argumentation. But the whole thrust of her analysis depended on the presumption that, if there was social injustice in *ancien régime* France and throughout Europe, governments were the major causes of the problem and had little to contribute toward their solution. Adams, on the other hand, believed that the source of the problem existed inside human beings—their jealousy and passion for distinction—which then created a craving for wealth in which the stronger and richer pressed their advantage and generated greater social inequality. Corrupt governments institutionalized these inequities, but did not create them. The sources of mischief would not go away once the corrupt government was toppled. They would fester and eventually insinuate themselves into the post-revolutionary society, replicating in new forms the old evils thought to be obliterated. Government for Adams, then, was not a mere impediment to the natural virtue of a disinterested citizenry. It was the crucial ingredient that disciplined human passions and thereby secured the revolution. "She will not admit," Adams lamented, "the only means that can accomplish any part of her ardent prophesies: forms of government . . . to restrain the passions of all orders of men."[18]

Third, and finally, since Wollstonecraft regarded government as an artifice that distorted and blocked the benign natural instincts of citizens, she gave little thought to its shape or structure. But then why should she, given her view that the primary accomplishment of any revolution should be to remove government? And once removed, she felt certain that liberated popular energies would opt for a simple and direct form of representative government, a single-house legislature that would reflect the collective opinions of the citizenry and conduct its necessary business with a minimum of bother.

Adams could barely contain himself. He covered Wollstonecraft's paragraphs with critical commentary. Her notion of a sovereign legislature representing all the varied interests of society was: "a savage theory. A barbarous theory. Indians, Negroes, Tartars, Hottentots would have refined it more." Her assertion that government should be simple was equally stupid. "The clock would be simple if you destroyed all the wheels," he wrote, "but it would not tell the time of day." Then he listed a long string of items, including a farmer's barn, a ship, a city, even the solar system, that would not function if deprived of their complexity. He concluded sardonically that the "simplest of all governments is a despotism in one." Wollstonecraft's naive assumption that the ultimate purpose of government was to "get out of the way" and thereby allow for the free expression of individual energies and opinions guaranteed disaster, since such a course assured that "jealousy, envy and revenge [will] govern with as absolute a sway as ever." The ultimate purpose of government, he insisted, was not to release individual energies but to constrain and balance them. In order to do that, "Power must be opposed to power, force to force, strength to strength, interest to interest . . . and passion to passion."[19]

One can almost see him hunched over Wollstonecraft's book in the library at Quincy, his hands shaking from the combination of palsy and excitement, the walls around him laden with books that had also received the same furious attention, most of the authors, including Mary Wollstonecraft, long since dead, but the ideas contained in the books still alive, simultaneously enlightening and deceiving nations and mankind, waiting for the shaky pen of the cantankerous patriarch to deliver its verdicts, the old man arguing with the books into the night.

THE TENDENCY TO define his own position against either an established or popular point of view did not necessarily mean that Adams only delivered bad news. His deep-rooted suspicion of all celebrities made him supportive of younger leaders traumatized by the larger-than-life depictions of his fellow American revolutionaries as they began to appear early in the nineteenth century. Especially after he emerged from his long effort at self-vindication, he enjoyed countering accounts of the American Revolution, or of what was becoming known as the "Founding Fathers," that verged on ancestor worship and inevitably left younger Americans feeling that all history was now epilogue. "I ought not to object to your reverence for your fathers," he wrote to Josiah Quincy in 1811, "meaning . . . those concerned with the direction of public affairs. . . . But, to tell you a very great secret, as far as I am capable of comparing the merit of different periods, I have no reason to believe we were better than you are." He sensed that romanticized versions of the American Revolution paralyzed what he called "the rising generation" with a patriotic storyline populated by demigods who spoke soliloquies reminiscent of the patriarchs in the Old Testament.[20]

Adams launched a personal campaign to shatter these sentimental tableaux and to assume a protective and almost grandfatherly posture toward the younger generation. The conduct of the American Revolution, he insisted, was less a religious crusade

led by saints than an unholy political mess managed, with vary-
ing degrees of effectiveness, by imperfect human beings. "Every
measure of Congress, from 1774 to 1787 inclusively," he wrote to
one young supplicant with stars in his eyes, "was disputed with
acrimony, and decided by as small majorities as any question
is decided these days." He reminded Rush to tell all the young
political aspirants in Pennsylvania that "the Majorities in Congress in '74 on all the essential points and Principles were only
one, two, or three votes . . . though they went out to the World
as wholly unanimous."[21]

Even though he was already on record as belittling the historical significance of the Declaration of Independence, the signing of
the Declaration was a symbolic event that so many correspondents
asked him about that Adams developed a veritable arsenal of critical weapons designed to smash idealized accounts. "I could not see
their hearts," he told one of the several hundred questioners about
the signing ceremony, "but, as far as I could penetrate the intricate
foldings of their souls, I then believed, and have not since altered
my opinion, that there were several who signed with regret, and
several others, with many doubts and much lukewarmness." He
reopened a correspondence with Thomas McKean, a former delegate from Pennsylvania at the Continental Congress who had also
been "present at the creation," to check his own memory. McK-
ean confirmed that many state delegations had been divided on
the question of independence and, as far as he could remember,
only a few actually signed the document on July 4. This encouraged Adams to denounce the famous painting of the scene by John
Trumbull, which hung (and still hangs) in the Capitol rotunda, as
a gross misrepresentation. Not only was Trumbull's painting bad

art—Adams objected to the misleading serenity of the scene and
called Trumbull's depiction of the Constitutional Convention "the
shin piece" because it seemed to focus the eye on the extended legs
and ankles of the signers—it was also bad history because there
was never one moment or even one day when all the delegates gathered to record their signatures to the Declaration. The war had
already begun by that date and members scurried in and out of
Philadelphia throughout the summer, affixing their names to the
now hallowed parchment whenever they happened to be in town.[22]

By contesting these patriotic fictions Adams hoped to blow
away the golden haze that was settling over the founding generation, including himself, and help provide the leaders of the rising
generation with more realistic expectations for themselves. "If you
should live to be an octogenarian," he informed one young man,
"you will know by experience the delight that is felt by those who
are stepping off the stage at the sights of such proofs of genius,
information and patriotism in those who are stepping on." In fact,
Adams claimed there was more intellectual talent available in the
new nation than there had ever been before. "I see a succession of
able and honorable characters," he told McKean, "from members
of Congress down to bachelors and students in our universities,
who will take care of the liberties which you have cherished and
done so much to support." The only problem, as he saw it, was
that the next generation of statesmen would be transfixed by the
idols being propped up by mindless devotees of patriotic mythology. He even hypothesized that one of the major reasons for the
successes enjoyed by the founders of independence and framers
of constitutions was the relative scarcity of available talent, which
allowed the ablest thinkers and leaders more readily to satisfy

their personal ambitions. The greatest danger facing the current crop of American leaders, he speculated, was not a lack but an overabundance of talent: "their numbers are so great, and their pretensions will be so high, that rivalries pernicious to the nation and her union may arise."[23]

Resisting inflated interpretations of the revolutionary generation was, in several senses, an old Adams custom, rooted in his intense hostility to utopian schemes of all sorts, whether they be Condorcet's or Wollstonecraft's depiction of a perfect democratic society in the future or historical treatments of godlike leaders of the recent American past. What was different, starting around 1812, was the absence of whining or moaning in the background, the elimination of most pleas for his own reputation, and the visible effort to enhance the status of others. Not that delivering praise was ever an easy or simple gesture for Adams. Praise, after all, like popularity, courted vanity. So it was usually dispensed in conjunction with a harsh message—the current generation could be encouraged if such encouragement was coupled with criticism of the fabricated stories of an earlier Augustan era—as if public opinion was a seesaw he was determined to keep in equilibrium much the same way he thought his own disposition and a well-structured constitution should be balanced. And when Adams first got wind of the surging historical reputations of southern, especially Virginian, participants in the Revolution, all the internal wires, fulcrums, levers, gears, and gyroscopes in his complicated psyche went into action.

The immediate cause of the reaction was the publication of a new biography of Patrick Henry. The author, William Wirt, was no superficial sentimentalist. Adams conceded that he was impressed with Wirt's scholarship, had always admired Henry himself, and that the book vividly, if somewhat melodramatically, recreated the texture of past events he had nearly forgotten. In fact, as he explained to John Quincy, Wirt's biography "called up so many Ghosts and they appear so much more venerable to me than they did when I lived and suffered with them, that I am almost as much terrified as the Old Lady of Endor was at the sight of Samuel." The ascendance of Patrick Henry's reputation, however, triggered Adams's intense suspicion that all the Virginia geese were being transformed into swans again, and that New Englanders were being forgotten altogether. He began, in earnest, to redress the balance.[24]

Adams launched a campaign to recover the memory of New England's special contribution to the Revolution. Since Jefferson and his southern friends had "made the Revolution a game of billiards," he wrote, "I will make it a game of shuttlecock. [Patrick] Henry might give the first impulse to the ball in Virginia, but [James] Otis' battledore had struck the shuttlecock up in air in Massachusetts . . . before Henry's ball was torched." This was a colorfully roundabout way of saying that James Otis had defied the authority of Parliament years before Henry did the same so eloquently in the Virginia House of Burgesses. But then Otis was not alone. "You say Mr. S. Adams 'had too much sternness and pious bigotry,'" he complained to William Tudor. Well, he lectured Tudor, your criticism merely documents your naiveté: "A man in his situation and circumstances must possess a large fund of sternness of stuff, or he soon will be annihilated. . . . Mr. [Sam] Adams was born and tempered a wedge of steel to split the knot . . . which tied North America to Great Britain." Successful revolutions required just that kind of intransigence. In fact, it took all kinds to make a revolution. He indignantly rejected the accusation that he had ever demeaned John Hancock for his foppish affectations: "I can say with truth," he pleaded with Tudor, "that I profoundly admired him, and even more profoundly loved him. If he had vanity and caprice, so had I. And if his vanity and caprice made him sometimes sputter . . . mine, I well know, had a similar affect upon him." Despite these petty disagreements—what Adams described as "little flickerings of little passions"—Hancock had been his abiding friend and (a gentle jibe here) a more stalwart supporter of independence than most of the slaveowning patriots living south of the Potomac.[25]

But the most intense campaign was waged in behalf of James Otis. Adams claimed that "Otis was the real father and founder of the American empire more certainly than Romulus was of the Roman." He knew that such an extreme statement would be greeted with incredulous laughter, because Otis was generally regarded as an early but minor voice opposing British sovereignty over the colonies, an eloquent but irascible character who eventually lost his mind and died before the Revolution actually began. But such criticism, Adams noted, did not bother him any more than "the barking of ladies' lap dogs [which] though they frighten sheep, only amuse me." He insisted that he believed Otis "to have been the earliest and the principal Founder of one of the greatest political Revolutions that ever occurred among men." When William Tudor completed a biography of Otis that Adams had long encouraged, Adams pronounced it "the most important volume of American Biography that I have ever read. . . ." He also encouraged John Trumbull to do a massive painting of Otis at the moment of his greatest triumph, arguing the Writs of Assistance Case before Thomas Hutchinson in the Boston State House in 1761, with a young John Adams taking notes in the background of the scene, "looking like a short, thick Archbishop of Canterbury."[26]

Just why Adams chose to make such an extreme case in behalf of such an unconventional figure as Otis is not difficult to discern. Part of the motivation was historically justified: Otis *had* been among the first to challenge the constitutional authority of Great Britain in language that undercut any and all attempts to exercise arbitrary power; the principle he defended in the Writs of Assistance Case was later enshrined in the first amendment to the United States Constitution. And as Adams himself acknowledged, he was committed to "puffing" New Englanders to offset the "puffing" of the Virginian dynasty. Most of all, however, Otis's reputation as an outspoken, vain, and difficult character not only illustrated his point that "the greatest Men have the greatest faults," and thereby struck a blow for a more realistic appraisal of the founding generation; it also served as a conveniently indirect reminder that another New Englander, also early to answer the tocsin against British rule and also infamous for his faults, deserved more credit than he was receiving from history.[27]

Eventually, even the inexhaustible Adams grew as weary of defending underappreciated heroes like Otis as he had already grown weary of openly defending himself or reducing the stature of his fellow revolutionaries to human size. Though he relished the fight, it was clearly a losing cause, since Americans obviously needed to believe in myths about their past just as religious devotees needed to believe in potent superstitions. He began, instead, to sound a new note when correspondents pestered him with the same old questions about the Revolution and the worthiest revolutionaries of his time.

"But what do we mean by the American Revolution?" he responded rhetorically to Hezekiah Niles in 1818. "Do we mean the American war?" Then, in an answer to his own question that has become famous, though understood by historians in several different ways, Adams proclaimed: "The Revolution was effected before the war commenced. The Revolution was in the minds and hearts of the people; a change in their religious sentiments of their duties and obligations."[28]

This was Adams's most familiar formulation, but it remains susceptible to different readings. It is possible to argue that Adams meant that the fifteen years preceding the outbreak of outright hostilities was the crucial era. This view would be compatible with his celebration of New Englanders like Otis, Sam Adams, and John Hancock, as well as his earlier autobiographical proclamations for himself. And there is some direct evidence to support this interpretation. In a letter to Jefferson, Adams first used language similar to the oft-quoted letter to Hezekiah Niles: "As to the history of the Revolution," he wrote Jefferson in 1815, "my Ideas may be peculiar, perhaps singular. What do we mean by the Revolution? The War? That was no part of the Revolution. It was only an Effect and Consequence of it. The Revolution was in the Minds of the People, and this was effected, from 1760 to 1775, in the course of fifteen Years before a drop of blood was drawn at Lexington."[29]

According to this interpretation, which became the dominant perspective among historians later in the nineteenth century and then again in the middle decades of the twentieth century, the American Revolution was essentially a constitutional clash between

Parliament, which was making a reinvigorated effort to impose its will on the western wing of its empire, and the political and economic leaders of the thirteen colonies, who defied Parliament's right to tax or legislate for them without their consent in highly literate pamphlet and newspaper broadsides. This version of American history put a premium on the role of prominent colonial leaders, on rational, even legalistic, arguments about the source of political legitimacy, and the controlled and surprisingly consistent political reaction within the leadership of the thirteen colonies. Again, Adams seemed to endorse this perspective on several occasions, claiming that the "accomplishment of it [the Revolution], in so short a time and by such simple means, was perhaps a singular example in the history of mankind. Thirteen clocks were made to strike together. . . ."[30]

The bulk of the evidence, however, indicates that Adams meant something different, especially as he grew older. He never abandoned his opinion that the years immediately preceding the war were crucial, or that the thoughts and actions of particular individuals caught in the revolutionary crisis made a difference. But his emphasis turned toward the more long-term and impersonal forces. When the Continental Congress gathered in 1774, he explained to Jefferson, it was like the convening of the Council of Nice: "It assembled the Priests from the E and W the N and the S, who compared notes, engaged in discussions and debates and formed Results. . . ." But the delegates merely embodied attitudes that had been developing in America for many years, in the local towns, villages, and remote byways of the countryside. Any "true history"—that bedeviling contradiction again—of the real causes of the Revolution would need to reach further back in time and much deeper into the local records of towns and families, where the elemental convictions that finally surfaced in the 1760s and 1770s were congealing. He agreed with Jefferson that "it is difficult to say at what moment the Revolution began," but in an important sense, "it began as early as the first Plantation of the Country." If one posed to him the question, "Who, then, was the author, inventor, discoverer of independence?" he would have to reply that the "only true answer must be the first emigrants"; the avowed revolutionary leaders of the 1770s were not prime movers so much as mere "awakeners and revivers of the original fundamental principle of colonization."[31]

His ultimate verdict—which was a premonition of the scholarly perspective on the Revolution dominant in the last quarter of the twentieth century—focused attention on invisible social, economic, and demographic forces operating at different speeds and in different patterns throughout the colonies. He told James Madison that the perennial question about "Who was the author . . . of American Independence" was silly and misguided: "We might as well inquire who were the Inventors of Agriculture, Horticulture, Architecture, Musick." It was not just that certain New Englanders deserved more acclaim than certain Virginians. Or that heroic icons like Washington, Franklin, and Jefferson should be remembered for their blunders as well as their success. The whole emphasis on "great men" was wrong. History was a panoramic process, better viewed through a telescope than a magnifying glass, best understood perhaps by older commentators who had acquired a seasoned sense of change over time and a perspective that carried the debate beyond myopic squabbles about who did what first or who merited the most credit. This was a way of thinking attractive to old man Adams for many reasons, not the least of which being that it was considered unfashionable.[32]

IN 1812, ADAMS described a magnificent three-year-old colt that he had just considered purchasing. It was "seventeen or eighteen hands high, bones like mossy timbers, ribbed quite to the Hips, every way broad, strong and well filled in proportion." The colt was also tame and gentle, as "good natured and good humored as a Cosset Lamb." Adams explained that the analogy to America came to him immediately: "Thinks I to myself, This noble Creature is the exact Emblem of my dear Country." Adams was hardly alone in believing that America was a spirited and sturdy colt-of-a-nation, blessed with nearly limitless natural resources, an exploding population and economy, a stable political system that both released and harnessed the energies of its citizenry, a nation destined at some time in the future to dominate the Western Hemisphere for a good stretch of human history. Nor was Adams alone in arguing that the foreign policy of the infant nation should be guided by the principle of neutrality. As he put it to Rush in the characteristic Adams formulation, he believed that the United States "should make no treaties or alliance with any European power; that we should consent to none but treaties of commerce; that we should separate ourselves as far as possible and as long as possible from all European politics and wars." These twin beliefs—that America was destined for greatness and that international neutrality was the wisest course—had been bedrock convictions within the political leadership of both major parties since the Washington presidency.[33]

But in two significant ways the Adams version of these

elemental convictions differed from the versions embraced by most
of his contemporaries. First, Adams refused to attribute the buoyant prospects of America to divine providence; he did not think
that Americans were a special people rendered immune by God's
grace from the customary ravages of history. He had always been
clear about this. Throughout his letters and formal political writings in the 1780s, for example, he had warned that "there is no
special providence for Americans, and their nature is the same
with that of others." The steady flow of letters from Quincy after
his retirement frequently reiterated the point. "There is no special
Providence for us," he wrote Rush. "We are not a chosen people that
I know of, or if we are, we deserve it as little as the Jews. . . . We
must and we shall go the way of all earth. . . ." Americans were just
as susceptible to vanity, folly, and delusion as any other people—
the notion that God watched over them being a singular example
of such superstitious stupidity—while the strategic strengths and
the "advantages we have over Europe," he noted caustically, "are
chiefly geographical."[34]

Second, Adams's notion of American neutrality was neither
as isolationist as the Jeffersonians preferred nor as pro-English as
the policies of most New England Federalists. "The government
of the United States from 1789 has been but a company of Engine
Men," he wrote Vanderkemp, complaining that the chief job of
every president, from Washington to Madison, "has been to spout
Cold Water upon our raw habitations . . . to prevent them being
scorched by the Flames from Europe." Neutrality was both a wise
and noble ideal, because America needed time to consolidate its
continental resources and resolve its sectional differences. But
Adams never believed that Europe would leave America alone,

or that the commercial interests of New England merchants and southern planters would allow for complete insulation from European problems: "Thus our beloved country," he confided to Rush, "is indeed in a very dangerous situation. It is between two great fires in Europe [i.e., England and France] and between two ignited Parties at home, smoking, sparkling and flaming, ready to burst into Conflagration." Despite the Atlantic Ocean and our "geographical advantages," America could never completely separate itself from the rest of the world and ought not to try.[35]

These variations on dominant American themes, or what we might call Adams's corollaries to the guiding principles of early American foreign policy (and what Adams himself simply called "my system"), gave him an unusual if not unique perspective on the events that led up to the War of 1812. "I am, I know, a singular Being," he wrote one congressman in 1813, "for Nobody will agree with me." But he nevertheless thought he was just as right now about the proper American policy as he had been in 1776 when he counselled war with England and in 1799 when he counselled compromise with France. He conceded to his old friend and physician Benjamin Waterhouse in 1813 that he might not have "the Foresight of the Tumble-Bug. Yet in my Conscience, I believe, I had seen more and clearer, than this Nation or its Government for fourteen years past."[36]

To his Federalist friends in New England, who were dedicated to preserving commercial relations with England at almost any cost, Adams delivered lectures against myopia. "It is not wonderful that some persons among us are so eager to rush into the arms of Great Britain," he chided, "but it is unaccountable that there should be so many. . . ." At some elemental level, the hostility toward England that had been generated in Adams's breast during the war for independence had never died. And, more importantly, he insisted that England's hatred for America was also still intact. "She has looked at us from our first settlement to this moment, with eyes of jealousy, envy, hatred and contempt," he claimed. As early as 1806 he predicted to John Quincy that a second war with England was likely: "Our Confusions will be very great, but she [England] will suffer most in the end," he declared, adding the hope that "Another war will transmit an eternal hatred of England to our American Posterity." But he realized that his prophecies were regarded as somewhere between treason and insanity by most of his New England friends. "Croak! Croak! Croak! Croak," he shouted in frustration to his son. "I can do nothing but croak, in the present state of things." He argued that he knew the English better than most, that Parliament was like an arrogant aristocrat who believed he had the right to impress American seamen and dictate terms about trade. Neither the Whig nor Tory leaders in London had a kind thought for America, he believed, and as for the mass of English citizens, "those millions of people who are not politicians, neither know, nor care, any more about us, than they do about the Seminole Indians."[37]

To the Jeffersonians, who also distrusted England but wished to avoid war at almost any cost, he gave sermons on military preparedness, especially the need for a larger navy. "The counsel which Themistocles gave to Athens, Pompey to Rome, Cromwell to England . . . and Colbert to France, I have always given and shall continue to give to my countrymen," he wrote as early as 1802; because "the great questions of commerce and power between nations and empires . . . are determined at sea, all reasonable encouragement should be given the navy." Then he added a slogan repeated over and over in his correspondence from Quincy: "The trident of Neptune is the sceptre of the world." American neutrality and aversion to war were both noble principles, he agreed, but the sincerity of the Jefferson administration's commitment to such principles was no guarantee of their ultimate triumph. Adams advocated a major naval build-up to protect the coastline and to secure control of the Great Lakes in the event of war, all the while negotiating just as strenuously in the hope that war might be avoided. It was the same position he had advocated during his own presidency when the danger was war with France. But this time Adams suspected that the English would spurn all American efforts at peaceful compromises.[38]

When Jefferson ordered an embargo on all American exports, designed to keep American commercial shipping out of the conflict between England and Napoleonic France, Adams went along with great reluctance, predicting that the embargo would prove more ruinous to the American economy than to the economies of the European belligerents. "I have never approved of Non Importations, Non Intercourses, or Embargoes for more than six weeks," he told Jefferson years later, suggesting that the real purpose of such measures was more psychological than economic; that is, the embargo produced pain and suffering within the American populace and thereby stiffened the will for war. "You and Mr. Madison had as good a right to your Opinions as I had to mine," he observed years later, "and I must acknowledge the Nation was with you. But neither your Authority nor that of the Nation has convinced me. Nor, I am bold to pronounce will convince Posterity." Although he sympathized with the burdens and respected the integrity of his successors to the presidency, noting that the "Talents, the Scholarship, the Genius, the Learning of Jefferson and Madison are not disputed," he worried about their discomfort with conflict and confrontations and what he called "their total Incapacity for practical Government in War. . . ."[39]

Nor did he attempt to hide his critical views from Jefferson himself. When negotiations failed and war finally broke out in 1812, Adams chided Jefferson for "the total Neglect and absolute Refusal of all maritime Protection and Defence. . . ." The war had now come and America was, just as he had warned, wholly unprepared for it. Jefferson tried to be gracious in response, congratulating Adams for his foresight "as having been an early and constant advocate of wooden walls," but then went on to explain that he had opposed a large naval force because England's fleet was too large and powerful for any American navy, no matter how enhanced, to risk combat on the open seas. Adams responded with a mini-lecture on military strategy: the United States had no intention of invading England, so a massive American navy capable of taking on the entire British fleet was unnecessary; the chief battles would be on this side of the Atlantic, mainly on the Great Lakes and coastline. "We must have a Navy now to command The Lakes," he observed, "if it costs us 100 Ships of the Line; whatever becomes of the Ocean." He believed that Jefferson had to assume responsibility for America's lack of readiness, for "if only a few Frigates had been ordered to be built," the war might have gone differently. "Without this," he wrote pointedly to Monticello, "our Union will be a brittle China Vase, a house of Ice or a Place [Plate? Palace?] of Glass." Jefferson wisely let the subject drop.[40]

Even before the fighting began, Adams had decided not only that it was inevitable but also that it was necessary, "necessary against England, necessary to convince France that we are something; and above all necessary to convince ourselves." The chief effect of the war, he predicted to Rush three years before it began, would be renewed American nationalism. "We hear very often declarations on the demoralizing tendency of war," he wrote, "but as much as I hate war, I cannot be of the opinion that frequent wars are so corrupting to human nature as long peaces." It was a tragic comment on mankind, he acknowledged, "that we cannot be virtuous without murdering one another," but such was the sad historical truth of the matter. A few months before the outbreak of hostilities, Adams repeated in almost poetic language his hope that war with England would recover the national spirit that had faded since the end of the revolutionary war:

> The winds begin to rustle, the clouds gather, it grows dark;
> will these airy forces rear up the Ocean to a foaming fury?
> A spirit seems to be rising; a spirit of contrition and shame
> at our long apathy and lethargy; a spirit of resentment of
> injuries, a spirit of indignation at insolence; and what to me
> is very remarkable, a spirit of greater unanimity than I have
> ever witnessed in this country for fifty years.[41]

Adams also tended to view the causes and the conduct of the War of 1812 through the prism of the American Revolution. He was critical of American military strategy, especially the decision to invade Canada, which proved a fiasco, because of British naval supremacy on the Great Lakes. But what he called "the great

Comedy of Errors" reminded him of the initial months of the Revolution: "I say we do not make more mistakes now than we did in 1774, '5, '6, '7, '8, '9, '80, '81, '82, '83," he reminded Rush. "It was patched and pie bald then, as it is now, and ever will be, world without end." He disclaimed any right "to reproach the present government or the present generation" for its conduct of the war: "We blundered at Lexington, at Bunker's Hill. . . . Where, indeed, did we not blunder except Saratoga and York[town], where our triumphs redeemed all former disgraces?" Even when the British army closed in on the national capital, Adams told friends not to panic. It was worse during the Revolution, he recalled, "when Congress was chased like a covey of Partridges from Philadelphia to Trenton, from Trenton to Lancaster. . . ."[42]

Lack of support for the war in pockets of Federalist New England reminded him of the foot-draggers and pseudo-Tories of old. In the Congress this timidity took the form of orchestrated delays, which he found nearly treasonable: "I expect to be tortured all winter, to read eternal Speeches in Congress repeating . . . over and over again a thousand times this common place nonsense," he complained. "The times require Ships and Cannon, not Sighs and Figures." His break with the Federalists, which for all intents and purposes had occurred in the last year of his presidency, was now rendered final and complete. When word reached him that New England Federalists were contemplating a convention in Hartford to consider boycotting the war and even seceding from the Union, he was indignant. These traitors should be "made to repent of it *in dust and ashes.*" The Hartford Convention would prove a fiasco, he predicted defiantly, claiming that it would produce only lukewarm opposition; or, as he put it more colorfully, it would resemble "The

Congress at Vienna, as least as much as an Ignis fatuous resembles a Volcano."[43]

Even the excruciatingly prolonged negotiations that eventually led to the Treaty of Ghent ending the war produced in Adams a sharp sense of *déjà vu*. For many of the issues at stake—the impressment of American seamen, British claims to trading rights in the western territories and fishing rights off the Newfoundland coast—were identical to the issues Adams had negotiated as head of the American delegation in Paris at the end of the Revolution. And the head of the American delegation at Ghent was none other than his son, John Quincy Adams.

When President Madison asked his advice about American concessions, Adams tried to be both candid and diplomatic: "All I can say is, that I would continue this war forever, rather than surrender one acre of territory, one iota of the fisheries, as established by the third article of the treaty of 1783, or one sailor impressed from any merchant ship. I will not, however, say this to my son, though I shall be very much obliged to you, if you will give him orders to the same effect." A few months later, of course, he was writing John Quincy with just the advice offered confidentially to Madison, recommending with relish what he called his own successful "mixture of fluency and impudence" as a diplomat. He warned John Quincy not to trade the coastal fisheries for control of the Mississippi: "Oh, how glad I am, that I am not in his [John Quincy's] place," he told Benjamin Rush's son. "I should have been tempted to say 'War! War, interminable, or eternal, rather than any such terms.'" When news of the signing of the Treaty of Ghent reached him, he was relieved that John Quincy would finally be coming home. But when the specific terms of the treaty revealed that both sides had agreed to the *status quo ante*, he was incensed, interpreting the stalemate as a personal affront to his efforts in 1783: "neither George third nor his Son have fulfilled his promises to my Country, made to me, as her Representative."[44]

It surely required "a singular Being" to take an entire peace treaty personally. But then, Adams was accustomed to uttering irreverencies out loud, just as he was accustomed to defying established opinions and presenting his strong and often passionate views in a defiant and argumentative format. That was the way he thought and felt and behaved. The most disarming aspect of his arguments about the causes and conduct of the War of 1812 turned out to be that, on virtually every major issue, events proved him correct. And, most disarming of all, this time he did not need to wait for posterity to clinch the verdict. But there was no need to worry about his foresightedness leading to sudden esteem, enhanced popularity, and vaunting vanity. He was safely insulated from such corruptions this time and did not need to take precautions against popularity. For no one, save John Quincy and a few close friends, was paying any attention.

CHAPTER FOUR

The American Dialogue

I consider you and [Jefferson] as the North and South
Poles of the American Revolution. Some talked, some
wrote, and some fought to promote and establish
it, but you and Mr. Jefferson *thought* for us all.
—Benjamin Rush to Adams, February 17, 1812

You and I ought not to die, before We have
explained ourselves to each other.
—Adams to Thomas Jefferson, July 15, 1813

T HE OUTBREAK OF WAR with Great Britain in 1812 allowed
all the oppositional tendencies of the Adams temperament to
align themselves properly, like the moons and planets in a favorable astrological forecast. Whether it was the arrival of a war he
had been predicting was inevitable and necessary, or the completion of his long series of self-justifying articles for the *Boston
Patriot*, Adams became discernibly more relaxed and outgoing. He
had discovered at last his fulcrum or centerpoint, a psychological
equivalent of his political ideal of balance.

The pace of his correspondence picked up and more of the Adams playfulness appeared in his prose. "I am as cheerful as ever I was," he wrote to Thomas McKean, "and my health is as good, excepting a quiveration of the hands." He then apologized in mock fashion for the word "quiveration," explaining that "though I borrowed it from an Irish boy, I think it an improvement in our language worthy a place in Webster's dictionary." When Robert Fulton, inventor of the steamboat, wrote to him about America's promising contributions to science and technology, Adams refused to sound his customary clarion call against theories of progress. "I am entirely of your opinion," he assured Fulton, "that the Diamonds in the quarries of science are inexhaustible . . . and I hope you will be a successful miner." He concluded on a buoyant note, announcing that if he was "only fifty years younger, I should be happy to dig with you." The correspondence with Benjamin Rush had always brought out his most exuberant energy, even when he was mired in despair over his declining reputation. But the letters to Rush now reached new heights of frivolity. When Rush began to send reports of his own dreams, Adams offered a diagnosis of the power of dreams to express deep-seated emotional urges, then challenged Rush "dream for dream." He described a recent nocturnal vision in which a grandiloquent Adams had delivered a calming speech to a menagerie of animals and ideologues in revolutionary France. The Adams bounce was back.[1]

Whether it was a cause or a consequence of Adams's newfound zest is impossible to know, but the reconciliation with Thomas Jefferson played a crucial role in carrying Adams past the morose resentment of his early retirement years. Beginning in 1812, Adams and Jefferson exchanged letters on a regular basis for fourteen years, until both legendary leaders died on the same day, which also happened to be the fiftieth anniversary of the Declaration of Independence. Of the 158 letters exchanged, Adams wrote 109, more than doubling the pace of the correspondence from Monticello and usually setting the agenda for the subjects discussed. From the perspective of posterity, it was a friendship made in heaven, interrupted by unpleasant political and party squabbles in the 1790s, now miraculously retrieved in time for the two patriarchs to stroll arm-in-arm toward immortality. "Jefferson is as tough as a lignum vitae knot," Adams exclaimed to Rush at the start of the exchange, marvelling at the clear and strong handwriting—no quiverations were allowed at Monticello—and admiring the famous Jefferson style: "Not one symptom of decay or decline can I discern in it."[2]

Once begun, the correspondence between the two patriarchs proceeded on this affectionate note. And once completed, it quickly became a landmark in American letters and eventually a classic, some would say *the* classic statement of the founding generation. Sensibilities as different as Woodrow Wilson and Ezra Pound have celebrated its intellectual significance. In the twentieth century, theatre companies and public radio stations have sponsored readings from the text; publishers have issued full and abridged editions in paperback; and schoolchildren are occasionally required to memorize the most evocative passages. Adams and Jefferson, as both men surely suspected, were sending letters to posterity as much as to each other.[3]

The fact that the letters were ever written at all was almost as much a miracle as the simultaneous death of the two patriarchs and constitutes what is probably the clearest sign of Adams's victory over his private demons and doubts. For Adams had to overcome the bitterness and resentment he had been harboring toward Jefferson from the start of the former's term as president and throughout his own early retirement years at Quincy. Jefferson was a "shadow man," he told friends, whose greatest talent was enigma. His character was "like the great rivers, whose bottoms we cannot see and make no noise." When Rush told Adams that he had dreamed that the Sage of Monticello and the Sage of Quincy were reunited, Adams countered that Rush should "take a Nap and dream for my instruction and Edification the character of Jefferson and his administration. . . ." There was no doubt, Adams concluded coldly, that such a dream would turn into a nightmare. When he was governor of Virginia and then again when he was president, Jefferson had exhibited "a total Incapacity for Government or War." The embargo had been a complete failure; the purchase of the Louisiana Territory, Jefferson's major achievement, had been accomplished in violation of his own beliefs about federal power; his persistent opposition to the decisions of John Marshall and the Supreme Court threatened the independence of the judiciary; he had left the nation "infinitely worse than he found it, and that from his own error or ignorance."[4]

Then there was Jefferson's status as a slaveowner. Adams claimed to give no credence to the scandalous stories about Jefferson's alleged relationship with Sally Hemings, his mulatto slave. As a fellow victim of similarly venomous vendettas, Adams empathized. But he went on to speculate that the allegation was "a natural and almost inevitable consequence of the foul Contagion in the human Character, Negro Slavery." Jefferson was seriously contaminated by that contagion and could not escape the prevalent suspicion that "there was not a planter in Virginia who could not reckon among his slaves a number of his children." Even though the Sally Hemings story was probably not true, Adams surmised with obvious satisfaction that it would remain "a blot on his Character" because it symbolized the inherently immoral condition in which all slaveowners, Jefferson included, lived.[5]

Finally, there was the matter of the past friendship between Adams and Jefferson. There is no question that the two men became close friends during the revolutionary struggle and the peace negotiations in Paris. Abigail even claimed that, in the 1780s, Jefferson was, as she put it, "the only person with whom my companion could associate with perfect freedom and reserve." And during the 1790s, even as the split between the Federalists and the Jeffersonian Republicans generated bitter and impassioned conflict that led to the creation of two political parties, the Hamiltonian wing of the Federalists worried constantly that Adams and Jefferson would draw on their vaunted friendship to strike a political compromise that might leave the High Federalists out of power. To be sure, when Jefferson spurned Adams's offer to play a major role in his administration, he committed the unpardonable sin, at least according to the Adams creed—he chose party over country and personal ambition over friendship. This wound festered and left a scar that, in some respects, never completely healed. But Adams was cordial toward Jefferson in the aftermath of the election of 1800, had him for dinner at the presidential mansion before the inauguration and, in the eyes of the High Federalists, evidenced less hostility toward the man from Monticello than toward his fellow Federalists. As Fisher Ames explained it, Adams had always retained "a strong revolutionary taint in his mind, [and] admires the characters, principles and means which that revolutionary system . . . seems to legitimate, and . . . holds cheap any reputation that was not then founded and top'd off." In short, the brotherly bond established in 1776 linked Adams and Jefferson in ways that Adams would never wholly repudiate.[6]

Throughout the early years of his retirement, however, as the anger over his defeat stewed and brewed inside him, Adams denied that a friendship with Jefferson had ever existed. "You are much mistaken," he explained to William Cunningham in 1804, "when you say that no man living has so much knowledge of Mr. Jefferson's transactions as myself." Adams claimed that he and Jefferson were never close: "I know but little concerning him." Then he went on to describe the almost constant personal interaction between the two men, from the Continental Congress in 1775–76, through the negotiations in Paris and the diplomatic efforts in London, then as fellow members of the Washington administration. The narrative conveyed just the opposite conclusion that Adams intended; no one in public life, save Madison, knew Jefferson so well and so intimately. But Adams held firmly to his denial of a close relationship. Although the Virginian "always proferred great friendship," he observed cynically, Jefferson had secretly supported and salaried "almost every villain he could find who had been an enemy to me." They were not now and never had been friends, Adams insisted, as if shouting the point more loudly would somehow make it true.[7]

Chinks in the Adams armor began to appear in 1809. Under the pressure of Rush's incessant prodding and his reported dream of a reconciliation between the two patriarchs, Adams reiterated his disingenuous claim that he felt "no Resentment or Animosity against the Gentleman and abhor the Idea of blackening his Character or transmitting him in odious Colours to Posterity." Then he

opened a small crack in his pride through which the old friendship might crawl. "If I should receive a Letter from him however,"
Adams observed curtly, "I should not fail to acknowledge and
answer it." A correspondence was not out of the question, he was
suggesting, but Jefferson would have to go first.[8]

The melting away of pride and resentment continued over the
ensuing months, helped along by Rush's persistent dreams and by
Adams's emerging capacity to poke fun at his own stubbornness.
Perhaps Jefferson should be excused for whatever mistakes he had
made, Adams conceded, because he was a mere youth: "Jefferson was always but a Boy to me. . . . I am bold to say that I was
his Preceptor on Politicks and taught him every thing that has
been good and solid in his whole Political Conduct." How could
one hold a grudge against a disciple? In this buoyant and jocular
mood it was even difficult to recall just what had caused the break
between the two men. "It lay as a confused recollection in my own
head," Adams wrote Rush, "that the only Flit between Jefferson
and me . . . was occasioned by a Motion for Congress to sit on
Saturday." Or was the source of the trouble the argument that he
and Jefferson once had with Washington about hairstyles? Jefferson preferred it straight and he preferred it curled. Or was it the
other way around?[9]

Then, in 1811, Adams was visited at Quincy by Edward Coles,
a Virginian close to Jefferson. In the course of the conversation
Adams let it be known that his political disagreements with Jefferson had never destroyed his affection for the man. "I always loved
Jefferson," he told Coles, "and still love him." When news of this
exchange reached Monticello, as Adams knew it would, Jefferson
responded heartily, if a bit less affectionately. "This is enough for

me," he wrote Rush, adding that he "knew him [Adams] to be always an honest man, often a great one, but sometimes incorrect and precipitate in his judgments." The major caveat, however, came at the end, when Jefferson told Rush that he had always defended Adams's character to others, "with the single exception as to his political opinions." This was like claiming that the Pope was usually reliable, except when he declared himself on matters of faith and morals. Here Rush performed his mischievous magic. He silently edited out the offensive passages and forwarded the favorable remarks to Quincy. That was how it stood at the close of the year, the two former friends and living legends sniffing around the edges of a possible reconciliation; but like wary old dogs, they were still reluctant to close the distance.[10]

In the end it was Adams who made the decisive move. The first letter went out from Quincy to Monticello on January 1, 1812, timing that suggests Adams had decided to revive the relationship as one of his resolutions for the new year. It was a short and cordial note, relaying family news and referring to "two pieces of Homespun" which he had sent along as a gift by separate packet. He apprised Rush soon thereafter, protecting his pride behind a barrage of jokes: "Your dream is out. . . . You have wrought wonders! You have made peace between powers that never were at War! You have reconciled Friends that never were at Enmity. . . . In short, the mighty defunct Potentates of Mount Wollaston and Monticello by your sorceries . . . are again in being." This was the playfully evasive and self-consciously nonchalant posture he maintained whenever the question of his reconciliation with Jefferson came up. There was nothing momentous or historic about the reunion, he insisted. There had never been any serious break between the two men most responsible for the Declaration of Independence. "It was only as if one sailor had met a brother sailor, after twenty-five years' absence," Adams quipped, "and had accosted him, how fare you, Jack?"[11]

There was a discernible awkwardness as well as a slight stumble at the start of the correspondence. Jefferson presumed, quite plausibly, that the "two pieces of Homespun" Adams was sending referred to domestically produced clothing, a nice symbol of the American economic response to the embargo; it also recalled the colonial response to British taxation policies in the 1760s, a fitting reminder of the good old days when Adams and Jefferson first joined the movement for American independence. And so Jefferson responded with a lengthy letter on the benefits of domestic manufacturing, only to discover afterwards that Adams had intended the homespun reference as a metaphor. His gift turned out to be a copy of John Quincy's two-volume work, *Lectures on Rhetoric and Oratory*. The exchange had begun on the same note that the friendship had floundered, an elemental misunderstanding.[12]

IT QUICKLY RECOVERED, as both men demonstrated that they required no instruction in rhetoric from John Quincy or anyone else. "And so we have gone on," wrote Jefferson in his lyrical style, "and so we shall go on, puzzled and prospering beyond example in the history of man." The "puzzled and prospering" phrase was vintage Jeffersonian prose, a melodic and alliterative choice of words conveying the paradoxical character of America's march toward its destiny. Not to be outdone, Adams shot back with an eloquent alliteration of his own. "Whatever a peevish Patriarch might say," he apprised Jefferson, "I have never seen the day in which I could say I had no Pleasure; or that I have had more Pain than Pleasure." The playful word duel continued throughout the correspondence. When Jefferson wrote: "My temperament is sanguine. I steer my bark with Hope in the head, leaving fear astern," Adams replied in kind: "I admire your Navigation and should like to sail with you, either in your Bark or in my own, alongside of yours; Hope with her gay Ensigns displayed at the Prow; fear with her Hobgoblins behind the Stern." Both men were, of course, splendid stylists, with Jefferson heading Adams's personal list of prominent Americans who knew how to write a sentence. (That was the major reason, Adams liked to remind his friends, he had chosen Jefferson to draft the Declaration of Independence in the first place.) Throughout the correspondence, however, and most especially at its start, the formality and elegance of the language suggests a level of self-conscious literary craftsmanship uncommon even for two of the most accomplished letterwriters of the era.[13]

Beyond their calculated eloquence, the early letters are careful, diplomatic, eager to avoid the political controversies which might still be tender topics for the other man: "But whither is senile garrulity leading me?" asked Jefferson rhetorically: "Into politics, of which I have taken leave. I think little of them, and say less. I have given up newspapers in exchange for Tacitus and Thucydides, for Newton and Euclid; and I find myself much the happier." Quite conscious of Adams's easily aroused irritability and sense of propriety, Jefferson felt compelled to wonder whether "in the race of life, you do not keep, in its physical decline, the same distance ahead of me which you have done in political honors and achievements." This gracious gesture, which indirectly endorsed Adams's earlier opinion to Rush that Jefferson was his protégé, prompted a gracious response from Quincy. Jefferson had now taken the lead on all counts, Adams acknowledged; Adams was only leading in the sense that he would be first to the grave.

Later on, Adams took refuge in one of the recurrent motifs that both men used as a safe haven throughout the correspondence—the dwindling list of surviving signers of the Declaration of Independence: "I may rationally hope to be the first to depart," he apprised Jefferson, "and as you are the youngest and the most energetic in mind and body, you may therefore rationally hope to be the last to take your flight." Like the last person to retire from the hearth in the evening, Jefferson would be the last one "to set up and rake the ashes over the coals. . . ." But danger lurked behind even the most careful remarks. If Jefferson thought the reference to Thucydides and Tacitus would keep the dialogue a safe distance from politics, Adams reminded him that even the classics, especially those particular authors, spoke directly to his own pessimism. The old nerve endings were still vibrating. "I have read Thucydides and Tacitus, so often, and at such distant Periods of my Life," he recalled, "that elegant, profound and enchanting is their Style, I am weary of them," claiming that their descriptions of Athens and Greece in decline were strikingly reminiscent of "my own Times and my own Life." Then he apologized for this outbreak of self-pity, joking that "My Senectutal Loquacity has more than retaliated your 'Senile Garrulity.'"[14]

A mutual sense of the delicacy and fragility of their newly recovered friendship explains in part the initial politeness and obvious care with which each man composed his thoughts and arranged his words. Their trust was newly won and incomplete;

nor, for that matter, would it ever be total. For example, when Adams asked Jefferson to assist in obtaining a judgeship for Samuel Malcolm, the former private secretary to Adams, Jefferson promised he would try. He then wrote Madison to say Malcolm was "a strong federalist" and therefore an inappropriate choice. Later he wrote Adams to express regret at failing to place Malcolm, claiming the request to President Madison had arrived too late.[15]

Adams was guilty of similar acts of duplicity. In 1819, he reported reading a copy of the Mecklenburg Declaration of Independence, a document purportedly drafted by a group of citizens in North Carolina in May of 1775 and containing language similar to Jefferson's later version of the Declaration. Jefferson responded immediately, contesting the authenticity of the Mecklenburg document, which seemed to cast doubts on the originality of his own famous draft. Adams promptly reassured Jefferson that he believed "the Mecklenburg Resolutions are a fiction" and that it had always seemed "utterly incredible that they should be genuine." Meanwhile, however, he was telling other correspondents just the opposite. "I could as soon believe that the dozen flowers of the Hydrangia now before my Eyes were the work of chance," he snickered, "as that the Mecklenburg Resolutions and Mr. Jefferson's declaration were not derived one from the other."[16]

The special character of the correspondence—the sheer literary quality, the classical references and proses, letters that take on the tone of treatises—followed naturally from their mutual realization that these private letters also had a public audience. Jefferson expressed amazement "that a printer has had the effrontery to propose to me the letting him publish it [the correspondence with Adams]," then wondered why "these people think they have a right to everything secret or sacred." Adams was more realistic, or perhaps more forthright. "This correspondence," he joked to Jefferson, "I hope will be concealed as long as Hutchinsons and Olivers," referring to the secret letters of Thomas Hutchinson and Andrew Oliver that were intercepted by American revolutionaries and published as evidence of a British conspiracy to abolish colonial liberties. The most important readers, however, were not contemporary snoopers, but subsequent generations. Adams said as much to Jefferson, envisioning the day when "your letters will all be published in volumes . . . which will be read with delight in future ages." Adams's obsession with his historic reputation, of course, was both obvious and notorious. Jefferson's concern was equally powerful, but more disguised and controlled. It seems fair to conclude that both men sat down to write the other in a more self-conscious frame of mind than they adopted when corresponding with less renowned friends and associates. This was not a casual correspondence. Words were chosen with one eye on posterity.[17]

WHAT GAVE THE correspondence its intellectual zest, and carried it beyond polite exchanges about old age, daily exercise discussions, and comparative reading lists, was Adams's inveterate effusiveness. No matter how hard he tried, no matter how often he reminded himself to avoid controversy, no matter how frequently he vowed to provide posterity with a more serene, scrubbed-up image of himself as the classical hero, Adams found it impossible to behave like a proper patriarch: "Whenever I sett down to write to you," he admitted to Jefferson in 1813, "I am precisely in the Situation of the Wood Cutter on Mount Ida: I can not see

Wood for Trees. So many Subjects Crowd upon me that I know not, with which to begin." It was the characteristically maddening and beguiling Adams impetuosity again. Soon, all the troublesome and forbidden subjects were breaking through with a velocity and ferocity that overwhelmed Jefferson's capacity to keep up.[18]

Jefferson, for example, had used the phrase "mighty Wave of public opinion" in passing, intending it as a favorable commentary on the benign power of the popular will. Adams repeated it mockingly, then unleashed a verbal barrage. Claiming that "these Letters of yours require Volumes from me," he went into a tirade against popular movements of several sorts: the Crusades, the French Revolution, the Thirty Years War, hurricanes in the Gulf Stream (!), corrupt elections, Christian and Muslim massacres, and a host of other catastrophes, creating a veritable wave of his own political rhetoric that was intended to wash over Jefferson's presumption that the will of the people was always benign. "Upon this Subject I despair of making myself understood by Posterity, by the present Age, and even by you," he thundered. On many occasions the "mighty Wave of public opinion," he went on, took the shape of a mob that committed terrorist acts against the public interest. Recalling a popular demonstration against the government in 1799, Adams chided Jefferson: "I have no doubt You was fast asleep in philosophical Tranquility, when ten thousand People, and perhaps many more, were parading the Streets of Philadelphia."[19]

Adams returned regularly to his outspokenly critical attitude toward popular movements. If not restrained by law, evangelical Christians in America would "whip and crop, and pillory and roast" just as they did throughout European history. "The multitude and diversity of them, You will Say, is our Security against them all. God grant it," he acknowledged. But the same emotional forces that propelled religious fanatics to commit unspeakable acts against humanity operated with equivalent ferocity in the political arena. "I wish that Superstition in Religion exciting Superstition in Politicks . . . may never blow up all your benevolent and phylanthropic Lucubrations," he warned Jefferson, but "the History of all Ages is against you." When Jefferson tried to respond in an accommodating way, agreeing that religious fanaticism had certainly proven destructive in Europe, Adams reiterated that irrational energies were not confined by any psychological embargo to the other side of the Atlantic. "I can only say at present," he concluded, "that it would seem that human Reason and human Conscience, though I believe there are such things, are not a Match, for human Passions, human Imaginations and human Enthusiasm."[20]

Of course, for Adams to insist on the power of the passions was like a devout Christian proclaiming the power of prayer. It came to him just as naturally, though surely more effusively, as silence and self-restraint came to Jefferson. A lifetime of introspection and daily entries in his diary had provided Adams with a palpable sense of his own emotional excesses. And his reading of history had confirmed that irrational forces usually shaped the behavior, not just of mass movements but also of aristocratic elites and individual despots. He could launch into a lecture on this theme with all the impetuous energy that graphically illustrated its point, thereby making his own passionate disposition an important part of his discourse on the irresistible power of human emotion.

Jefferson was not temperamentally disposed to find the discourse interesting. He tended not so much to deny the influence of the emotional and irrational as to believe that they were best ignored. He was as constitutionally cool as Adams was warm. An inveterate record keeper who logged all his letters, kept track of daily weather changes, and maintained elaborate files on his library, Indian languages, and garden plantings, Jefferson never kept a diary or any account of his deepest feelings. Introspection struck him as self-indulgent. In 1816 he made the mistake of declaring this opinion to Adams, wondering why otherwise intelligent people allowed themselves to probe their private feelings and become preoccupied with depressing emotions like gloom and grief. "I wish the pathologists then would tell us," Jefferson asked rhetorically, "what is the use of grief on the economy, and of what good it is the cause. . . ."[21]

It was as if he had dropped a match in a munitions factory. Adams felt obliged to deliver a series of lectures on "the uses of grief," a subject on which he claimed to be one of America's experts. Grief, he explained, was not just a futile form of sorrow. Under its spell men are driven into "habits of serious Reflection. . . ." It "sharpens the Understanding and Softens the heart." The furrows depicted in the portraits and statues of great men "were all ploughed in the Countenance, by Grief."[22]

Jefferson tried to drop the subject: "To the question indeed on the Utility of Grief, no answer remains to be given. You have exhausted the subject." But Adams had just gotten started. There were many more "uses of grief," all of which required enumeration. Then there were the equally important "abuses of grief," which required documentation with examples drawn from the classics, Christianity, and even the misuse of Washington's reputation by the High Federalists under Hamilton to sustain support for their banking schemes. Grief, it turned out, was a many-sided and many-splendored emotion. Jefferson tried to fight off the last lecture-of-a-letter on the subject by concluding that the uses and the abuses of grief seemed to cancel themselves out, allowing him to cling to his original contention that "we may consider its value in the economy of the human being, as equivocal at least." Adams could not have disagreed more, since he regarded the controlling of human passion as the ultimate function of government. But he let the matter drop.[23]

By then, however, the pattern was set. Adams was writing over two letters for every one of Jefferson's, setting the intellectual agenda of the correspondence so that it accorded with his most passionate preoccupations. "Answer my letters at your Leisure," he advised Jefferson as it became clear that the stream of words from Quincy was threatening to flood Monticello. "Give yourself no concern," Adams added, explaining that the correspondence had become a major emotional outlet for him, "a refuge and protection against Ennui." Jefferson apologized for his failure to keep up, claiming that he received over twelve hundred letters each year, all of which required answers. Adams replied that he received only a fraction of that number, but chose not to answer most of them so he could focus his allegedly waning energies on Jefferson, whom he called the only person "on this side of Monticello, who can give me any Information upon Subjects that I am now *analysing* and *investigating:* if I may be permitted to Use the pompous Words now in fashion." Adams declared that he was not going to take a "stand upon Epistolary Etiquette . . . though I have written two Letters, yet unnoticed I must write a third." If Jefferson felt somewhat overwhelmed, Adams assured him that he was only writing "a hundredth part of what I wish to say to you." And after all,

Adams pleaded to his famous friend, "You and I ought not to die, before We have explained ourselves to each other."[24]

THERE WAS NEVER any realistic possibility that a truly mutual understanding of their deep-rooted differences would emerge fully in the correspondence. Adams invested himself in the exchange much more than Jefferson; it obviously meant more to him and received a fuller measure of his intellectual attention. (Indeed, Adams gave the correspondence with Jefferson almost the same kind of intense attention that Jefferson gave to the founding of the University of Virginia at that same time.) In addition to the inherently unbalanced character of the exchange, its self-conscious theatricality and the patriarchal role-playing in which both men engaged meant that genuine debate and complete closure were not the highest priorities. But the initial clash over the role of popular movements in history, and then the semi-comical argument over how to regard basic human emotions like grief, constituted clues into the deeper mystery of what was, in fact, their profound disagreement over the proper meaning of the American Revolution.

Part of the disagreement, to be sure, was temperamental; if asked to choose weapons, Adams would have selected a broadax while Jefferson would have picked a stiletto. But the honesty of their personal affection suggested that each man recognized the missing elements in his own personality in the character of the other. They were the proverbial opposites that attracted. Beyond or beneath the temperamental differences, however, were buried several fundamentally incompatible political convictions and two opposing versions of republican ideology. No matter how polite and seductively civil their letters were designed to appear—and they *were* self-consciously designed for just that effect—the correspondence between the two wise men of the revolutionary generation was an earnest American dialogue over just what they and their generation had wrought.

It is tempting, and perfectly plausible, to read the correspondence between the two patriarchs as an elegant and amiable conversation between elder statesmen, moving from topic to topic like accomplished dancers doing a minuet. It would be more accurate, however, to understand the correspondence as a dialogue between intellectual combatants representing two different visions of the American republic, periodically retreating to safe and uncontroversial subjects in order to avoid risking another rupture in the friendship.

Aging, for example, was a safe subject. Both men worried about senility, what Adams called "dying at the top," and shared their sense of dismay when meeting old friends whose mental faculties had deteriorated. Each time one of their fellow signers of the Declaration of Independence died, they exchanged recollections of the remaining survivors. In 1821, when William Floyd of New York passed on, Adams noted that "We shall all be asterised very soon," then concluded with a Latin inscription and a question: "Sic transit Gloriola (is there such a Latin Word?) mundi." Jefferson concurred that the time for their generation was running out. As for the term "gloriola," he recalled that Cicero had once used the word, which, translated loosely, meant "little bit of glory," an appropriately modest description of their generation's contribution to American history.[25]

Language was another safe refuge. Adams enjoyed using

words like "quiveration" and "gloriola," often accompanying their usage with denunciations of British dictionaries, especially the famous dictionary by Samuel Johnson, which Adams regarded as a fossilized list compiled by a pedant. In 1820 *The North American Review*, New England's leading magazine of letters, criticized Jefferson for using such new words as "location" and "centrality," which had not yet earned their way into common usage. Jefferson wrote Adams to confirm their mutual sense that "Dictionaries are but the depositories of words already legitimated by usage," and to declare proudly that the two old patriarchs were still young enough to serve as wordsmiths in "the work-shop in which new ones [words] are elaborated." Adams did not believe, as Jefferson sometimes predicted, that an entirely new American language would eventually evolve independent of English, but both men relished their role as linguistic revolutionaries, viewing the language as a vibrant, ever-changing human creation shaped in the hurly-burly of public opinion.[26]

There were, of course, other safe harbors besides aging, language, and the classics, but the trouble was that Adams was congenitally predisposed to steer even the most innocuous subject out into the rough waters of politics if Jefferson inadvertently happened to leave the way open. That, in fact, is how the most extensive and revealing debate over political principles in the correspondence actually began. Jefferson accidentally launched the debate with a familiar, and he must have thought, completely unexceptional formulation:

The same political parties which now agitate the U.S. have existed thro' all time. Whether the power of the people, or

that of the *aristoi* should prevail, were questions which kept
the states of Greece and Rome in eternal convulsions; as they
now schismatize every people whose minds and mouths are
not shut up by the gag of a despot. . . . To me it appears that
there have been differences of opinion, and party differences,
from the first establishment of governments, to the present
day . . . every one takes his side in favor of the many, or of
the few.[27]

Adams had already declared himself an avowed enemy to all political parties, whose only concern, as he saw it, was "that they shall
lose the Elections, and consequently the Loaves and Fishes. . . ."
His first instinct was diplomatic, to agree with Jefferson's characterization of the eternal struggle between the few and the many,
a distinction as old as Aristotle. "Precisely," he wrote back to
Jefferson, adding that this was why he had always insisted that
"While all other Sciences are advanced, that of Government is at
a stand; little better understood; little better practiced now than
3 or 4 thousand Years ago." Having dispensed with the civilities
and acknowledged the points of agreement, they then proceeded
to expose how much they disagreed.[28]

The truth was that Adams and Jefferson were about as far
removed from one another on the question of "the few and the
many" as any members of the revolutionary generation. Jefferson's formulation sounds so familiar to our ears because it pres-
ents the political choices in a modern political vocabulary that was
destined to dominate American political culture and eventually
become a rhetorical posture adopted by all major political parties:
"the power of the people" was hallowed and sacred; governments

became despotic whenever a privileged elite defied the will of the majority; the only legitimate republican government was rooted in popular consent; as Jefferson put it, "governments are republican only in proportion as they embody the will of the people, and execute it."[29]

Adams sensed the dramatic gap that separated him from Jefferson without ever being able to fathom fully where his own thinking had veered off in another direction. He recalled an evening in Paris in the 1780s when Jefferson, a youthful John Quincy, and he were being harangued by Lafayette on the power of the people and the future of what was being called "democracy." He was astonished then, and remained perplexed ever after, at what he called "the gross ideology of them all." But he acknowledged to Jefferson that "Your steady defence of democratical Principles, and Your unvariable favourable Opinion of the french Revolution laid the foundation of Your Unbounded Popularity." Meanwhile, his opposition to these ideas "laid the foundation of that immense Unpopula[r]ity, which fell like the Tower of Siloam upon me."[30] Somehow, from that moment onward, Adams had developed the reputation as a crypto-monarchist, a defender of aristocratic privileges, an enemy of the common man and his aggregate symbol, "the people," a reputation which Adams justifiably claimed was misrepresentative. Somehow, even though the French Revolution had followed a disastrous course that Adams correctly predicted, Jefferson's association with romantic convictions about "the power of the people" that had legitimized the bloodshed and human misery in Europe made him a political hero in America. It forever remained a mystery to Adams how this had happened.

Only a part of the mystery got resolved in the correspondence with Jefferson, which served too many purposes to allow for systematic discussions of all contested political principles. Clearly, however, the core of the difference that divided the two patriarchs had something to do with incompatible conceptions of "democracy." The term needs to be put in quotations in order to remind us that it had not yet achieved the powerful meaning that it would in the course of the nineteenth century, indeed was about to achieve during the presidency of Andrew Jackson. Neither Adams nor Jefferson referred to themselves as "democrats." For both of them, the operative term remained "republican." But beneath this apparent agreement lay a fundamental difference of opinion with enormous implications for their subsequent political reputations and respective places in American history.

Put simply, Adams did not believe there was such a thing as "the people"; he could never bring himself to think about popular sovereignty in the reverential fashion required by the emerging democratic tradition that Jefferson was coming to symbolize. "The fundamental Article of my political Creed," he announced to Jefferson, "is, that Despotism, or unlimited Sovereignty, or absolute Power is the same in a Majority of a popular Assembly, an Aristocratical Counsel, and Oligarchical Junto and a single Emperor."[31] This put him at odds with the new democratic religion, which took as an article of faith the belief that what Jefferson called "the will of the people" was unquestionably benign; it was inherently impossible for "the people" to behave despotically. Adams had no trouble endorsing the Lockean doctrine that all political power *derived* from the people. He had helped lead a revolution against an English king and Parliament based squarely on that principle. Moreover, he had been a leader in the Continental

Congress in insisting that all the state constitutions be ratified by popular conventions called explicitly for that purpose, perhaps the clearest expression of the doctrine that all political power is derived from the people. But he had never been able to convince himself that there was an undifferentiated body of popular opinion "out there" with an abiding will of its own. And he was similarly incapable of regarding popular movements as beyond criticism. On these central tenets of the emerging democratic faith, he remained an agnostic.

His way of defending what was already becoming a sacrilegious position, outside the mainstream of American political discourse, was to attack. A useful weapon was his new word "ideology," which he had first encountered in a speech by Napoleon but which was first employed in a systematic fashion by Destutt de Tracy, a French *philosophe* Jefferson admired enormously. Adams read Tracy, then wrote Jefferson that he was delighted with this strange new term "upon the Common Principle of delight in every Thing We cannot understand." What is "ideology," he asked rhetorically. "Does it mean Idiotism?" he joked. "The Science of Non compos Menticism? The Science of Lunacy? The Theory of Deleriism?" The belief in the separate and independent existence of an entity called "the people" struck Adams as a typical act of ideology, the confusion of a romantic sentiment lodged in the mind of theorists and propagandists with a social reality. Moreover, the elevation of this illusory entity to the status of a sacred icon effectively blinded Americans to the political dangers that could just as easily come from misguided majorities as conniving minorities. Whenever he heard political leaders justify a policy by referring to "the people," he suspected that something duplicitous and deceitful was brewing. Adams objected to Jeffersonian rhetoric because it tended to rhapsodize about the omniscience of popular majorities in much the same way that medieval defenders of papal and monarchical power had claimed a direct connection to the divine. For Adams, the threat to the American republic could just as easily come from the left as the right; democratic majorities were just as capable of tyranny as popes and kings.[32]

The differences between the two sages became even clearer when Adams, seizing on Jefferson's use of the Greek word *aristoi*, launched what proved to be the most extensive exchange on political philosophy in the entire correspondence: "I recollect," Adams noted nostalgically, "near 30 years ago to have said car[e]lesly to You, that I wished I could find time and means to write something upon Aristocracy. You seized upon the idea and encouraged me to do it, with all that friendly warmth that is natural and habitual to you." Adams claimed that he had been "writing on that Subject ever since," the only problem being that "I have been so unfortunate as never to make myself understood."[33]

Whether it was a function of perversity, or utter obliviousness to the political vocabulary of the post-revolutionary era, Adams had always demonstrated outright genius at making himself misunderstood on the seminal political issues of his time. His criticism of Jeffersonian rhetoric about "the people" often came across as a denunciation of representative government. His obsession with the necessary role of the aristocracy and its ravenous appetite for power often made him sound like a proponent of privilege and an enemy of equality. And since the idea of equality happened to be the most alluring idea of the age, his reputation as a traitor to the republican cause always retained a tinge of plausibility.

Part of his problem was surely psychological; he was temperamentally averse to endorsing, or even appearing to endorse,
political principles which were, or even appeared to be, faddish or
fashionable. He only felt comfortable as the irreverent dissenter,
delivering jeremiads to naive optimists, lectures on perseverance
to the faint of heart, warnings about mob violence to defenders of
popular rule. His obsession with aristocracy was yet another example of what might be called his enlightened perversity, his way of
contesting the egalitarian presumptions of the political creed that
Jefferson, more than any other American, would come to symbolize, by employing language that defied those very presumptions.[34]

"Your *aristoi*," he warned Jefferson, "are the most difficult Animals to manage, of anything in the Whole Theory and practice
of Government." Adams had a way of describing the resourcefulness of aristocratic families in European and American history that
seemed to render the likelihood of an egalitarian politics virtually
impossible. Whether it was the feudal barons of medieval France,
the landed gentry of Elizabethan England, the merchant class of
colonial New England, or the great planter families of the Chesapeake, the preponderance of political power, as Adams saw it,
invariably rested in the hands of a few wealthy individuals and
families. "Now, my Friend, who are the *aristoi*?" Adams asked rhetorically. "Philosophy may Answer 'The Wise and Good.' But the
World, Mankind, have by their practice always answered, 'the rich
and beautiful and well born.'" And even philosophers, he chided,
when marrying their children, "prefer the rich the handsome
and the well descended to the wise and good." The power and
influence of a wealthy family might wane, but it would "soon be
replaced by an equally wealthy successor." Or, as Adams put it,

"Aristocracy, like Waterfowl dives for Ages and rises again with brighter Plumage."[35]

In one sense, Adams was not saying anything especially novel, for that matter nothing that did not follow from James Harrington's *The Commonwealth of Oceana* (1656), a classic treatise on the affinity between property and political power—one of those books Adams had in his library and covered with admiring marginalia. The notion that the wealthier segments of society had exercised a disproportionate share of political power throughout history was hardly news, even to a champion of equality like Jefferson.[36]

Where Adams and Jefferson parted company, and Adams parted company with the emerging liberal tradition in America, was in the diagnosis of the sources of social inequality. Adams thought it was natural and unavoidable rather than artificial and correctable. "Inequalities of Mind and Body are so established by God Almighty in his constitution of Human Nature," Adams apprised Jefferson, "that no Art or policy can ever plain them down to a Level." The thread of social inequality was woven "in the Constitution of human nature," he repeated, "and wrought into the Fabrick of the Universe." No matter how much "Philosophers and Politicians may nibble and quibble," he concluded, "they never will get rid of it." Adams claimed that he had "never read Reasoning more absurd, Sophistry more gross, in proof of the Athanasian Creed, or Transubstantiation, than the subtle labours . . . to demonstrate the Natural Equality of Mankind."[37]

Jefferson realized that Adams was contesting one of the central tenets of the Jeffersonian faith. He responded with his longest letter to date, acknowledging that "we are both too old to change opinions which are the result of a long life of inquiry and reflection," then offered his contrasting opinion "on the suggestion of a former letter of yours, that we ought not to die before we have explained ourselves to each other."

He conceded that European society had been dominated by aristocratic families, but such domination was a function of artificial privileges as well as social conditions in which men were "crouded within limits either small or overcharged, and steeped in the vices which that situation generates." In America, on the other hand, feudal privileges such as primogeniture and entail had long been outlawed and the existence of an unspoiled continent meant that "everyone may have land to labor for himself if he chuses." Adams's worries about aristocratic power were appropriate for Europe and for the past, but not for America and the future, where opportunity to advance was as available as the abundant land.

Along the way Jefferson distinguished between the natural aristocracy, based on virtue and talent, and the artificial or pseudo-aristocracy, "founded on wealth and birth, without either virtue or talents." Adams's strictures against aristocracy, he thought, were really warnings against the artificial aristocracy, which Jefferson agreed was "a mischievous ingredient in government, and provision should be made to prevent its ascendancy." Given the favorable laws and social conditions in America, as well as an educational system that was accessible to and rewarded talent, one could reasonably expect that "rank, and birth, and tinsel-aristocracy will finally shrink into insignificance. . . ."[38]

Jefferson's clear articulation of the assumptions underlying his vision helped Adams to focus his own disagreement more sharply than ever before. The chief problem was not that Adams clung tenaciously to outmoded definitions of an aristocratic order, but rather that he could not persuade himself that a wholly new chapter in human history had opened in America. Although he used the word "order" instead of "class," his heresy derived from his refusal to accept the Jeffersonian vision of a classless American society, a vision he regarded as illusory. "No Romance could be more amusing," he wrote Jefferson, than the belief that the elimination of feudal restrictions and the availability of land would lead toward greater social equality. Unless one believed that human nature itself had somehow changed when it migrated from Europe to America, the removal of encrusted restrictions would only ensure a *more* ferocious scramble for wealth and power and a *more* unequal distribution of property. "After all," he observed, "as long as Property exists, it will accumulate in Individuals and Families." Unless Jefferson wanted to do away with the very notion of private property, releasing Americans into the marketplace or the wilderness would only assure the unequal distribution of goods: "I repeat it, so long as the Idea and existence of PROPERTY is admitted and established in Society, Accumulations of it will be made, the Snow ball will grow as it rolls."[39]

Finally, Adams cautioned Jefferson that "Your distinction between natural and artificial Aristocracy does not appear to me well founded." One might be able to separate wealth from talent in theory, but in fact, and in society, they were inextricably connected, like the world itself, "a mixture of the Sublime and the beautiful, the base and contemptible, the whimsical and the ridiculous." Adams went into a frenzy over Jefferson's sentimental presumption that wisdom and virtue, if somehow miraculously unmoored from all physical and economic conditions, would sail victorious into the American sunset: "The five Pillars of Aristocracy," he argued, "are Beauty, Wealth, Birth, Genius and Virtues. Any one of the three first, can at any time, over bear any one or both of the two last." But it would never come to that anyway, because the qualities Jefferson regarded as artificial and those he regarded as natural were, in fact, all mixed together inside human nature, then mixed again within society, in blended patterns that defied Jefferson's geometric dissections.[40]

Adams eventually let the subject of aristocracy in America drop. The correspondence again moved into less contentious territory—the character of Napoleon, Plato's metaphysical murkiness, the problematic status of medicine as a science. Both the dialogue and the friendship that underlay it survived the sharp clash over elementary political values and moved ahead. Despite their irreconcilable differences over the seminal political questions of the era, the friendship remained rock solid. In 1818, when asked about his relationship with Jefferson, Adams declared firmly that "He is the last & oldest of my confidential bosom friends, let party faction & politics say what they will."[41] Adams might have used the persistence of the friendship as an instructive example of his point about the power of the passions: sheer affection always overpowered mere reason.

But the momentary clash was itself an example of what Benjamin Rush meant when he referred to the two patriarchs as "the North and South Poles of the American Revolution." The tension that had existed between Adams and Jefferson from the 1790s onward went far beyond the personal jealousies and bickerings generated by specific political conflicts over particular episodes like the quasi-war with France, the need for an enlarged American navy, or the controversial election of 1800. Adams and Jefferson had come to embody fundamentally different versions and visions of what the American Revolution meant. Conventional political categories—left versus right or liberal versus conservative—cannot adequately capture the issues at stake. The labels most recently employed by historians—modern versus classical—are more helpful, but still do little justice to the layered differences of intellect and temperament that would permit each man to wear both labels on different parts of his intellectual anatomy.

If both could legitimately claim to be republicans, and they could, the correspondence exposed the ideological breadth of the term as well as the intriguing affinity the two men felt in large part because of the way their mutual contradictions interacted. In his private life, most especially with trusted friends, Adams released his passionate energies in bursts of unbridled opinion. In his political thought, all his different formulations were bound together by the belief in control, balance, the modulated supervision of social change. Jefferson reversed the dichotomy, controlling his own private feelings so effectively that no one, then or since, could claim to know him fully, while simultaneously advocating a politics of release, an ideology of individual liberation from all forms of exterior constraint or control. Such paradoxical patterns defy one-dimensional labelling and call into question the very relevance of generic categories of description.

Whatever we choose to call them, the political values that Jefferson championed, indeed that his name came to represent, became central tenets of the American liberal tradition; the values Adams embraced became important ingredients for critics of that tradition on both the conservative and radical sides of the political spectrum. And that posture—critical realist of seductive Jeffersonian illusions—was the one Adams found most comfortable throughout his correspondence with that man at Monticello. Jefferson embodied deep and sincere convictions about a truly open-ended America, a fundamentally new kind of society which had liberated itself from the burdens of the past and from the class divisions of Europe; which required only a minimalist government, whose only function would be to remove artificial barriers to individual initiative; which could justifiably claim to represent an undifferentiated, nearly spiritual entity called "the will of the people." No matter how powerful these convictions were to become in nineteenth-century America, Adams regarded all of them as illusions.[42]

DURING THE LAST ten years of the correspondence Adams remained the instigator and primary energy source of the exchange, but even Adams preferred to seek out subjects on which disagreement was unlikely. The proliferation of banks became a convenient rallying point, since both men worried that men who merely "moved money around" without creating anything substantial with their labor were parasites. Jefferson expressed agreement when Adams broke into angry soliloquies on the evils of the banking business, which he called "an infinity of successive felonious larcenies."[43] Or when James Madison retired after two terms as president, both men welcomed him into the fold of senior patriots. Adams thought that Madison's administration "has acquired more glory, and established more Union, than all three of his Predecessors, Washington Adams and Jefferson, put together." But he worried that, because "our good Brother Madison" did not have "Children and Grand Children and great grand Children" around him, he would be unhappy. Jefferson said not to worry: "Such a mind as his, fraught with information, and with matter for reflection, can never know ennui."[44] Or when John Quincy was elected president in 1824, the proud father expressed his concern that "our John" would be devoured by competing political factions. "I call him our John," he explained to Jefferson, "because when you was at Cul de sac at Paris, he appeared to be almost as much your boy as mine." Jefferson responded graciously, expressing confidence that public support would rally around the new president, avoiding any mention of his nearly total disagreement with all of John Quincy's presidential programs.[45]

Minor disagreements presented no threat to the friendship. Jefferson thought that France and French ideas, despite the excesses of the French Revolution and the havoc of the Napoleonic Wars, were destined to dominate the European continent. Adams claimed to be "charmed with the fluency and rapidity of your Reasoning," but predicted that Great Britain, not France, would remain the major European power throughout the rest of the century. In 1820, when Jefferson was attempting to establish the curriculum of his newly founded University of Virginia, Adams impishly suggested that "it would . . . be advisable to institute . . . Professorships of the Philosophy of the human Understanding, whose object should be to ascertain the Limits of human knowledge already acquired." But then the disciple of doubt acknowledged that the disciple of optimism would himself "have doubts of the propriety of setting any limits, or thinking of any limits of human Power, or human Wisdom, and human Virtue." And since Jefferson had repeatedly expressed his opinion that Europe was a swarm of contagious diseases that ought not be allowed to contaminate the American social environment, Adams wondered why he would recruit the faculty for his beloved university from England and the Continent. "The Europeans are all deeply tainted with prejudices," he reminded Jefferson, "all infected with Episcopal and Presbyterian Creeds, and confessions of faith." Jefferson conceded the point, but explained that Europe also happened to be the home of the best scholars.[46]

Adams even felt sufficiently comfortable with the friendship, and with his own demons of ambition, to joke about the glaring difference between Jefferson's ascending reputation and his increasing anonymity. "All the Literary Gentlemen of this part of the Country have an Ambitious Curiousity to see the Philosopher and Statesman of Monticello," he noted in 1819. Since few visitors approached Jefferson for an introduction to the Sage of Quincy, Adams claimed to be in the awkward posture of granting requests without being able to pay back Jefferson in kind. He was like one of those despised bankers who loaned out money without any gold or hard currency to back it up.[47]

Even hostile voices from the past could not shake their mutual resolve to go to their graves as friends. In 1823, the son of William Cunningham published selections from Adams's correspondence with his father. These letters dated from the early years of his retirement, when Adams was still reeling from his defeat of 1800 and full of anger at Jefferson. Adams was worried that his old resentments, now under control, had come back to haunt his newfound serenity with Jefferson. But the response from Monticello was a model of gracious charity:

Be assured, my dear Sir, that I am incapable of receiving
the slightest impression from the effort now made to plant
thorns on the pillow of age, worth, and wisdom and to sow
tares between friends who have been such for nearly half a
century. Beseeching you then not to suffer your mind to be
disquieted by this wicked attempt to poison its peace, and
praying you to throw it by. . . ."[48]

Adams demanded that Jefferson's letter be read aloud at the
Quincy breakfast table, calling it "The best letter that ever was
written . . . just such a letter as I expected, only . . . infinitely better expressed." The whole Cunningham episode had merely solid-
ified their friendship, he observed triumphantly, by revealing that
"the peevish and fretful effusions of politicians . . . are not worth
remembering, much less of laying to heart." He concluded his
response to Jefferson with a "salute [to] your fire-side with cordial
esteem and affection," and signed it "J.A. In the 89 years of his age
still too fat to last much longer."[49]

The one significant subject that defied even the seasoned
serenity of their latter years was slavery. Adams had alluded to it
indirectly in 1816, when he confided to Jefferson that "there will
be greater difficulties to preserve our Union, than You and I, our
Fathers Brothers Friends Disciples and Sons have had to form it."
Then, in 1819, while Congress was debating the extension of slavery into the newly recognized territory of Missouri, Adams felt
bold enough to broach the subject directly: "The Missouri question I hope will follow the other Waves under the Ship and do no
harm," he wrote, adding that he realized it was "high treason to
express a doubt of the perpetual duration of our vast American

Empire." But he worried that the sectional conflict over slavery had the potential to "rend this mighty Fabric in twain . . . [and] produce as many Nations in North America as there are in Europe." Finally, in 1821, after the so-called Missouri Compromise allowed for the extension of slavery in the western territories, Adams offered his most candid assessment of the national dilemma: "Slavery in this Country I have seen hanging over it like a black cloud for half a century. . . . I might probably say I had seen Armies of Negroes marching and countermarching in the air, shining in Armour." Then he reiterated his long-standing position. "I have been so terrified with this Phenomenon," he explained to Jefferson, "that I constantly said in former times to the Southern Gentlemen, I cannot comprehend the object; I must leave it to you. I will vote for forcing no measure against your judgments." Jefferson never responded to Adams's comments and never mentioned the subject of slavery in his letters to Quincy.[50]

Silence had, in fact, become Jefferson's official position on slavery. After making several bold proposals for the end of the slave trade and the gradual abolition of slavery early in his career, Jefferson had maintained a mute posture since the 1780s, claiming that the intractable subject defied even his leadership. "I have most carefully avoided every public act or manifestation on that subject," he wrote to George Logan in 1805, promising that "should an occasion ever occur in which I can interpose with decisive effect, I shall certainly know & do my duty with promptitude & zeal." In the meantime, he observed, "it would only be disarming myself of influence to be taking small means." But the propitious moment never arrived. In 1814, Edward Coles, the staunch Jeffersonian who eventually endorsed emancipation, begged the

Sage of Monticello to break his silence, claiming that "This difficult task could be more successfully performed by the reverend father of our political and Social blessings than by any other succeeding Statesman." By then, however, Jefferson pleaded old age. "No, I have outlived the generation with which mutual labors and perils begat mutual confidence and influence," he explained. Ending slavery was a glorious cause, he acknowledged, but had been passed on to "those who can follow it up, and bear it through to its consummation."[51]

As much as he insisted that American society should not be divided into classes, Jefferson thought that American history should be separated into generations. In other contexts his belief that there were discrete generational units which came into the world and went out together had extremely radical implications, for it led Jefferson to the rather awkward conclusion that one generation could not make laws for the next. "No society can make a perpetual constitution, or even a perpetual law," he claimed, because to do so would defy the Jeffersonian principle that "The earth always belongs to the living generation." Or as he put it to Adams, "When we have lived our generation out, we should not wish to encroach upon another." Taken literally, for that matter taken at all seriously, this was a prescription for anarchy that Jefferson never tried to implement. On the issue of slavery, however, Jefferson's belief in generational sovereignty served the conservative purpose of justifying, indeed requiring, silence and passivity from the revolutionary generation on the most ominous problem facing the new nation. "Nothing is more certainly written in the book of fate than that these people [i.e., slaves] are to be free," he announced in his autobiography, written in 1821. But it was

equally obvious to him that emancipation would require a revolution in public opinion that Jefferson felt was a long way off,
the work of the next generation, or perhaps an even more distant
cohort of American leaders several ages away.[52]

Adams agreed with Jefferson that slavery constituted the most
nearly intractable problem faced by the revolutionary generation.
"The Subject is vast and ominous," he noted in 1817: "More than
fifty years has it attracted my thoughts and given me much anxi-
ety. A Folio Volume would not contain my Lucubrations on this
Subject. And at the End of it, I should leave my reader and myself
as much at a loss, what to do with it, as at the Beginning." However, Adams did not agree with—for that matter, he did not comprehend at all—Jefferson's belief in generational sovereignty. For
Adams, history was not a dead burden of accumulated weight that
each generation was free to toss aside; it was a combination of mis-
haps and successes, ignorance and wisdom, from which future leaders should learn. The problem with slavery, Adams acknowledged,
was that it constituted the one subject on which he, Jefferson, and
the rather remarkable generation of leaders they symbolized had
little wisdom to offer.[53]

Just what Adams thought that limited wisdom was became
clear in the national debate over the extension of slavery into Missouri, which prompted different reactions from the two patriarchs
that were so loaded with emotion and implication that each man
chose to avoid mentioning his thoughts to the other. Adams saw the
issue as clearcut. "Negro Slavery is an evil of Colossal magnitude,"
he wrote to William Tudor, "and I am therefore utterly averse to
the admission of Slavery into the Missouri Territory." He thought
that the procedural question—whether the federal government or

the state legislature had the power to make the decision—was of merely secondary importance. He hoped that "the Legislature of Missouri, or the [Territorial] Convention, may have the Wisdom to prohibit Slavery of their own accord," but whether or not they did, the federal government had established its right to rule for the territories when it approved the Louisiana Purchase. "I think the Southern gentlemen who thought it [the Louisiana Purchase] constitutional," he explained to his beloved daughter-in-law Louisa Catherine, "ought not to think it unconstitutional for Congress to restrain the extention of Slavery in that territory." The primary issue for Adams was the moral imperative against slavery and, even more telling, his clear sense that the revolutionary generation had never intended that the evil institution spread beyond the South. (This was eventually the position that Lincoln took in the 1850s.) In 1820, Adams was alerting several of his correspondents, though not Jefferson, that "we must settle the question of slavery's extension now, otherwise it will stamp our National Character and lay a Foundation for Calamities, if not disunion."[54]

Jefferson seemed to resent the very existence of the debate, as if the eloquent silence he had maintained on the unmentionable subject should become national policy. Although he supported what he called the rights of slaveholders to live in Missouri, his major complaint was the growth of federal power—the issue Adams considered secondary—which he began to describe as an encroachment on southern rights reminiscent of British intrusions in the pre-revolutionary years. "In the gloomiest moments of the Revolutionary War," he wrote in 1820, "I never had any apprehensions equal to what I feel from this source." His pronouncements became more pessimistic and morbid, outdoing even Adams at his most apocalyptic: "I regret that I am now to die in the belief that the . . . sacrifice of themselves by the generation of 1776, to acquire self-government and happiness," he warned, "is to be thrown away by the unwise and unworthy passions of their sons, and that my only consolation is to be that I live not to weep over it." Even his beloved University of Virginia, which he had originally conceived as a national center of learning, became for Jefferson a bastion of southern ways to protect Virginia's rising generation against the seductive infidelities of Harvard and Yale, where abolitionists, bankers, unscrupulous merchants, and Federalist fanatics acquired their bad manners and destructive ideas.[55]

"I look back with rapture to those golden days," Adams wrote to him in 1825, "when Virginia and Massachusetts lived and acted together like a band of brothers and I hope it will not be long before they may say redeunt saturnia regna."[56] But the golden age Adams referred to was gone for Jefferson, blasted into oblivion by sectional politics and what seemed to him a northern conspiracy to make the unmentionable subject of slavery the dominant topic of the new age. Although Jefferson surely knew that Adams was one of the conspirators, just as he knew that John Quincy embodied a political persuasion that threatened the survival of slavery and states' rights, he sustained his commitment to the correspondence to the end, avoiding the troublesome topics, concealing his mounting bitterness and despair, maintaining pretenses. The friendship symbolized by the correspondence would thus serve as a testimony to posterity about the way it had once been within the extraordinary but now nearly defunct generation that he and Adams symbolized.

Adams never knew the depth of the tragedy Jefferson felt nor the irony of their shifting circumstances. From 1820 onward,

Jefferson—America's most attractive apostle of optimism—was trapped in a spiralling despondency. He had lost the faith that his very name was destined to epitomize and instead became an example of the paranoia and pessimism that Adams had eventually overcome. Wracked by rheumatism and a painful intestinal disorder that would eventually kill him, even his physical condition deteriorated more rapidly than that of his older friend at Quincy. Jefferson's personal debts continued to mount, for he had never mastered the reconciliation of his expensive tastes with the financial facts of his household economy. His addiction for French wines and French luxuries, like his affinity for French ideas, never came to grips with the more mundane realities. When an old friend whom he had unwisely loaned a huge sum of money defaulted, the liability fell on Jefferson's estate, prompting a lamentation that was saved from total despair by the inimitable Jeffersonian style: "A call on me to the amount of my endorsements for you," he wrote his indebted friend, "would indeed close my course by a catastrophe I had never contemplated." Infirm, insolvent, and depressed that the future he always trusted had somehow taken a wrong turn, Jefferson lived out his last days amidst two hundred slaves he could not free without encumbering his heirs with even greater debts, without his magnificent library, which he had been forced to sell for cash, on the deteriorating grounds of the once proud Monticello, which was decaying at the same rapid pace as his own political optimism.[57]

CHAPTER FIVE

Erudite Effusions

I am willing to allow your Phylosophers your opinion
of the universal Gravitation of Matter, if you will allow
mine that there is in some souls a principle of absolute
Levity that buoys them irresistably into the Clouds . . .
an uncontroulable Tendency to ascend. . . . This I take
to be precisely the Genius of Burr . . . and Hamilton.

—Adams to Benjamin Rush, April 12, 1807

The Town of Quincy have been pleased to Elect me
a Member of the [Massachusetts Constitutional]
Convention—and wonderful to relate . . . I am
sufficiently advanced in my dotage to have accepted
the Choice. And if I should fall like Chatham in
attempting to utter a few sentences, it would be
pronounced by the World . . . *EUTHANASIA*. I feel not
much like a maker or mender of Constitutions, in
my present state of imbecility. . . . But I presume one
shall not be obliged to carry wind-mills by assault.

—Adams to Louisa Catherine Adams, October 21, 1820

A T ITS BEST, the dialogue with Jefferson had the character of a good conversation, its pace and rhythm dictated by the more ebullient Adams temperament, its content determined by the play between Adams's compulsion for candor and Jefferson's desire for discretion. One might conjure up the picture of a stately Jefferson, gazing calmly into the middle distance, while Adams, slightly frenzied, briskly paces back and forth, periodically tugging on Jefferson's lapels, slapping him on the back, whispering admonitions into his ear, filling up the Jeffersonian silences with talk.

Since conversations are, by their nature, informal exchanges without an explicit agenda, it would be foolish to expect the dialogue between Adams and Jefferson to provide a comprehensive account of either man's mature thought. Nevertheless, certain features of the political landscape as Adams saw it came into sharper focus in the correspondence with Jefferson than they ever had before. Jefferson was like one of those books he argued with in the margins, except Jefferson could argue back, forcing Adams to clarify the core values of what he called "my system." It was not just that Adams needed an opponent to discipline his inherently effusive intellectual energies, though that was surely so. Or that Adams possessed a dialectical temperament that tended to define its deepest convictions in opposition, like a lawyer defending a client, though that was true as well. The Adams affinity for dialectic and dialogue had even deeper roots. Although he had written four volumes to explain his "system," Adams was perhaps the most unsystematic great thinker of the era. For Adams, thought was more a series of pulsations than a connected set of geometric lines, more a set of explosions that went off in his consciousness than a logical syllogism. He revealed more of his political thought in dialogues with others than in his informal political treatises because the episodic character of a conversation matched nicely with his impulsive, hit-or-miss, indeed episodic, mode of thinking.

The correspondence with Jefferson had drawn out of him fresh expressions of his reasons for mistrusting the liberal faith as Jefferson embodied it. But the deepest and most comprehensive expression of the convictions underlying Adams's own political thought occurred in his correspondence with another, less famous, Virginian. The dialogue with Jefferson exposed the extent of Adams's discomfort with the beguiling optimism of the Jeffersonian vision, most especially the formulations that grew out of the French philosophical tradition and that eliminated altogether the need for an active role for government in shaping and controlling social policy. At the same time he was writing Jefferson, however, Adams unburdened himself in a series of candid letters-as-lectures that constituted his clearest and fullest explanation of what he meant by an American aristocracy.

It began somewhat mysteriously. In September of 1813 Adams told Jefferson that he had "scarcely sealed my last letter to you . . . when they brought me from the Post Office a Packett, without Post Mark, without name date or place. . . ." The package contained an unsigned manuscript over 600 pages in length. "I gravely composed my risible Muscles and read it through," he reported to Jefferson, and discovered that he was reading "an attack upon me by name for the doctrines of Aristocracy. . . ." Adams was stretching the truth with Jefferson. He later admitted that he "never read the book" but only "dipped here and there," claiming that the prose style defied comprehension and that "no one will ever read it through."[1]

Adams immediately suspected that the anonymous author was John Taylor, a disciple of Jefferson who had served in the Senate while Adams was vice president. "Taylor was an eternal talker," Adams recalled, "the greatest talker I ever knew, excepting George the Third." The manuscript read the way Taylor talked, full of "fire and fluency" that eventually lost itself in esoteric abstractions. Jefferson agreed with Adams's speculation, recalling that Taylor was known for his "quaint, mystical and hyperbolic ideas . . . [and] affected, new-fangled and pedantic terms. . . ." Adams confirmed the diagnosis: "The Style answers every characteristic, that you have intimated." Taylor must be the man. A few months later, in April 1814, Adams wrote the first of what would eventually become thirty-two lengthy letters to Taylor. Rather than feel insulted that his political views were under attack again, Adams felt honored that his previous publications were still taken seriously. "I thought my Books, as well as myself were forgotten," he joked to Jefferson: "But behold! I am to become a great Man in my expiring moments."[2]

THE MANUSCRIPT JOHN TAYLOR had sent to Adams was published in Fredricksburg in 1814 under the title *An Inquiry into the Principles and Policy of the Government of the United States.* Although it eventually came to be recognized as a minor classic in the agrarian tradition, when it first appeared few readers noticed its existence and fewer still found it relevant or readable. Apparently Taylor had been sitting on his plantation in Caroline County,

Virginia, for the past twenty years, studying and arguing with the three-volume work Adams had written in the late 1780s under the title *A Defence of the Constitutions of Government of the United States of America.* Taylor, in effect, had actually done what Adams kept telling his friends and correspondents they ought to do, indeed, the entire political leadership of the United States ought to do; namely, to go back and read his *Defence,* along with the separate collection of essays he had published in 1790 under the title *Discourses on Davila,* which he claimed should be "considered as a fourth volume of the Defence. . . ." If only they would do so, he claimed incessantly, they would discover in one place the seeds of his system, and simultaneously understand why he had been right about the chief sources of danger to America's experiment with republicanism. He told Rush, for example, that the Federalist leader Fisher Ames, whom he called "that pretty little warbling Canary Bird," often "Sang of the Dangers of American Liberty," but that a younger John Adams "had preached in 'The Defence' and the 'Discourses on Davila' and held up in a Thousand Mirrors all those Dangers and more twenty years before him." Moreover, Ames, like so many other Federalist leaders, failed to comprehend that "the sordid Avarice which he imputes to the whole Body of the American People belongs chiefly if not exclusively to his own Friends, the Aristocrats or rather the Oligarchs who now rule the Federal Party."[3]

Meanwhile, on the other side of the political spectrum, the disciples of Jefferson—and Taylor fell into this camp—could have avoided their near-fatal infatuation with unfettered democracy, their naive belief that the people are capable of "nothing but Innocence, Purity, Virtue, Humanity, Liberty and Patriotism."

Perhaps the most remarkable feature of his political writing in the 1780s, Adams bragged to Mathew Carey, was "the date of their composition and publication," for he had warned against the despotic consequences of unlimited democracy before the French Revolution had shown "its face of Blood and Horror, of Murder and Massacre, of Ambition and Avarice. . . ." Adams went so far as to claim that the most scathing critique of the French Revolution, Edmund Burke's *Reflections on the French Revolution,* had actually been based on his own *Defence.* In 1787, he had given a copy of the first volume of his *Defence* to the English diplomat David Hartley, Adams recalled to Vanderkemp, who had in turn passed it along to Burke, who was then allegedly inspired to compose his classic work. As a result, Adams claimed—with pride and with a covering joke to mask his vanity—whenever Burke was asked if he thought George Washington was the greatest man of the age, he purportedly replied: "I thought so . . . 'till I knew John Adams."[4]

Throughout his retirement years, Adams returned regularly to his personal copies of the *Defence* and *Davila* to record his private pleasure at their prescience. "This dull, heavy volume," he noted in the margins of *Davila* in 1812, "still excites the wonder of its author." He remained proud that he had found "the courage to oppose and publish his [i.e., Adams's] own opinions to the universal opinions of mankind." But instead of assuring his reputation, "the work . . . operated to destroy his popularity" and became a piece of proof "that he was an advocate for monarchy, and labouring to introduce a hereditary presidency in America." A year later, in 1813, he reviewed his political writings again, commenting that "Americans paid no attention or regard," and concluding that their failure to heed his warnings would very probably lead to increasing sectional divisions and even civil war.[5]

From the very beginning, for that matter, he had expected to be misunderstood. "If it is heresy," he had written to Franklin the year the *Defence* was published, "I shall, I suppose, be cast out of communion." And to James Warren he had predicted in the same year that "This Book will make me unpopular. . . ." It was the classic Adams formulation. He had spoken the unpopular truths to a hostile world, just as he had done the right thing in the quasi-war with France despite the political costs. But posterity would eventually vindicate his judgment. "The time will come," he assured himself, "after I am dead, when the System of it in general must be adopted, with bitter repentance that it was not heeded sooner."[6]

The truth was much messier. Both the *Defence* and *Davila,* it is true, contained much of the political wisdom Adams had to offer his countrymen. But they were really not so much books as notebooks, not so much coherent expositions of the Adams "system" as collections of quotations from other authors interspersed with his own erudite effusions. In the preface to the first volume of the *Defence,* Adams explained that it had been "necessary to write and publish with precipitation," apologizing that he was too pressed for time "to correct the style, adjust the method, pare off excrescences, or even obliterate repetition." When offered the opportunity to revise the entire work in 1794, however, he declined. After his retirement to Quincy he regularly lamented the inchoate character of his political publications, worrying that "nothing I ever printed or wrote in my whole life is fit for the inspection of Posterity," and justifying the incoherence on the grounds that they were "all written in a hurry, distracted with care, despirited by discouragements—never transcribed, never corrected, and not even ever revised."[7]

The problem was not so much lack of time as temperament. In his formal writings as in his conversation, Adams careened off one subject into another like the proverbial loose cannon on a slippery deck. The artifice required to implement a large design over many pages was not in him. More than any other member of the revolutionary generation, Adams wrote as he talked. His written thoughts, like his spoken thoughts, had an excited, volatile, rambling quality that defied orthodox versions of coherence or control. Moreover, he tended to seize whatever was at hand to document his convictions, then be led by that source into topics extraneous to his original point, thereby carrying the reader down long, often interesting but false trails, building up alongside his odyssey-of-an-argument massive mountains of only slightly relevant detail. Fully three quarters of the pages in the *Defence* and over half of *Davila* were lifted verbatim from other books, only a small portion of which were indicated by quotation marks.[8]

In effect, Adams the inveterate conversationalist built into his published writings unacknowledged conversations with other authorities. Where Adams's voice ends and another begins, however, is often impossible to determine, leaving most unsuspecting readers to wonder who is addressing them, where they are being led, and why they should put themselves in the hands of an author whose obsessions have so obviously overwhelmed his respect for their sensibilities as well as their patience. If there continues to be lively debate among twentieth-century scholars over Adams's prominence as a political thinker, there is virtual unanimity that his published political writings demonstrate his deficiencies as a formal political philosopher.[9]

For any modern reader with the stamina to plow through the *Defence,* it is difficult at first to understand why Adams put such an emphasis on its contents or why John Taylor spent twenty years denouncing its doctrines. On its face the *Defence* was a long-winded refutation, in the familiarly obsessive Adams mood and mode, of the French philosopher Turgot's claim that the legislatures established in the newly created American state governments should be simple, single-house affairs. Adams's *Defence* was literally that, a defense of the bicameral legislatures adopted by most of the states and eventually enshrined in the federal Constitution. "The United States are large and populous nations . . . and they are growing every day more disproportionate," Adams had argued, "and therefore [are] less capable of being held together by simple governments." Adams advocated "mixed governments," that is, governments composed of three separate branches, meaning a strong executive, an independent judiciary, and a legislative branch divided into an upper and lower house, again just as most of the colonial charters and state constitutions had required. "It may be laid down as a universal maxim," he had written, "that every government that has not three independent branches" would eventually degenerate into a despotism. The history of republican governments in Europe demonstrated clearly that simple, unbalanced constitutions quickly deteriorated into either "an absolute monarchy; or an arrogant nobility. . . ." The latter was actually the most dangerous, because emboldened aristocrats had shown a tendency to "annihilate the people, and, attended with their horses, hounds and vassals . . . run down the king as they would hunt a deer, wishing for nothing so much as to be in at the death."[10]

Very much a product of the 1780s, and of his reading of English and European history, the *Defence* demonstrated that Adams, along with several other American political thinkers of the time, recognized that the revolutionary faith in public virtue so prevalent during the 1770s was inadequate as a basis for political stability once the war with England was won. "We may preach till we are tired of the theme," Hamilton had written in 1782, "the necessity of disinterestedness in republics, without making a single proselyte." Adams concurred that it was foolish to expect Americans to become more capable of self-denial and public spiritedness than any other people in history. To believe that the American people would behave virtuously was to think like the French Utopians, who expected a political revolution to change human nature. "The best republics will be virtuous," he noted in the *Defence,* "and have been so; but we may hazard a conjecture, that the virtues have been the effect of the well ordered constitution, rather than the cause."

Adams joined with a host of commentators on the American scene to argue that "the people in America have now the best opportunity and the greatest trust in their hands, that Providence ever committed to so small a number, since the transgression of the first pair. . . ." Although it was a propitious moment, the act of framing new constitutions for the American republic was, he insisted, a decidedly human project taking place on this earth and not in the Garden of Eden: "It will never be pretended that any persons employed in that service [i.e., framing constitutions] had interviews with the gods, or were in any degree under the inspiration of heaven." He went out of his way to dispel the mythology of America as an exception to the rules of history or the revolutionary generation as instruments of divine providence. And the chief lesson that Adams claimed he had learned from his reading of history was that "without three orders, and an effectual balance among them, in every American constitution, it must be destined to frequent unavoidable revolutions." Although Adams made the matter sound rather mechanistic—separate branches of government and a bicameral legislature automatically yielding a balanced constitution—nothing about the basic message defied the common wisdom then being implemented in the separate state constitutions or in the national convention in Philadelphia. When, years later, James Madison, the chief architect of the United States Constitution, asked Adams about foreign critics of the American system of government, Adams emphasized the same features. "When a writer on government despises, sneers, or argues against mixed governments or a balance in government," he wrote to Madison, "he instantly proves himself"—the favorite Adams stigma—"an ideologian."[11]

A close reading of the *Defence*—something very few could manage in the 1780s, given the sprawling, inchoate character of the work and the quirky schedule of its publication—revealed that Adams had been correct to worry that his apparent agreement with the broad outlines of American constitutionalism masked a fundamental disagreement that would set him against the emerging mainstream of American thinking about politics. The seeds of his aversion to liberalism, in short, were already planted in the *Defence*. Madison, in fact, had been one of the first to notice the lurking problems posed by Adams's analysis. "Men of learning find nothing new in it," he cautioned Jefferson, who had initially congratulated Adams for his contribution to the debate over constitutional frameworks, while "Men of taste [find] many things to criticize." Always a sharper and more sophisticated political thinker than his mentor at Monticello, Madison was hoisting the warning flags. Some of Adams's ideas, he was telling Jefferson, were not worthy of applause.[12]

But until John Taylor published his own sprawling but comprehensive critique in 1814, no one had identified the deepest sources of Adams's political alienation. Adams himself tended to focus on two specific recommendations in the *Defence*, the power he proposed for the chief executive and the role of the Senate or upper house, believing that his chief sin had been to insist on investing more authority in those branches than the bulk of his compatriots found necessary.

And, indeed, Adams's preference for a strong executive was part of the problem. At several places in the *Defence*, Adams seemed to endorse empowering the executive, which he also called "the first magistrate," to a degree that seemed dangerously reminiscent of the sovereign powers of European kings. He advocated "a first magistrate . . . invested with the whole executive authority," and he specifically recommended that the Constitution "give that first magistrate a negative on the legislature," a right of veto which could not be overturned by a two-thirds majority. During his term as vice president he incurred the wrath of most members of Congress and became the butt of jokes in the press for advocating royal titles for the president. He was dubbed "His Rotundity" for insisting that Washington be referred to as "his Majesty." Throughout his retirement years, he clung tenaciously to his belief that the Americans' justifiable disenchantment with the arbitrary

policies of George III, whom, after all, he had played a leading role
in overthrowing, ought not blind them to the need for executive
power. "The Supreme head or the executive of a great nation must
be inviolable," he noted in the margins of one book, "or the laws
will never be executed." In 1811 he told Josiah Quincy that "the
President has, or ought to have, the whole nation before him, and
he ought to select the men best qualified . . . without being shack-
led by any check, by law, constitution, or institution."[13]

Critics who accused him of secretly harboring a fondness for a
divine right theory of the American presidency, or for a hereditary
rather than elective chief executive, immediately found themselves
drowning in a flood of Adams invective. "I never in my life went
to such a length," he complained to Rush, insisting that he was
a republican to the core and not a royalist. But critics noted that
his attitude toward European monarchs was disturbingly empa-
thetic: "Talleyrand once [in 1789] asked me, what I thought of the
[French] King," he recalled to John Quincy. "I answered that he
was Daniel in the Lyons Den. If he ever escaped alive, it must be
by Miracle." He repeated a version of the recollection to Jefferson
as late as 1823, acknowledging that "I am no king killer merely
because they are kings—poor creatures they know no better—
they believe sincerely and conscientiously that God made them to
rule the world."[14]

Not only was Adams willing to invest the presidency with
powers that many readers of the *Defence* found downright monarchical, he also exhibited a curious fascination with the role of the
Senate. At Philadelphia, the delegates to the Constitutional Convention had eventually seen fit to create an upper house in order
to provide the smaller states with a legislative body in which there

would be equal representation rather than representation proportional to populations. But Adams's motives for favoring the creation of a senate were entirely different and seemed to smack of an affection for a European-styled aristocracy. "The rich, the well-born, and the able, acquire an influence among the people that will soon be too much for simple honesty and plain sense," he wrote in the *Defence*. He argued that these natural aristocrats "must, therefore, be separated from the mass and placed by themselves in a senate," an arrangement, he claimed, "that is, to all honest and useful intents, an ostracism."[15]

The notion that the people of the United States ought to conceive of senators as some kind of elected aristocracy struck most readers as odd. The belief that empowering such creatures by electing them into the Senate was a means of *limiting* their influence struck most readers as bizarre. Nevertheless, there it was in the *Defence,* not just an incidental point made in passing, but one of Adams's major preoccupations. In every society known to man, he assured his readers, "an aristocracy has risen up in a course of time, consisting of a few rich and honorable families, who have united with each other against both the people and the first magistrate." Best to put these talented but troublesome creatures in one place, the Senate, and watch them carefully. He seemed to be saying that the Senate was simultaneously a podium for the natural aristocrats and a prison.[16]

He had, in fact, been harping on this theme from the time he was a young man. In 1765, in his *Dissertation on the Canon and Feudal Law,* his polemic against arbitrary power was based on the ominous warning that priests and lords constituted an oligarchic gang that used its privileges to tyrannize the rest of society.

The mechanistic and rather silly idea that one could harness the potentially disruptive energies of the aristocracy by housing it in the upper branch of the legislature actually came from John Louis DeLolme, a Swiss writer whose *The Constitution of England* first suggested the scheme, which was obviously a rationale for the English House of Lords. Adams acknowledged DeLolme's influence in the *Defence,* then clung unrepentantly for the rest of his life to the view that the Senate was, or at least should be, a combined haven and detention center for America's elite. While his social analysis of the role played by aristocratic or elite factions in both Europe and America had profound implications, his description of the Senate as an institutionalized solution to the problem of elite power was more a gimmick than an idea and more a measure of his desperation at finding an answer to what he regarded as the central dilemma of political science. Meanwhile, readers of the *Defence* could plausibly conclude that Adams's obsession with aristocracy implied an affinity for coats-of-arms and hereditary privileges. His view of the Senate, well, that was sheer lunacy.[17]

THE THRUST OF John Taylor's long-winded and much-delayed critique of Adams's *Defence* was to argue that, apart from specific disagreements about the power of the presidency and the role of the Senate, Adams's entire way of thinking about politics was hopelessly out of date and, in the end, fundamentally un-American. Taylor apologized for the twenty-year delay in getting his own thoughts into print, claiming that he had waited "until age had abated temporal interests and diminished youthful prejudices." He acknowledged that, given his own and Adams's advancing years, his published thoughts "are almost letters from the dead." Although the tone of Taylor's remarks was not personal—he was properly respectful toward one of the nation's patriarchs and claimed to have "a high opinion of his virtue and talents"—the message of Taylor's book was devastating. If Taylor was right, Adams was an intellectual anachronism who had missed the political significance and meaning of the American Revolution.[18]

For his part, Adams let it be known that he was not going to defer gracefully or apologetically, nor had age diminished his vaunted capacity to defend himself. "You must allow me twenty years to answer a book that cost you twenty years of meditation to compose," he warned Taylor. One could hear the rounds clicking into Adams's chambers and the salvo being aimed toward Caroline County. He expressed the hope that Taylor's work would not burden him with "the absurd criticism, the stupid observations, the jesuitical subtleties, the stupid lies that have been printed concerning my writings, in this my dear, native country, for five and twenty years. . . ." If so, Taylor should expect no quarter from the self-professed "Hermit of Quincy."[19]

The core of Taylor's critique was to charge that Adams was the prisoner of a classical way of thinking about politics that was no longer appropriate for post-revolutionary America. What Taylor called "the numerical analysis" was the classical assumption that all political arrangements were variations on the same eternal theme: namely, the proper balancing of the interests of the one, the few, and the many. In the *Defence,* this ancient formula had caused Adams to adopt the old classical categories of monarchy, aristocracy, and democracy. Because Adams's mind remained trapped "within the magick circle of the numerical analysis," he had failed to recognize that the American Revolution had changed everything. "Monarchy, aristocracy and democracy" were not timeless truths, but "rude, and almost savage political fabricks." Constructing a new constitution for America with these elements was "like . . . erecting a palace with materials drawn from Indian cabins." Adams might be excused for thinking in the old way and offering readers "a cloud of quotations . . . collected from the deepest tints of ancient obscurity." After all, he had been abroad in France and England for most of the 1780s, when American political thinking "had advanced more rapidly . . . than the philosophy and policy comprising his references had in twenty centuries." But, excuses aside, Adams continued to live and think within a classical paradigm that had been blown to pieces by the democratic and egalitarian implications of the very revolution he had done so much to foster.[20]

Although it is doubtful that Adams fully digested what Taylor was saying, from a historical perspective Taylor's critique was important because it laid bare for the first time the underlying reasons for Adams's alienation from the American political mainstream. The very language and categories of analysis Adams relied upon had become strange and nearly treasonable in American political culture. To talk calmly of monarchy and aristocracy as elemental ingredients in the social equation was to challenge implicitly the inherently democratic character of the new American government. To suggest by such language that there were enduring social divisions, orders, factions, or classes—Adams used all these terms—was to question the existence of a rough version of social equality in America and, even worse, to imply that the goal of equality was a pipedream.

For Adams, the balancing of power within the Constitution between the branches of government was a man-made response to the inherent divisions within society. But no such divisions existed within America, Taylor argued, and whatever inequalities or differences of wealth or status did remain were vestiges of the old European order, merely temporary and evanescent clusters of interest so numerous and so ephemeral that they effectively checked one another. In short, Taylor was telling Adams that the most important checks and balances, which in Adams's classical scheme were performed by a government designed to control the boistrous energies of society, in America were naturally and efficiently performed by the dynamics of society itself. All of Adams's endless prattling about the dangers of aristocracy only exposed how hopelessly trapped he remained in classical categories of analysis. Instead of being "natural and unavoidable," aristocracies were in truth "artificial or factitious, and therefore avoidable." A strong and active government was not necessary to constrain these pockets of power and privilege, because in America those that did exist disciplined themselves.[21]

Adams was ready with a response. "In fine, is it not humiliating," Adams scolded Taylor, "to see a volume of six or seven hundred pages written by a gentleman of your rank, fortune, learning, genius and eloquence, in which my system, my sentiments . . . are totally misunderstood and misrepresented?" But as soon as Adams began training his verbal artillery on Caroline County, it became abundantly clear that he still did not fathom Taylor's primary accusation. The charge that his entire way of thinking about politics was rooted in classical categories and an outdated vocabulary was translated in Adams's mind to the charge that the art of shaping governments had not changed since the days of the Greeks and Romans. "I have said no such thing," he retorted to Taylor. "I know the art of government has changed, and probably will change again." Then, however, he added that "these arts are founded in certain principles of nature, which have never been known to change; and it is the duty of philosophers, legislators and artists to study these principles." And the reiteration of these political principles quickly led Adams back to the one, the few, and the many, the abiding clash of monarchy, aristocracy, and democracy, the very categories Taylor identified as the problem. In response to Taylor's charge that Adams had relegated the democratic element to an inferior status, when in fact it was the *only* element worthy of discussion in the American government, Adams denied the charge in a way that only confirmed its correctness: "That is not my doctrine, Mr. Taylor," he wrote. "My opinion is, and always has been, that absolute power intoxicates alike despots, monarchs, aristocrats, and democrats, and jacobins, and *sans culottes*. I cannot say that democracy has been more pernicious, on the whole, than any of the others."[22]

Ironically, it was precisely because Adams remained wedded to a classical conception of politics that he also remained immune to the seductive illusions that had established themselves as central assumptions in post-revolutionary American political culture. His most piercing insights derived from the fact that, in Taylor's terms, he was an anachronism. Some of the crucial points of disagreement had revealed themselves in the exchange with Jefferson over the role of popular majorities, but the diplomacy demanded by that relationship prevented the kind of clear resolution possible with Taylor: "We make ourselves popular,

Mr. Taylor, by telling our fellow citizens that we have made discoveries, conceived inventions and made improvements," Adams observed with wry disdain for the presumption that America had somehow become an exception to the lessons of history. "We may boast that we are the chosen people; we may even thank God that we are not like other men; but, after all, it would be but flattery, and delusion, the self-deceit of the Pharisee." If Taylor accused Adams of being irrelevant, Adams accused Taylor of being "an ideologian," an Americanized version of those French dreamers whose rhapsodic romances led directly to Robespierre and then Napoleon.[23]

"That all men are born to equal rights is true," Adams declared defiantly, rebuking Taylor for suggesting that he had ever thought otherwise. But to teach that "all men are born with equal powers and faculties, to equal influence in society . . . is as gross a fraud . . . as ever was practised by monks, by Druids, by Brahmins, by priests of the immortal Lama, or by the self-styled philosophers of the French Revolution." Taylor had also implied that Adams's obsession with aristocracy masked an affection for European-styled titles and privileges in America. This too was ridiculous. "You seem to think aristocracy consists altogether in artificial titles, tinsel decorations of stars, garters, ribbons, golden eagles and golden fleeces, crosses and roses and lilies, exclusive privileges, hereditary descents, established by kings or by positive laws of society," Adams lectured. But that was not the kind of aristocracy Americans needed to worry about and certainly not the kind of elite he had ever sanctioned.[24]

Taylor, like Jefferson and the French ideologues, seemed to believe that enduring social inequalities were created by governments and man-made laws. They were, Adams declared, not created at all. They were inherent:

> I have seen, in the Hospital of Foundlings . . . at Paris, fifty babes in one room;—all under four days old; all in cradles alike; all nursed and attended alike; all dressed alike; all equally neat. I went from one end to the other of the whole row, and attentively observed all their countenances. And I never saw a greater variety, or more striking inequalities. . . . They were all born to equal rights, but to very different fortunes; to very different success and influence in life.[25]

If America really was, as Taylor seemed to believe, the land of social equality, then the gods had arbitrarily conspired to suspend the laws of biology, the principles of history, and even the much-praised "power of the people." For if it was true, as Taylor would surely concur, that "the supreme . . . power is placed by God and nature in the people, and they can never divest themselves of it," then it was equally true that all popular movements in recorded history demonstrated a need "to distinguish the one and the few from their own average and level." The more democratic the society, the stronger the desire to create social gradations. "You may depend upon it," wrote Adams, anticipating Alexis de Tocqueville's analysis of American democratic culture, "the people themselves, by their own observation and experience and feelings . . . made these distinctions before kingcraft, priestcraft, or noble-craft had anything to do with them." After the enslaved blacks of Santo Domingo had overthrown their white masters, Adams noted, they immediately came under the power of despots of their own color. "Bananas and water they still enjoy," he observed, "and a whole regiment would follow a leader who should hold a saltfish to their noses."[26]

Finally, Adams chose to drive home his point about the illusory character of Taylor's egalitarian ideology with the kind of personal attack he would never have made on Jefferson. How could it be, he asked rhetorically, that the loudest criticism of his writings on aristocracy should come from a slaveholder with vast estates and vast wealth, much of it inherited from his wife's side of the family? Taylor was a distinguished Virginian, Adams noted wryly, who had then "married well, obtaining both an amiable consort, and a handsome fortune." He was, in short, a perfect example of the kind of aristocrat Adams was talking about. "If you complain that this is personal," Adams explained, "I confess it, and intend it should be personal, that it might be more striking to you." If Taylor was offended by the analysis, Adams promised to "give you full leave to ask me any questions relative to myself, my ancestors, my posterity, my natural or political friends." Although he did not say it outright, Adams clearly insinuated that celebrations of American social equality were hardly credible when they came from privileged leaders of the Virginia aristocracy whose status depended on inherited estates and a labor force of enslaved blacks.[27]

But then, Adams's observations on the inevitability of social inequality created problems for his reputation that went beyond credibility. Adams kept insisting that he was not celebrating the enduring social divisions within America at all; he was only calling attention to their existence, refusing to believe the lovely lie that the American environment acted as a kind of solvent that dissolved away all social distinctions and class differences. Nor did he wish to stigmatize Virginia's planter class. If one were to study the history of any New England town, he acknowledged, one would almost always discover that two or three families owned most of the good land and dominated the town government long before and again after the American Revolution. Whether one liked this state of affairs was beside the point. The real point was to recognize that social inequality and elite power were as much a part of the social fabric of America as Europe. Pretending that they did not exist was utter delusion. Believing that they could be eliminated altogether was utopian nonsense. "All that men can do," he apprised Taylor, was to design governments that "modify, organize and arrange the powers of human society," striving to achieve a political balance that would regulate social divisions "in the best manner to protect, secure, and cherish the . . . natural rights of mankind." It served no purpose other than obfuscation to pretend that the endlessly challenging task of governing consisted solely in uttering magic words like "democracy." As Adams was fond of explaining, democracy was like "a young rake who thinks himself handsome and well made. . . . Democracy is Lovelace, and the people are Clarissa."[28]

If Adams was correct in accusing Taylor and other proponents of democracy of using the magic word in a misleading way, he himself had a maddening tendency to expand and contract his definition of aristocracy without warning, sometimes referring to the oligarchic segment of the government, sometimes referring to elite members of society, sometimes referring to any constellation of political or economic power, sometimes even referring to beautiful and articulate women at a dinner party. Since the problem of aristocracy was his favorite political obsession, he seemed to see it wherever he looked: "Every government is an aristocracy in fact,"

he wrote Rush. "The despotism of Genghis Kahn was an aristocracy. The government of the most popular French convention . . .
was an aristocracy. The most democratical canton in Switzer-
land was an aristocracy. The most leveling town meeting in New
England is an aristocracy." If six women were to gather together, he
explained to Taylor, and four of them were beautiful and talented
while the other two were ugly and ill-tempered, it was extremely
likely that the former would succeed at marriage, improve their
station, and therefore illustrate the principle of aristocracy. In the
political realm, it was even easier to identify an aristocrat: "I will
tell you in a few words what I mean by an aristocrat," he told
Taylor. "By an aristocrat, I mean every man who can command
or influence TWO VOTES; ONE BESIDES HIS OWN." Nor did it make
any difference how the influence was achieved. It could be "by
his virtues, his talents, his learning, his loquacity, his taciturnity,
his frankness, his reserve"—Adams was in mid-flight now, just
warming up—it could also be "his face, figure, eloquence, air,
attitude, movements, wealth, birth, art, address, intrigue, good
fellowship"—now the conclusion of the litany would drive home
the darker side of aristocratic power—it could even be "drunken-
ness, debauchery, fraud, perjury, violence, treachery, pyrrhonism,
deism or atheism, for by every one of these instruments have votes
been obtained or will be obtained." Taylor could hardly be faulted
for wondering how such a sprawling, all-inclusive version of aristocracy retained any coherent meaning at all.[29]

On the other hand, Adams could hardly be faulted for the elu-
siveness of his American aristocracy, since it now seems clear that
it was a concept that he employed in response to the equally protean, many-faceted, and elusive concept of American democracy.

Aristocracy had become Adams's antidote for exuberant liberal expectations in several forms: the notion that popular majorities invariably elected the best representatives; the notion that legislative assemblies represented the considered will of the people; the notion that equality of opportunity would usually lead to at least a semblance of social equality; the notion that economic competition in the marketplace would generate a roughly equitable distribution of goods; the notion, first formulated by Madison in *Federalist 10*, that the vastness of the American continent assured the interaction of so many factions and interest groups that no monopoly of economic and political power was likely to develop or to require government supervision. Each of Adams's different explications of aristocracy was a counter to these liberal assumptions—Adams thought them presumptions. If he often shifted his ground or the angle of his argument about the role of aristocracy, it was because his target—the emergent liberal values of nineteenth-century America—was devilishly difficult to pin down. It was hard to be precise when questioning a set of convictions whose credibility derived in part from being so self-evident as to require no defense.

If Adams's aristocracy was a many-faceted creature that kept changing its character in order to counter the protean illusions about democracy, the nub of his argument was more straightforward; namely, that in all societies for which there was any kind of historical record, political power and wealth tended to go hand in hand; and a few people invariably accumulated more wealth and power than the others. The central problem of American politics was to make political use of the aristocracy while still controlling its influence, to design governments and then use government's authority to assure that the energies of the elite flowed toward public ends. One way to assure that this did *not* happen, indeed one way to assure domination by a plutocracy or oligarchy, was to pretend that aristocracy had become extinct in America.

Fortunately, specific manifestations of aristocracy kept popping up on the national landscape, offering Adams the opportunity to define his "aristocratic principle" in practical terms. The Essex Junto was one of his favorite examples. This was a collection of conservative leaders, the spiritual heirs to the Hamiltonian wing of the Federalist Party, which was based in Essex County, Massachusetts, and saw itself as the chief defender of New England mercantile values. During his presidency this was the powerful faction that had opposed his policies toward France and contributed to his defeat in 1800. Adams noted that these High Federalists "are possessed of so much Wealth and so great a Portion of the Talents of the Country" that they embodied "an exclusive and monopolizing Spirit." On the other hand, many of these die-hard Federalists also possessed "so many Virtues, and good Principles, and are so nearly right . . . that I am convinced, without them, the People of America cannot preserve themselves from Anarchy," a concession Adams offered despite his personal distaste for Fisher Ames, their titular leader, and his keen sense that "of all Men in the World, I have the least obligation to them."[30]

But then the High Federalists were a dying breed that Adams correctly believed had committed political suicide by opposing the War of 1812 and endorsing the secession of New England from the Union at the Hartford Convention in 1815. More worrisome was the new "monied aristocracy" made possible by the proliferation of banks and paper money. "The banking infatuation pervades all America," he wrote Rush in 1810, warning that "an Aristocracy is growing out of them that will be as fatal as the feudal barons, if unchecked in time." For Adams, the banking industry was the northern equivalent of southern slavery; both institutions were "engines of aristocracy" that converted the labor of the many into huge profits for the few. "Every Bank in America is an enormous Tax upon the People for the Profit of Individuals," he declared, plundering "the Madness of the Many for the Profit of a Few." Banks, he told Rush, had replaced whiskey as the chief source of intoxication in America and were in the process of "undermining all principles, corrupting all morals. . . ." Far from being exemplars of probity, bankers were "swindlers and thieves," skilled at the art of "making immense fortunes . . . in a twinkling of an eye, by a financiering operation which substitutes a paper money whose immense depreciations go into the pockets of a few individuals. . . ."[31]

In his lengthy critique of Adams's doctrine of aristocracy, Taylor had devoted nearly a hundred pages to a like-minded argument. Taylor was also upset with what he called "finance capitalism," meaning the emergence of banking houses, insurance companies, paper money, and rampant speculation. In Taylor's formulation, the banking industry also "divides the nation into two groups, creditors and debtors . . . and fills each with malignity towards the other." While bankers claimed to be serving the financial interest of the public, they manipulated interest rates to make "a minority of the nation rich and potent, at the expense of the majority, which it makes poor and impotent." Adams told Jefferson that Taylor's massive book confounded him for many reasons, but the major reason was that "the Conclusion of the whole is that an Aristocracy of Bank Paper, is as bad as the Nobility of France of England," a point that Adams said he "most assuredly will not controvert. . . ." In fact, neither Taylor nor any of the Virginia agrarians could outdo him in his hatred of banks. "Our whole banking system I ever abhorred," he trumpeted, "I continue to abhor, and shall die abhorring." Much to his chagrin, he was going to die in what he and Rush agreed had become a "bebanked, bewhiskied, and be-dollared nation."[32]

There are at least two fundamental misconceptions at work here, both of which need to be corrected if Adams's political thinking is to be assessed fully and fairly. The first is Taylor's misconception, shared by most of the Jeffersonians, that Adams supported the banking program of Hamilton and the High Federalists. Clearly, he did not. As president he had not tried to dismantle the Hamiltonian banking scheme. For that matter, Jefferson had also renewed the Bank of the United States during his presidency. But Adams, like Jefferson and Taylor, harbored a deep-seated distrust of banks as sanctuaries for corrupt profiteers, gambling houses where the public trust was systematically put at risk and sold to the highest bidder. The second misconception, following logically from the first, is that because he shared fully in the rhetoric against these new financial institutions, because he condemned banks and bankers in language that was just as hostile and even more colorful than Taylor's, then he must have concurred with the Jeffersonian—soon to be Jacksonian—remedy: banks were the snakes in the American Eden and must be destroyed. This was an attitude rooted in the pre-capitalistic values of traditional republicanism, so it seems plausible that Adams, the epitome of republican ideology, would find it compelling.

The truth is more intriguingly paradoxical. Adams agreed

with Taylor's criticism of banks in one important respect; namely, banks were "engines of inequality" that transferred wealth from the middling and poorer classes into the hands of the already rich. As Adams put it: "Who can compute the vast sums taken out of the pockets of the simple and hoarded into the purses of the cunning . . .?" Taylor, who spoke for the agrarian interests of the Jeffersonians in the South, dramatized the financial exchanges as an "ambuscade" that stole from "the family of the earth" and rewarded "the family of cunning." Both men, along with Jefferson, also viewed the profits of bankers as inherently immoral, because they manipulated money and interest rates without doing any productive labor themselves.[33]

But Taylor regarded all banks as conspiratorial agencies operating in collusion with government to defy and distort the natural laws of the marketplace. He was one of the first to articulate the sectional perspective of southern farmers as victims of a northern banking conspiracy sanctioned by the federal government. Supporters of Andrew Jackson, then again, later in the century, southern Populists would seize upon this vision to stigmatize banks and bankers as symbols of an unholy alliance between capital and government. Given their assumptions about the inherently equitable distribution of goods that would occur in an unfettered marketplace, the appearance of vastly unequal pockets of wealth could only be the consequence of government-sanctioned meddling. Taylor's solution, like Jackson's after him, was to sever all connections between banking and the federal government.[34]

Adams, on the other hand, never believed in the benign operation of the marketplace. Left to its own devices, he thought that the marketplace would no more discipline itself than would

Jefferson's version of "the people." Indeed, that was the major problem presented by what Adams called "the multitude of swindling banks"—they were essentially gambling houses that enhanced and accelerated the worst features of the marketplace. Adams did not object to banks because they were distorting the natural rhythms of a burgeoning capitalistic economy. He objected that government regulations were not in place to assure that the flow of money and property served the public interest rather than private interests. Rather than free banks altogether from federal control, he thought that all banks should be public institutions under the control of the national government: "My own opinion has invariably been, that there ought to be but one Bank in the United States," he wrote in 1811, "and that a National Bank with a branch in each State. . . . This ought to have been a fundamental Article in the Constitution." Banks, in short, were like all other aristocratic elements in American society—dangerous yet indispensable creatures. "An attempt to annihilate them," he warned, "would be as romantic an adventure as any in Don Quixote." Banks could never be eliminated, but ought never to be freed to pursue their avaricious ends; they must be regulated by law to serve national economic goals. If Taylor's views on banks foreshadowed the Jacksonians and the Populists, Adams's views foreshadowed the regulatory legislation of the Progressives and the New Deal.[35]

Of course, allusions to future political movements invariably distort the historical integrity of Adams's political thinking, which was very much a product of late-eighteenth-century conditions that cannot be translated easily, sometimes at all, into the idioms and arguments of our modern world. It is, however, striking to realize how much the classical categories that were the primary units of his political thought literally *forced* him to think about American society in terms that did not fit the emerging liberal consensus of his own day but are eerily relevant to ours. His insistence on three separate orders—monarchy, aristocracy, and democracy—made him unreceptive to any homogenized or undifferentiated conception of "the people." His grounding in classical history made him wary of, then downright hostile to, the claim that America's more egalitarian social conditions or expansive environment rendered it an exception to the lessons of history. His obsession with aristocracy and the role of elites made him contemptuous toward egalitarian expectations of several sorts, most especially the expectation that the marketplace could discipline human energies without the aid of government. Finally, his classical orientation made it impossible for him to think about government in the same negative way that most of his fellow Americans had come to understand it. For Adams, government was not, indeed could not be, a separate sphere of limited authority divorced from the dynamics of society or the marketplace. It was an organic expression of the forces that comprised American society; not, if you will, "them" but "us"; not a foreign body distantly overseeing the activity of millions of private citizens, but the public will itself, and therefore an inherently collectivistic enterprise whose goals transcended any merely individualistic ethos.

IF THE BUILDING blocks out of which Adams shaped his thinking about politics came from the classics, his deepest insights into the human motives that inhabited and eventually animated the classical categories came from introspection. If Adams's temperament was inherently oppositional or dialectical, revealing itself most fully in dialogue or debate, the ultimate dialogue was with himself. In his early and middle years that dialogue went on in his diary, but he stopped making entries during his presidency and never resumed them again after his retirement. In one section of his *Discourses on Davila,* however, he had recorded his most candid opinions on the emotional source of all political behavior, especially the underlying motives for aspiring political leaders and erstwhile aristocrats. Originally published in serial form in 1790, soon after his return to America from England, *Davila* was republished as a book in 1813, but attracted little notice. Although no John Taylor made it the focus of extended study, Adams himself returned to it regularly. "Americans paid no attention or regard to this," he noted in the margins in 1813, "and a blind mad rivalry between the north and south is destroying all morality and sound policy as a result." It is doubtful that *Davila* by itself could have prevented the Civil War, but there is no doubt that it contained the most personal and penetrating comments on the psychological roots of his political "system" that Adams ever wrote.[36]

The main theme of *Davila* was introduced through a story that Adams told of a starving pauper and his dog. Friends eventually advised the pauper to avoid death by eating the dog's food. But the pauper refused, asking rhetorically, "who will love me then?" Adams claimed that the pauper's reaction cut to the core of human motivation. "In this *'who will love me then?'* there is a key to the human heart," Adams observed, "to the history of human life and manners; and to the rise and fall of empires." For it was in the heart, not the head, that Adams found the most powerful forces shaping individual and group behavior, the primary elements in his political chemistry. Nor was Adams content to locate the emotional wellspring, then follow the analysis of classical or modern theorists. "I have been somewhat a student of Machiavel," he wrote Vanderkemp, "but he has always been disagreeable to me because I never could know whether he was in jest or earnest." *Davila* did feature a long quotation from Adam Smith's *Theory of Moral Sentiments,* which Adams was clearly reading at the time of composition, but he cited Smith for the same reason he loaded down all his published writings with acknowledged and unacknowledged quotations—the book was at hand—and in his frenzied fashion of composition, he seized whatever sources were around him to document his point.[37]

In *Davila,* however, the point about the inner workings of the heart clearly came not from a book but from the heart Adams knew best, his own. There were many human emotions, he observed, but none was "more essential or remarkable, than the *passion for distinction,*" that is, the craving "to be observed, considered, esteemed, praised, beloved and admired by his fellows. . . ." This need to be noticed could express itself in several forms. When it took the form of "a desire to excell another, by fair industry, and the practice of virtue [it] is properly called *Emulation.*" When it changed course and "aims at power, it is *Ambition.*" It could also express itself in a variety of guises that received separate names, including "jealousy," "envy," and "vanity." But the separate names only referred to the different targets of what was a single human passion. "It is a principal end of government to regulate this passion," he argued, "which in turn becomes a principal means of government." And this bedrock human passion, he was at pains to emphasize, was not a desire for wealth or power. The quest for material distinction was merely a secondary passion that served as a means to the ultimate end, which was the need for attention and affection.[38]

Merchants, bankers, and other members of "the moneyed aristocracy" were actually driven by emotional forces that wealth itself, no matter how huge the supply, could never satisfy: "Why do men affront heaven and earth to accumulate wealth, which will forever be useless to them?" The answer was psychological, not material or economic. It was *because riches attract the attention, consideration, and congratulations of mankind.*" Avaricious businessmen who pursued more and more sums of money were rather pathetic creatures, for they were trying to purchase affection with a currency that would never fetch much in the only emotional exchange that mattered: "Riches force the opinion on man that he is the object of the congratulations of others," Adams wrote. "His imagination expands, and his heart dilates at these charming illusions. His attachment to his possessions increases as fast as his desire to accumulate more; not for the purposes of . . . utility, but from the desire of illustration." Over a century later Thorstein Veblen would develop a similar theory of economic behavior and give it the memorable label "conspicuous consumption." Adams had early on encountered the same psychological dynamic inside his own soul, where the lingering vestiges of New England Puritanism also made him familiar with the futility of amassing wealth as a way of persuading oneself, and others, that salvation was assured.[39]

Adams was less interested in the theoretical or theological origins of the insight than its political applications. He claimed that "the science of government, may be reduced to the same simple principle," namely, the act of "conducting, controlling, and regulating the emulation and ambition of the citizens." There was no way, he was at pains to insist, that the drive for "the attention, consideration, and congratulations of our fellow men" could ever be eradicated. "Nature has taken effectual care of her own work," he declared; it has "wrought the passions into the texture and essence of the soul, and has not left it in the power of art to destroy them."

Here was another instance in which Adams warned against the folly of any political scheme that attempted to remake human nature. Moreover, the primacy of this particular passion helped explain why he could never accept political prescriptions built on the principle of social or economic equality. It was not just that human beings were born with inherently different talents and abilities. It was also that the deepest compulsion in the human soul drove men to distinguish themselves from others, to accrue property, status, and honors in ways that defied all egalitarian ideals. Adams put the point succinctly in a letter to a grandson: "In all the democratical governments I have ever read [about], heard or seen, there is little real love of equality," he wrote in 1821. "In all governments, in every individual, there is an eternal struggle to rise above somebody or other, or to depress somebody or other who is above him. . . ." The egalitarian schemes of those French *philosophes* and their American counterparts within the Jefferson camp had the singular disadvantage of running against the deepest grain of human motivation.[40]

It was not only folly to oppose the elemental urges of mankind, it was also counterproductive. The passion for distinction had been woven into the fabric of human nature for a purpose. "Nature has ordained it, as a constant incentive to activity and industry," Adams proclaimed, "that . . . men might be urged to constant exertions of beneficence." Because of the irresistible impulse to win the approval of others, "men of all sorts, even those who have the least of reason, virtue or benevolence, are chained down to an incessant servitude to their fellow creatures; laboring without intermission . . . slaves to mankind." The social consequences of this powerful drive would, he predicted, become most visible in America, because "the lowest can aspire as freely as the highest. . . ." Adams was careful not to claim that the relatively open and uncrowded conditions in America would allow for the emergence of social equality. In fact, he thought that greater freedom in this richer environment would produce greater inequality. But he did think that the combustible combination of the drive for distinction with the more wide open American environment would generate unprecedented levels of productivity.[41]

The pursuit of profits and wealth, no matter how successful, was only one way to satisfy the craving for respect. Adams thought that most Americans would opt to release their ambitious energies along this avenue, in part because it was the most visible and obvious course and in part because the economic opportunities were more prolific in America. A smaller number would choose to distinguish themselves outside the marketplace, pursuing what Adams called "reputation." Many members of this group were likely to be successful merchants and businessmen who realized that wealth itself was inadequate to quench their thirst for recognition and who eventually graduated to a higher plateau, where they could release their passions in philanthropic causes. Public officials, men of letters, and military men also lived at this level; they could be expected to talk in terms of "a sense of duty, a love of truth," but their deeper and often unconscious motives were decidedly selfish. "It is the *notoriety*, the *celebration*," Adams argued, "which constitutes the charm that is to compensate the loss of appetite and sleep. . . ."[42]

The most successful players on this plateau might expect public recognition in the form of titles, statues, and even a place in the history books. "The wisdom and virtue of all nations," Adams explained, "have endeavored to regulate the passion for respect and distinction, and to reduce it to some order in society, by titles marking the gradations of magistracy. . . ." By creating separate honors to aim for, the government encouraged greater exertions on behalf of the public and was simultaneously able "to prevent . . . collisions among the passions of many pursuing the same objects." One of the reasons Adams proposed fanciful titles for the leading public officials in America—a proposal that his critics denounced as evidence of his aristocratic and un-American sensibility—was to ensure an adequate supply of honorific rewards. Since America lacked the kind of aristocratic titles and emblems that had grown up over time in Europe and Great Britain, Adams thought they should be created for distinguished public servants in order to guarantee that the drive for distinction would be attracted into government and public service and not fall back into the merely material rewards of the marketplace.[43]

On the other hand, Adams himself acknowledged that the quest for titles or statues or a place in the history books was an irrational drive: "For what a folly is it!" he observed. "What is it to us what shall be said of us after we are dead? Or in Asia, Africa, or Europe while we live. There is no greater possible or imaginable delusion. Yet the impulse is irresistible." What made it irresistible he did not say. Like a primordial instinct, it was simply there, festering away in the souls of all human beings. Perhaps it was some hidden urge to deny one's mortality, to live on in the imaginations of others. Perhaps it was some conditioned reflex that God had built into nature in order to guarantee public spiritedness. Whatever the ultimate source of the urge, Adams was clear about two points: first, he knew its power first hand and could testify personally to its dominance over purely rational approaches to life; second, given the undeniability of the passion for distinction, the proper function of government was not to pretend that such forces did not exist, but rather to assure they were "directed to virtue, and then encouraged by generous applause and honorable rewards."[44]

Finally, some men were born at opportune moments in history, when nations were being founded or great crises that would shape the future of the world were in process. These rare historical moments often called forth the deepest reservoir of human ambition, the most ferocious form of the passion for recognition. "This," wrote Adams—surely with a keen sense that he was describing his own generation and, he hoped, himself—"is the tribe out of which proceed your patriots and heroes." Men like Jefferson and Taylor, who had fashioned a political rhetoric that stigmatized aristocratic power, were inadvertently condemning the very group of American leaders—the revolutionary generation—which had been responsible for creating the American republic. History only afforded a few opportunities to satisfy such leaders. "But there are but a few, and God knows but a few," Adams noted, with the combination of talent and ambition to "aim at approbation as well as attention, at esteem as well as congratulation. . . ." Only those leaders with the deepest craving for fame were candidates for this highest calling; and society sanctioned the full release of their egotistical impulses because circumstances demanded and required nothing less. "I have read in a book that Alexander did much good," Adams recalled wryly, "and in another book that Caesar did great work, and in others, that English liberties are all owing to Cromwell; and I believe all these paradoxes."[45]

The paradox derived from the fact that such leaders, like banks, were both indispensable and dangerous, that the very passion for fame and glory, once released, was also extremely difficult to control. Hamilton and Burr were his favorite examples of the built-in danger. Adams had given this lecture on self-control to himself countless times in his diary. In *Davila* it was elevated to the highest level of political theory: "But for our humiliation," he warned, "we must still remember, that . . . the passion, although refined by the purest moral sentiments, and intended to be governed by the best principles, is a passion still; and therefore, like all other human desires, unlimited and insatiable." He inserted a quotation from Samuel Johnson that put the question nicely: "Heroes proceed! What bounds your pride shall hold?" The autobiographical answer to that question he had always given to himself was clear: constant doses of humility, endless lectures on self-discipline. But at the national level more than trust in such personal admonitions was required. "The answer to that question can be nothing other than this," he concluded, "that as nature has established in the bosoms of heroes no limits to those passions; and as the world, instead of restraining, encourages them, the check must be in the form of government." This meant limited terms of office, checks and balances, and a constitution that explicitly precluded even the most charismatic and virtuous official from standing above the law.[46]

Whereas Madison thought that the vast size of the American

republic served as a safeguard against despotism by assuring that the greater variety and number of interest groups would collide with one another in a continental version of Adam Smith's marketplace, Adams worried about the geographical size of the United States and the growing population. "National passions and habits are unwieldy, unmanageable, and formidable things," he warned, and when "exposed to the observation of greater numbers of people, the effects . . . become more serious, interesting, and dangerous." His primary concern was that the vastness of the American republic would enlarge the size of the political theatre in which ambitious leaders played their roles, expanding the arena in which their urge to distinguish themselves could function, feeding that urge with continental conquests. Alexander Hamilton and Aaron Burr troubled him in this connection, since they were energetic leaders with "an uncontroulable Tendency to ascend," and the western territories afforded them every opportunity to stage adventurous expeditions. He also worried that personal rivalries for national attention would break down regionally, with sectional leaders vying for political power in elections that produced "slanders and libels first, mobs and seditions next, and civil war, with all her hissing snakes, burning torches, and haggard horrors at last." Frequent elections, like so many other features of his political thinking, were double-edged weapons: on the one hand, they prevented entrenched power from becoming permanent; on the other hand, they multiplied the occasions when vanity could distort the national interest. But he offered such scenes as warnings rather than prophecies. They were also reminders that the American experiment with republican government over such a vast tract of land was an unprecedented undertaking of great promise and great risk, with the greatness on both scores deriving from the unprecedented scope America offered for the expression of humankind's most elemental drives.[47]

Davila was like his other attempts at political theory, only more so: a disorderly collection of profound insights, both the disorder and the profundity deriving from the same source inside the Adams personality. Adams admitted as much to himself. Whenever he made marginal notes in his personal copy of *Davila*, he admitted disappointment at its rambling and disjointed form. "The Style has little fluency," he scribbled in 1813, then added with obvious pride, "but the sense is as immortal as human nature."[48]

The lack of what Adams called "fluency"—the ricochet style of *Davila* and the *Defence*—inadvertently expressed one of his deepest political convictions: namely, that comprehensive theories of politics were invariably too neat and rational to capture the maddening messiness of the real world. True, Adams did believe there was such a thing as human nature. He had studied it in written histories and, more tellingly, had confronted its emotional imperatives inside himself. But he did not believe that conventional forms of political philosophy did much justice to the complex irrationalities of the human condition. He associated elaborate theories of politics with French *philosophes* like Turgot and Condorcet, whose mental fabrications bore only a tenuous connection to history's machinations. As Adams saw it, political theory of the grandiose sort was invariably "ideology," an organized collection of seductive hopes and wishes, a systematic way of going wrong with confidence. History and the human heart that propelled it could not be reduced to a set of accessible political prescriptions, which were, after all, merely pieces of theoretical wisdom, and therefore a contradiction in terms.

If the dishevelled condition of his political writings conveyed an important insight into the limitations of language and political theory, it also obscured his legacy. Adams was fond of telling friends and family that his reputation suffered for the lack of "puffers," what we would call publicists or lobbyists. (The deeper problem, of course, was that, even if such creatures had made themselves available to Adams, he would never have listened to them.) What he really needed was a skillful editor, someone to play the role of monitor of his political writings, a role Madison played with Jefferson, someone to rescue his erudition from his inveterate effusiveness. For if Adams should not be seen, indeed did not wish to be seen, as a political theorist or philosopher, he does merit recognition as one of America's most notable political thinkers.[49]

What might a thoughtful editor have selected as the central features of the Adams political legacy? Well, the core impulse of his political thought was adversarial, contrarian, and dialectical, an exact intellectual expression of his personal temperament. For this reason all scholarly attempts to locate logical inconsistencies in his thought, or to accuse him of shifting his ideological position after the American Revolution, are misguided ventures that fail to grasp the animating principle of his political mentality. While a firm believer in the classical political categories, he was obsessed with a *dynamic* version of the classical ideal of balance. This meant that he could be counted on to oppose the reigning *Zeitgeist*, whether it was blowing toward the left or the right. Dramatic shifts of emphasis were an integral part of his avowed system. He regarded all political movements and social trends as addictions; like the vanities and ambitions coursing through his own soul, they required countering correctives lest they fly out of control. He was unparalleled among his peers in understanding the doctrine of checks and balances in ways that went beyond erector-set rationality.

Finally, Adams was the supreme political realist of the revolutionary generation. His lifelong habit of mistrusting himself effectively immunized him against illusory solutions to the problem of political power provided by both the older classical and newer liberal traditions. The classical belief in virtue, while a noble ideal, struck him as a naive and at best short-lived hope, for it asked more of human nature than could possibly be sustained. Meanwhile the various liberal antidotes to the virus of political power—an enlightened people, a benign marketplace, the expansive borders of an enlarged republic—struck him as a wholly inadequate, or as seductive delusions that usually made matters worse. Among America's dominant political theologians, he remained the avowed agnostic and therefore the most astute analyst of political power's inherent intractability. In the end, he could not bring himself to believe that there were any ultimate answers to the overlapping problems of self-government or national government, at least none that did not contain within themselves the seeds of their own destruction.

CHAPTER SIX

Intimacies

Among all the great characters that it has been my
lot to meet . . . I have never met with a mind of such
varied powers, such acute discrimination, and which
if I may use the expression, was so intrinsically sound;
with a memory so fertile, so clear, and so perspicuous.
Every thing in his mind was rich, racy, and true.

—Louisa Catherine Adams, Diary, June 2, 1839

I have as great a Terror of learned Ladies, as you have.
I have such a consciousness of Inferiority to them, as
mortifies and humiliates my self-love, to such a degree
that I can scarcely speak in their presence. Very few of
these Ladies have ever had the condescention to allow
me to talk. And when it has so happened, I have always
come off mortified at the discovery of my Inferiority.

—Adams to Francis Vanderkemp, April 8, 1815

As THE RETIREMENT YEARS at Quincy rolled on and Adams
entered his eighties, his vision of public affairs remained connected to incessant explorations of his own boisterous personality.

When he looked backwards into history or outward into the emerging nation he had helped to establish, he saw the same emotional ingredients throbbing and pulsating and influencing events as when he looked inside himself. Politics for him remained psychology writ large, a heaving collection of irrational urges that moved across the social landscape like the ambitions and vanities he felt surging through his own soul. More than any member of the revolutionary generation, Adams thought of statecraft as a public application of the skills required for self-management, regarded political analysis as a public version of introspection.

The emotions or passions were not merely abstract concepts to think or write about in splendid isolation from their effects; they were forces he experienced personally. As Bernard Bailyn has so nicely put it, Adams "felt the world, directly and sensitively, before he thought about it," so that his most profound and perceptive insights into what we call political theory were not, for him at least, theoretical at all. They were vivid projections onto a larger social screen of the images he saw inside himself; or, more accurately, they were intellectual expressions of the emotions he felt most deeply. His mind and heart were wired together in such a fashion as to preclude purely abstract expression; thought and feeling were so intermingled inside him that he was literally incapable of rational detachment.[1]

One reason Adams kept rereading his *Discourses on Davila* with approval throughout his retirement was that its central argument— that emotional rather than rational forces inevitably shaped history and the men who made it—confirmed his personal experience with his own interior demons; it also somewhat sanctioned his own temperamental volatility. And one reason Adams had to contend with a reputation for unpredictable outbursts unbecoming a classical hero of the American republic was that he remained maddeningly and irreverently outspoken in public as well as private situations.

"I have one head, four limbs and five Senses," he responded mockingly to one of the innumerable inquiries about his physical condition in old age, adding that he was "Five feet seven or nine Inches, I really know not which." As for his reputation for emotional outbursts that resembled tantrums, he claimed that his political enemies had exaggerated the tendency: "My temper in general has been tranquil except when any Instance of extraordinary Madness, Deceit, Hypocricy, Ingratitude, Treachery or Perfidy has suddenly struck me. Then I have always been irascible enough, and in three or four Instances too much so." This was a concession he would never have made in the earliest years of his retirement. As he entered his eighties, he wanted the world to know that, whatever storms still brewed inside him, they were now under control and that "Anger never rested in the bosom."[2]

Anger, of course, was only one kind of emotion. There were many others, which Adams could readily exhibit whenever roused to action by what he considered an impertinent remark about his political values or an uninformed question about the meaning of the American Revolution. Then his verbal artillery would blast away and the words would explode on the page or in the air, usually in a long series of capitalized or emphasized abstractions that defined a whole range of emotions. Years earlier, during his most active service on behalf of the American Revolution, Adams had confided to his diary that he was, by nature, a calm and even languid character. Then he added: "Yet some great Events, Some cutting Expressions, Some mean Hypocrisies, have at Times, thrown this Assemblage of Sloth, Sleep, and littleness into Rage a little like a Lion." What impressed visitors to Quincy who called upon the septuagenarian patriarch was the abiding ferocity of his feelings, the sheer energy and animated intelligence that remained vibrant and powerful even as his physical condition succumbed to the inevitable ravages of old age. As one visitor put it, there was not "the smallest chip of an iceberg in his composition."[3]

The last portrait done of Adams, painted by Gilbert Stuart in 1823, captured the lionlike fury, with its steely-eyed gaze and rumpled hair that floated around his head and down to his shoulders like a mane. "Stuart caught a glimpse of the living spirit shining through the feeble and decrepit body," observed Josiah Quincy, adding that it fixed the final image of the old man "at one of those happy moments when the intelligence lights up the wasted envelope. . . ." Despite the wrinkled skin, reddened eyes, arthritic hands, and stooped posture, the spirit of the man remained incandescent, always at risk of becoming inflammable.[4]

The older he got, the more Adams tried to fit himself into the role of the stoic Roman statesman, living out a life of rustic simplicity as depicted in Cicero's *De Senectute*. "I can read Cicero's de Senectute, because I have read him for almost seventy years," he wrote in 1820, "and seem to have him almost by heart." But the heart was always the problem for Adams, whose temperament precluded stoicism in much the same way that fire melted ice. In his eighty-fifth year, while rereading Cicero's advice on self-control and seasoned serenity, he acknowledged that his admiration for the stoical message was at odds with his visceral reaction to the text. "I never delighted much in contemplating commas and colons, or in spelling or measuring syllables," he admitted—and this from a

Bronze casting of John Adams, based on plaster "life mask" of 1825, depicting Adams as the American Cicero. *John Adams (1735–1826), 1940, John Henri Browere & Roman Bronze Works, bronze, H: 29 x W: 21.5 x D: 10.5 in., Fenimore Art Museum, Cooperstown, New York, Gift of Stephen C. Clark. N0201. 1961. Photograph by Richard Walker.*

writer whose cavalier approach to punctuation and spelling defied generations of accomplished editors—"but now, while reading Cato, if I look at these little objects, I find my imagination, in spite of all my exertions, roaming in the Milky Way. . . ." Even the punctuation in a Latin sentence, it seems, could set him off, catapulting his mind beyond simple translation and into some

idiosyncratic realm where his own eccentricities were free to roam.
He had always been, and always remained, too passionate and
slightly out of control to fit neatly into the classical mold, too sen-
tient and singular a being to appear properly enigmatic.[5]

Even as he grew into a very old man, his efforts to adopt Ciceronian poses usually failed miserably, victims of his penchant for
candor and the tendency to transform dignified requests for his
wisdom into jokes. In response to a touchingly laudatory letter
from John Jay, Adams refused to accept the praise or behave like
a sage. "I am too feeble and have been confined to the house the
greatest part of the winter," he wrote to Jay in 1821, "but I hope to
crawl out like a Turtle in the Spring." One visitor who expected to
encounter a sedate and sober old man came away shaking his head
and reporting that, unlike all other professed sages, Adams "could
not keep his mouth shut." When a correspondent asked him the
secret of his longevity, he replied that every day he drank lots of
cider, water, lemonade, and "no more than a pint of wine," and
always tried to have chocolate for breakfast. Then he pleaded for
relief from such questions, claiming that "the history of my Physical habits according to the best estimate I can make, would fill a
Volume in folio as large as the life of Richard Baxter."[6]

In 1820, when a friend apprised him that the new Maine constitution set an age limit for judges, he dashed off a comic retort
that self-consciously mocked his own reputation for vanity as well
as the infamous Adams vituperative style: "I consider this as a personal affront to me as an Old Man," he joked; it was also a repudiation of the wisdom of the ages and of the classics and, if these
revered authorities carried no weight with the voters of Maine, they
should be informed that the Master of Montezillo had declared the

new law "against the Precepts and practice of the Bible." His daily exercise habits inspired the same self-deprecating exuberance. As he told Charles Francis, his grandson and eventual editor, he liked to ride his horse, Rosenante, two or three miles a day, but would much prefer to ride around his property on a less majestic and much shorter beast: "Six and thirty years ago as your father can tell you," he recalled in 1815, "I rode over a great part of the Asturian & Pyrenian mountains in Spain, on a beautiful mule, and I would give more for that little animal for any use now, than for the best horse at the new market races." The erstwhile Cicero of American politics kept behaving like Sancho Panza.[7]

Adams's inveterate effusiveness, the sheer volume of emotional energy that he expended in talk, letterwriting, friendships, and even in solitary thinking, deserves more than casual notice as an intriguing aside that supplements, in merely ornamental fashion, an intellectual assessment of his thought and character. His emotional intensity, and the free-flowing manner in which it expressed itself, was a central feature of his personality. It was the major reason he found it impossible to produce a coherent statement of his political philosophy in a single volume or treatise; it underlay his inability to craft his autobiography with the manipulative artifice of a Franklin or—to peer into the future of the Adams family— with the ironic orchestrations of his great-grandson, Henry; it shaped, often in a decisive way, the opinions of friends, enemies and, even more tellingly, associates who did not know him well, by creating an impression of unpredictable volatility and almost dangerous honesty; and it prevented him from being conveyed to the world or to posterity in the guise of a classical hero with a dignified deportment, deliberative demeanor, and a temperament

sufficiently elusive to serve as a Rorschach test for subsequent generations. In all these ways, the passionate energy of his personality
was the electrical current that animated his very being and defined
what even he came to call his "singular character."

THE VERY SAME emotional excesses that so often got him into
trouble in public life—his candor, flat-out style of argument, and
proclivity to engage whenever challenged—usually had the opposite effect in his private life. Most of those who came within his
orbit, even when that orbit was delineated by his withering criticisms and hostile opinions, ended up concluding that Adams was
irresistibly likable. For example, in 1824 John Taylor saw fit to
compose an affectionate final letter to Adams. "During a long illness from which I am not yet recovered," Taylor wrote, "the reveries
which usually amuse sick people visited me; and among them the
idea of writing a farewell letter to you." Taylor knew better than
most how difficult and contentious Adams could be. But as he lay
dying, Taylor felt the urge to record his respect and affection for
the man whose political theory he had spent twenty years attack-
ing. However much they might disagree about politics, however
irascible Adams had been in responding to Taylor's criticism of his
Defence, Taylor wanted to go to his grave acknowledging Adams's
personal greatness. His farewell letter "will not be suspected of
adulation," wrote Taylor, given their long record of disagreement
and Taylor's fatal illness; it was intended only "to file among your
archives some facts, which may meet the eye of a historian, as well
as to give some pleasure to a patriot."

Among the facts was Taylor's assessment that Adams ranked

"next to Washington" in the American pantheon, a rather remarkable placement for an avid Jeffersonian to make, especially one whom Adams had confronted in thirty-two long, accusatory, and explanatory letters. But the candor, the unvarnished sincerity and human engagement that Adams displayed in the extended conversation with Taylor won over the Virginian's heart despite their irreconcilable differences as political thinkers. The bond Taylor claimed to feel defied logic or reasoned argument. Having encountered the palpable vivacity of the essential Adams, it was simply impossible not to like him.[8]

Usually, however, it was Adams who defied conventional expectations to reach out for a personal connection in spite of public disagreement. The resumption of the friendship with Jefferson illustrated this tendency, which Jefferson then responded to with his characteristic geniality. But the rekindling of the Adams-Jefferson relationship was but the most famous example of a decided pattern that recurred regularly throughout the latter years at Quincy. In 1820, for example, Adams wrote Louisa Catherine that there were "reports in circulation here that Mr. Randolph of Roanoke is in a state of insanity. . . ." The reference was to John Randolph, the eccentric Virginia congressman, avid defender of states' rights, slavery, and agrarian values—Randolph might be described as a slightly deranged man-child whose eloquent tantrums on the floor of the Congress on behalf of what he gleefully acknowledged was a lost cause became the prototype for the doomed Cavalier of southern fiction. Adams admitted that Randolph "has appeared through his whole public life to be possessed of a Demonical Spirit of Malice and Vengeance without cause against me." And this was no Adams exaggeration.

(Randolph had expressed the hope that the entire male side of the Adams family should be tortured to death by Indians.) Nevertheless, Adams confided to his daughter-in-law that "I have ever considered him [Randolph] gifted by nature with some amiable qualities and therefore have always felt a kind of respect for him." He asked Louisa Catherine to convey his wish for a quick recovery and a resumption of the inimitable Randolph style.[9]

Perhaps Adams recognized some piece of himself in the eccentric Virginian, a tendency toward wildly idiosyncratic urges that could easily, as it had in Randolph, expand into a near-maniacal temperament. More likely, the Adams gesture of friendship, for forgiving past political differences, for responding to the elemental humanity inside old enemies as well as old allies, was an established and instinctive habit that required no special explanation.

Just two months before he asked after Randolph's health, for instance, he bemoaned the death of John Wentworth, a Harvard classmate Adams described as "my friend of 70 years standing." Wentworth had sided with the British during the Revolution, served as the last royal governor of New Hampshire, then fled to Nova Scotia as an exile. But Adams still felt an emotional bond with him. "In spite of Political and National Alienations," he wrote, "which I find do not reach the heart, I feel the death of Wentworth—as I should a brother." The same sentiments applied to David Sewall, who after Wentworth's death remained his sole surviving Harvard classmate. "Our political sentiments," Adams observed to Sewall, "are of no consequence to the community. You & I agreed very well at College. . . . We have ever since, as I hope, agreed in private friendships. But we have gazed at the great political system of the universe, through different telescopes."

That made little difference, however, as long as their mutual trust allowed them to begin letters with a hearty "How do you do?"[10]

In the classical scheme of things such a capacity to reach past political and ideological disagreements reflected the maturation of the mind, the older and wiser man's development to a stage where cool reason finally established control over unruly passions; serenity, in the form of sober judgment and calm acceptance of life's petty vicissitudes, was an inherently rational condition that usually came with age, when the youthful fires had died down and reasoned decisions at last had the opportunity to assume their place of natural supremacy. But much as he enjoyed making self-congratulatory references to Cicero, Adams never evolved to this allegedly "higher" stage of personal maturity. One of the central ironies of his character was that America's most notorious defender of a classical conception of politics possessed an inherently passionate, non-classical disposition: "The astonishment of your Family at my vivacity is very just," he had written to Rush just before his closest friend's death, adding that "when a man's vivacity increases with years it becomes frenzy at last."[11] His vaunted vivacity remained the dominant feature of his personality.

Adams never conquered his passions. They were, in fact, the basis for and source of his infectious amiability. Adams did not overcome long-standing political differences with old friends like Jefferson, Wentworth, or Sewall because of some newfound Ciceronian self-control. Quite the opposite, he retrieved such relationships because he could not control himself. "Had you and I been forty days with Moses on Mount Sinai," he gushed to Jefferson, "and admitted to behold, the divine Shekinah, and there told that one was three and three, one: We might not have had the courage to deny it, but We could not have believed it." The urge to share such playful thoughts was spontaneous, the irresistible result of what Adams himself called his "sauciness." He could forgive and forget, not because he had achieved stoic detachment, but because he had never lost a child-like impulse to share his deepest personal feelings. When, much earlier in his life, Jonathan Sewall commented that "Adams has a heart formed for friendship," he was making what turned out to be more than a casual observation. Once Adams had established a bond of trust with another, there were no well-placed way stations in his soul where candor could make convenient stops while discretion assessed the implications. Friendship filled too basic a need, satisfied too compelling an impulse, to make it subservient to cautionary restraints.[12]

Of course, trust could easily get him into trouble. Four years after Benjamin Rush's death his son, Richard Rush, asked Adams about the possible publication of the Adams-Rush correspondence. This would have exposed Adams to a cascade of criticism and humiliation, since his letters to Rush contained his most outrageous bursts of indignation and his most indiscreet judgments on his fellow members of the revolutionary generation. "The correspondence between your Father and me has been for forty years together too intimate and too free, to see the Light at present," Adams explained. When Richard Rush suggested that perhaps an edited version might not offend, Adams countered that "My Letters to him are of a rougher and coarser Constitution" than public taste, no matter how skillful the editing, "could withstand." Adams rejected any censored version, insisting that he "would not have one line of them suppressed." Fortunately, Richard Rush concurred, so Adams was spared the embarrassment of explaining opinions that, even in the twentieth century, possess the power to shock.[13]

Not so fortunately, Adams sent off many letters to less reliable correspondents, strangers or casual acquaintances who were trusted with controversial opinions, which were then published without his permission in local newspapers. The most damaging episode involved William Cunningham, a Federalist polemicist who had engaged Adams in an exchange of letters in the early years of his retirement. The correspondence contained some of Adams's most critical assessments of Jefferson, accusing him of "a mean thirst of popularity, an inordinate ambition, and a want of sincerity." When Cunningham announced that he intended to publish the letters, Adams was flabbergasted. "The correspondence and conversations that have passed between us have been under the confidential seal of secrecy and friendship," he claimed, warning that "Any violation of it will be a breach of honour and of plighted faith." But Cunningham's son eventually published the letters in 1823, as part of a scheme to discredit John Quincy's prospects for the presidency by exposing the elder Adams as an "aristocratical and despotic" creature, whose reputation would have been best served "if his public labours had ceased, with the termination of the revolution. . . ." This was a harsh and prejudicial judgment based on statements Adams had made in offguard moments and in his most resentful moods. But it represented the kind of price Adams paid for trusting near strangers with his unbridled, often excessive, opinionated declarations.[14]

The most glaring example of his out-of-control style had been the heated exchange with Mercy Otis Warren in 1807. If Warren had seen fit to publish any of the Adams harangues against her treatment of his role in the American Revolution, it would have confirmed the most critical judgments of his worst enemies. But

Warren was a long-standing friend of the family, who kept the offensive letters private. Probably under prodding from Abigail, Adams began to repair the damage he had done with Warren, so that by 1814 the friendship was fully reinstated. Instead of asking explicitly for her forgiveness, he leapt to her defense when several newspaper accounts questioned her authorship of *The Group*, a propagandistic play she had written during the American Revolution but which skeptics claimed could not have been written by a woman. Adams testified that a woman had, indeed, written the play and that Warren was the woman, in his view the most intellectually accomplished and politically astute woman of his generation. These male skeptics, he assured Warren, were like the Tory disbelievers of old; he reminded her that "Through the whole Revolution the Tories sat on our skirts and were a dead weight to us." Warren then invited Adams to come down to Plymouth for a family visit to seal the reconciliation. He declined, but wanted her to know that his rejection should not be interpreted as a qualification of his renewed affection for her. "Three score and nineteen years have reduced me to the situation, the temper and humor of Mr. Selden," he explained, "who Clarendon says, would not have slept out of his own bed for any office the King could have given him."[15]

The recovered friendship with Mercy Otis Warren fit the same pattern as the renewed relationships with Jefferson, John Taylor, and former college friends like Sewall and Wentworth. In each case deep political and ideological disagreements proved less powerful than Adams's craving for emotional affinity. But the Warren friendship was different in one obvious and important way: it was a friendship between a woman and a man. While not unprecedented in late-eighteenth- and early-nineteenth-century

America, it was far from commonplace. And given the character of the friendship between Adams and Warren—the presumption of intellectual equality, the tendency on the part of Adams
to treat Warren as a fellow member in the small gallery of greats
who helped to make the American Revolution, the infrequency of
any gender-based decorum, chivalric patronizing, or gentlemanly
poses—the friendship seems rare indeed. Obviously the life-long
relationship with Abigail had educated Adams to the possibility
that women could possess first-rate minds and strong personalities worthy of his respect. But the friendship with Warren had
started in the years before the American Revolution, before the
lifetime experience with Abigail could have worn away some of
his traditional assumptions about the purportedly proper relationship between women and men. Even when he was lambasting her
for her treatment of him in her *History,* Adams always interacted
with Warren as if she were on the same plane as Jefferson, Rush,
Taylor, and his other prominent friends. No other male member
of the revolutionary generation treated Warren with this kind of
presumed equity. And no other male member of the revolutionary generation seemed capable of the kind of unalloyed, unro-
mantic intimacy with strong-willed American women that Adams
achieved with Warren.

It would be misleading to explain his relationship with Warren as evidence that he was an early advocate of sexual equality
in anything like the modern sense. Adams explicitly opposed the
extension of the suffrage to women during his speech at the Massachusetts Constitutional Convention. And he had only critical
things to say about Mary Wollstonecraft's argument for women's
rights in her *Vindication of the Rights of Woman,* which he regarded

as another utopian tract infected by the same dangerously seductive ideas she had championed in her glowing endorsement of the French Revolution, which he despised. On the other hand, his attitude toward women whom he knew personally, friends like Warren and the female members of the extended Adams family, was often remarkably egalitarian. And he was prepared to accept, even encourage, intellectual achievement by women within the circle defined by family and close friends. There was, in effect, a line drawn through his thinking about women that separated his public from his private positions. It was not just that Adams endorsed the notion of "separate spheres," the emerging belief that women should be granted considerable authority within the parameters defined by their domestic duties. It was rather that he found it difficult to enforce any kind of gender-based subordination of women once they entered his private world of friends and family; that is, once he established a personal and emotional bond with them.[16]

Warren obviously crossed that line and entered that world. The fact that Warren was a woman became incidental, even irrelevant, once the bond of intimacy had been established and the Adams impulse for friendship began to flow. His urge to connect simply overwhelmed other constraints. With Jefferson, the bond of friendship had proven sufficient to overcome their significant ideological differences. With Warren, the bond was sufficiently powerful to overwhelm his conventional convictions about the proper role for women and, even more telling, what he admitted with typical Adams candor was his nervousness whenever around intellectually accomplished women. As he confessed to Vanderkemp in 1815:

I have as great a Terror of learned Ladies, as you have. I have such a consciousness of Inferiority to them, as mortifies and humiliates my self-love, to such a degree that I can scarcely speak in their presence. Very few of these Ladies have ever had the condescention to allow me to talk. And when it has so happened, I have always come off mortified at the discovery of my Inferiority.[17]

Although this was probably a playful exaggeration, and a remark referring primarily to the aristocratic French women he had encountered during his diplomatic years, Warren's deft and deadly response to the Adams tirades against her *History* in 1807 fit his description of the "learned Ladies" perfectly. He seemed to believe that accomplished women like Warren possessed emotional and instinctive powers unique to their sex, and that, when combined with the intellectual virtues of a liberal education, generated energies that few men could match. The fusion of affective and intellectual strengths was, of course, not a uniquely feminine capability—Adams himself came at the combination from the male side of the gender equation, though with him the balance of emotion and intellect was often precarious, sometimes pugnacious, and always masculine in its directness and ferocity. Nevertheless, he told John Quincy, the new nation he had helped to found, if it was to live up to its highest ideals, ought to adopt a symbolic nomenclature that enshrined womanly rather than manly qualities. "We have no word in our language that implies the exact idea of the Patria of the Romans, the Fatherland of the Dutch or the Patrie of the French," he explained in 1815. "Why should we not introduce Matria, instead of Patria? Mankind in general love their

Mothers, I believe, rather more tenderly than their fathers, & perhaps have more reason for it."[18]

Meanwhile, despite the insecurity that, by his own admission, made him feel mortified in the presence of intellectual women, Adams endorsed the principle that women should receive the same education as men. When Emma Willard wrote him in 1819 to request his support for a school designed to introduce young women to the classics and a college-level curriculum, he agreed wholeheartedly. Mothers and wives ought to be educated like men, he explained, because they had the responsibility to educate the rising generation of male leaders for the American republic. Nor was this merely agreeable rhetoric on his part. He preached the same message to the female members of his own family: "The female mind is estimated at a much higher gradation in the scale, than it was a hundred years ago," he wrote to his granddaughter. "May you, and your contemporaries, exert yourselves to raise it still higher."[19]

The contrast between Adams's and Jefferson's thinking on the question of female education is instructive. Although Jefferson claimed to give education more thought than any other subject during his retirement years, he admitted that the education of women "has never been a subject of systematic contemplation with me," adding that the matter "has occupied my attention so far only as the education of my daughters required." Jefferson had encouraged his daughters to study music, the fine arts, and the more refined topics, "which might enable them, when they became mothers, to educate their own daughters. . . ." He presumed that mothers would have no responsibility for educating their sons, unless the fathers "should be lost, or incapable, or inattentive." Adams, on the other hand, thought that mothers should be responsible for educating all children, sons and daughters alike. He apprised his granddaughter that she would be derelict in her duty as a mother if she failed to introduce all her children to philosophy, literature, and history. This meant, he informed her, that she herself had to develop a familiarity with Locke's *Essay on Human Understanding,* Dugald Stewart's *Elements of the Philosophy of the Human Mind,* then the works of Descartes, Berkeley, Hume, Condillac, and Turgot. Some of these authors advocated dangerous ideas, he warned, but the republican mother needed to master these ideas in order to assure that her children would be exposed to them in a safe and proper fashion. While part of him feared women like Mercy Otis Warren, then, another part of him proclaimed that she was the ideal that subsequent generations of American women should strive to emulate.[20]

ADAMS THOUGHT ABOUT the emotions or passions in much the same way he thought about aristocracies: they were powerful forces for good and ill, damnably difficult to control, most efficacious when confined within well-guarded compartments or well-delineated spheres of action. The political compartment in which he hoped, rather vainly, to confine the inevitable aristocrats of American society was the Senate. The social sphere in which he believed it safe to release emotional emergies included close friends like Rush, Jefferson, and Warren; but the main and safest arena was the family. Of course, being Adams, vows of caution and restraint were incessantly violated, indiscretions regularly escaped the private circle of friends and family and burst into public view, where they did damage and exposed him to criticism. But within the family, which was after all the place where he lived out the entirety of his long retirement, the disarmingly honest habits of his heart could play themselves out without fear of ridicule; there his compulsion to connect enjoyed its most natural habitat.

"Why you seem to know nothing about me," he teased old friend Vanderkemp; "I have grandchildren and great grandchildren, multiplying like the seed of Abraham. You have no idea of the prolific quality of the New England Adamses. Why, we have contributed more to the population of America, and cut down more trees, than any other race." There was truth in the joke, since the four children whom he and Abigail had brought into the world generated separate branches of their own, which in turn produced yet another permutation of direct descendants and in-laws. Moreover, a strikingly large number of this extended family ended up living at the Adams homestead in Quincy. The procession of children, grandchildren, eventually great-grandchildren, improvident in-laws, and stray relatives began with Sally Smith, the widow of the alcoholic son, Charles; Sally moved in with her two daughters in 1801, followed soon thereafter by youngest son, Thomas Boylston, along with his wife and the inevitable grandchildren, then by the three grandchildren by John Quincy and Louisa Catherine, who used the Adams homestead as a permanent depository for children during their diplomatic postings in Russia and Europe. And this was just the start. When the staff of servants, maids, cooks, and gardeners was added to the compliment, the household had the day-by-day feel of a hotel occupied at all times by at least three generations of Adamses. Or perhaps it would be more accurate to say that the social and physical context in which Adams lived out his life mirrored his own psychological complexity—part farm, part orphanage, part salon, part retirement village, part shrine, all bustle.[21]

Within this ever-shifting domestic context, Adams could afford to indulge his craving for emotional expression; targets for his passionate release of affection presented themselves on a daily basis; and energies that would otherwise have been bottled up, then exploded onto the world in frantic bursts, flowed out of him more evenly and calmly. "Love to Louisa and her dear Boys," he exclaimed to John Quincy in 1815, remembering how the presence of his grandchildren in the house buoyed his spirits:

> Oh! how I want John to divert me and George to assist me! Charles is a little Jewell too! how delighted I should be to have them all about me. Yet they would devour all my Strawberries, Cherries, Courants, Plumbs, Peaches, Pears and Apples. And what is worse they would get into my Bedchamber [and] disarrange all the Papers on my writing Table.[22]

He relished the role of over-indulgent grandfather, apprising a young man who married his granddaughter, Abby, that only he was permitted to call her "Hussie"; the fact that Abby was only sixteen years old gave him no pause, he declared, since she had announced that she wanted to marry and produce another great-grandchild for "Mr. President." The young man was about to discover the greatest joys of domestic life, Adams observed, which were "Peace, Nourishment, Copulation, and Society."[23]

Schooling, of course, received his intense scrutiny and most frequent comments. "I am afraid you will be offended at my freedom," he wrote to grandson George, "but you are in your hand writing, at such an immense distance behind your two Brothers that I cannot abstain from urging you to . . . sett your Commas, Semicolons, Colons and points 'exactly' right." This was an urging that younger members of the Adams tribe usually mocked, given their grandfather's notoriously eccentric way with punctuation. After George and John were sent off to England to join their parents in 1815—John Quincy was negotiating the Treaty of Ghent at the time—the benevolent patriarch wrote his grandchildren to continue the practice, one might say the Adams family obsession, of recording their impressions in a journal:

> I wish you to have a pencil book, always in your pocket, by
> which you may note [?] on the spot any remarkable thing you
> may see or hear. . . . A journal, a diary, is indispensable. . . .
> Without a minute diary, your travels will be no better than
> the flight of birds through the air; they will have no time
> behind them. Whatever you write preserve. I have bushels of
> my silly notes, written in fits of impatience and humiliation.
> "These fair creatures are thyself." And are now more useful
> and influential on self examination than all the sermons of
> the clergy.[24]

He established a daily schedule that assured not only a balanced blend of physical and intellectual exercise but also a regular period of interaction with various members of the third generation of Adamses. Most mornings he was up at dawn, then out in the garden or fields working with his hands when weather permitted. The afternoon was reserved for correspondence, reading, and banter, all of which required the presence of grandchildren, nieces, nephews, and young in-laws to take dictation, copy letters, or read to him when his ever-failing eyesight gave out. We can catch only glimpses of the easy intimacies established in this comfortable context, since proximity made a written account unnecessary and therefore the most important emotional connections eluded even the most self-revealing family correspondence in American history.

But glimpses do survive; and they suggest an old man at peace with himself at last, dispensing wisdom and love with what might be termed a relaxed intensity in a setting that allowed his affections to flow. He regularly referred to John Quincy's sons as "my dear boys," claiming that "George is a rage, John a Hero, and Charles, both I hope. . . ." He shared with George an essay in the *Essex Register* that, as he put it, contained "a story about me . . . which represents me as a more blustering coxcomb than I ever was in my Life." He threatened to recall "all my Posterity, Children, grand children and great grand children," then "give them a hall at Montezillo" where they could help him hammer out more accurate account of his "best blusterings." In the early 1820s, as part of his campaign to bolster the reputation of New Englanders in making the history of the country, he gathered together the sermons, journals, and histories of several Puritan patriarchs, then orchestrated daily reading sessions for all the youngsters in his bedchamber. When they complained, he acknowledged that the old books exhibited "superstition, fanaticism, quaintness, cant, barbarous poetry, and uncouthness of style . . . ," but argued that watching his progeny take turns reading out loud generated in him "as ardent an interest as I ever felt in reading Homer or Virgil, Milton, Pope, or Shakespeare." There is even a glimpse of Abigail intruding into these grandfatherly scenes, scolding him for spoiling the youngsters with candy and fruit; once, while he was dictating a letter in which he lamented being "coaxed by a fascinating Woman into a Subscription" for a book he did not really want, she leaned over and jotted at the bottom: "'ah poor Man, dalilah has shorn his Locks.' Not his wife, however." In this atmosphere of casual intimacy his candor was a precious gift, not a political liability; his eccentricities were the butt of loving jokes, not public ridicule; his craving for approval and affection was constantly and routinely satisfied, not blocked and congested into pathetic bundles of self-pity; his compulsions expressed themselves in acts of affection rather than flashes of anger. "I assure you in the sincerity of a Father," he wrote John Quincy in 1815, that "the last Fourteen years have been the happiest of my life."[25]

"YOUR HUSBAND IS a phenomenon equally strange and uncommon," Adams wrote to Louisa Catherine in 1823. "I have ransacked my old imagination and memory to find out some comparison to which he may be likened," he added, then concluded that John Quincy was most like "an Indian warriour, suffering under the most cruel torments of his Enemies," enduring the torture without any discernible change in his facial expression, chanting a prayer to the gods that went: "I go to the place where my father is gone. His soul shall rejoice in the fame of his Son. . . ." It was the most revealing statement Adams ever made about John Quincy, for it simultaneously expressed his enormous paternal pride and his equally powerful worry that his son would repeat the mistakes he had made—dedicating himself to an impossible ideal of virtuous public service that never received the popular support it deserved. And it acknowledged that there was something "strange and uncommon" about his most learned and accomplished child, something flawed or missing or overdeveloped in his character that made happiness in this world highly problematic, something that, as an over-active parent, he might have misguidedly helped to create. This overlapping pride and worry became the dominant feature of Adams's emotional life during his last decade, as John Quincy, always the apple of his eye, became the central object of his most troubled affections.[26]

On the one hand, the correspondence between father and son continued the tradition of paternal advice and patriarchal super-vision begun when John Quincy was a boy. "My advice to you is, study Epictetus in Greek as I did, more than fifty years ago," Adams wrote in 1815, recommending patience to a son then nego-tiating the terms of the Treaty of Ghent that ended the War of 1812. "My Son, you must be cool, candid & respectfully frank with those Britons," he advised that same year, suggesting that British threats to continue the war should not be taken seriously and offering his own shrewd assessment of the strategic reasons for playing a strong hand: "They have not the power, & the more they attempt it the more they will be convinced of their error. They seem not to be sensible, that if they drive us to extremities, which they cannot, we should meet the friendship of their Enemies over the whole globe. And whatever they may think, they have enemies enough." Thoughts of his son jousting with English diplomats about American fishing rights off Labrador and Newfoundland and the impressment of American seamen conjured up memories of his own role in negotiating the very same issues in 1783. He was sure, he confided jokingly to John Quincy, that this time, like last, an Adams would prove "too fluent for them." On the other hand, he was worried that John Quincy would win the peace at the expense of his political reputation at home: "Such are the collisions of Interests, Passions, Prejudices, & Sacrifices, between the two Nations, that I am apprehensive, you will lose in England, as I did, all the popularity you have acquired by such hazards, much labors, such services!"

But the fearful commiserations were less frequent than the fatherly advice, often delivered in a bittersweet style that mocked his own capacity to teach his learned son any lessons he did not already know perfectly well. "Where shall the beginning, the middle and the end of an oration be," he asked rhetorically, "when the orator has nothing to say?" After the negotiations at Ghent had ended, he could not resist reviewing the old refrains: remember that history is "a book of parodoxes," that "extreme distress will ever alone bring forth the real character of this Nation," that popular opinion is forever fickle: "The People of the United States are the most conceited people that ever existed on this Globe," he remarked in 1816, "the most proud, vain, ambitious, suspicious, jealous . . . and I am as guilty as any of them. Have a care of them!"[27]

From his side of the father-son relationship, John Quincy posted many long and detailed letters from Paris, London, St. Petersburg, Ghent, Washington, and most of the diplomatic stops in between, full of textured descriptions of sights and sounds that he knew his father would remember from his own travels, periodically laden with personal convictions that he knew his father would share. "Have traversed the Kingdom of Sweden and the *sovereign princedom* of the Netherlands," he wrote from Ghent in 1814 just before the peace negotiations began, "and here I am in the city of Charles the 5th waiting with my four colleagues, until it pleases the mistress of the world, as She now fancies herself, to send deputies for the purpose, as she imagines, of receiving our submission." He knew that his father, sitting home at Quincy, would smile at the caustic reference to England. And he concluded on an ironic note calculated to join together their mutual toilings in the same long-term cause: "I am well assured that the work to which we have been called, that of conciliating American and British pretensions, will be found *more unnatural* than your and my wandering life."[28]

In addition to the exchanges of diplomatic information and the expressions of self-satisfaction that the Adams line was continuing to conduct the foreign policy of the United States, the extensive correspondence between father and son also had playful moments. In 1819, for example, when John Quincy was negotiating the terms of the Transcontinental Treaty with Spain, which established expanded borders for the United States in the huge territory west of the Mississippi River, Adams wrote his son to empathize with the diplomatic difficulties, claiming he could share the sense of accomplishment because he was himself "now involved in a controversy about a half a dozen acres of land and a hundred cord of wood" in Quincy. Or when John Quincy asked several questions about family genealogy, the patriarch chided his son for caring about such things; it was a sign, he joked, that even his son was "growing old." Genealogical charts were wholly unnecessary and silly, Adams explained, since a walk through "Quincy Church Yard will furnish you with proof that your blood has not run through scoundrels, and that is all I desire."[29]

John Quincy was also capable of good-natured chidings; in fact, he was more capable of unreserved and playful verbal joustings with his father than with any other human being. After the senior Adams wrote him a lecture-of-a-letter on the abiding values of Christianity, John Quincy retorted with a defense of his different version of the same elemental principles: "As for you, my dear father . . . although you have been all your life doing as you would be done by, yet your theory and practice do not always coincide. . . . If after sixty years of assiduous study and profound meditation you have only come to the result of trusting the Ruler with the skies, and adhering to the sermon upon the mount, I may be permitted to adopt the same conclusions by a shorter and more compendious process."[30]

But beneath the expressions of paternal advice and affection, and the corresponding expressions of filial loyalty and respect, lay a more troubled refrain. Although Adams was extremely proud of his son, although he often basked in the reflected glory of John Quincy's remarkable accomplishments as Secretary of State and his eventual ascension to the presidency, his protective parental instincts were stronger than his ambitions for the family name. "For my personal part," Adams wrote in 1813, "I should not much care if, like Mr. Jay, you should retire and study prophecies or translate Demosthenes, provided that you are so near me that I would see you once a day or even once a week." This became the dominant message in his letters to John Quincy:

One thing is clear in my mind and that is, that you ought to be at home; if there, you should be obliged to live on Turnips, Potatoes, and Cabbage as I am. My sphere is reduced

to my Garden and so must yours be. The wandering life that
you have lived, as I have done before you, is not compatible
with human nature. It was not made for it.[31]

In the midst of John Quincy's diplomatic maneuverings at Ghent,
alongside the strategic advice about American naval power and the
effects of the war on the British economy, he advised his son "to
retire to Quincy, as I have done, 'the world forgetting, by the world
forgot'"; there he would be able to "dedicate the rest of your days
to your children, to Literature, to Science & let the Dogs bark
as they will." And when President Monroe was considering John
Quincy for the job of Secretary of State, Adams told his son that
he would "rather have you retire to Montezillo, renounce all public
employment forever, and lay your bones here with your Ancestors
than remain where you are [in Washington], annihilating yourself
and ruining your children."[32]

As Adams himself acknowledged, his motives were partially
selfish. John Quincy was, as he often put it, "the greatest comfort
of my life," and he wanted his favorite son near him during his
few remaining years. But, in addition to his craving for company,
Adams understood the internal demons that were driving his son's
pursuit of political distinction. He understood them intuitively
because they were very much like his own vanities and ambitions.
And he understood them historically because, as a father, he had
helped to instill them in John Quincy, along with an almost other-
worldly sense of duty: "You come into life with advantages which
will disgrace you if your success is mediocre," he had written to
his then young son in a typically fierce Adams injunction. "And
if you do not rise to the head not only of your Profession, but of

your country, it will be owing to your own *Lasiness, Slovenliness,* and Obstinacy."[33]

Now the son was rising, achieving a level of political success far from mediocre, living out his father's fondest hopes. Of course, Adams did share vicariously in John Quincy's fame; but he also felt compelled—he could not help himself—to protect his son from suffering the same kind of pain and disappointment he had experienced in public life. On several occasions, after offering political or diplomatic advice on the specific issues John Quincy was handling, Adams concluded letters with a plea for personal reserve and a cool, enigmatic style that would leave his son less exposed to criticism or recrimination. But then he often added: "I believe your nature is as incapable of it as mine"; or, "I know your nature, like mine, will find this posture impossible." In short, he saw himself in John Quincy: an extraordinarily erudite and learned young man whose boundless ambition was harnessed to a life of public service by a deeply internalized and equally boundless sense of duty. The new nation obviously needed such talented public servants, who were prepared—in John Quincy's case one might even say conditioned since childhood—to spend themselves in a worthy cause. Eventually, however, they would be used up and discarded, especially if they were disposed to cling tenaciously to personal principles rather than adapt to shifting political realities. If, then, there was an irreconcilable tension between public success and private happiness, the elder Adams kept urging his son to choose the latter. Even as John Quincy's name began to be bandied about in official circles as a candidate for the presidency, his father fretted more than he approved. "What a rattling & cackling and clattering there is about the future presidency," he noted in 1823; "it seems like a Conclave of Cardinals intriguing for the Election of a Pope." His persistent message to John Quincy was cautionary and protective: "Political calms cannot be of long duration in this Country," he warned. "My advice . . . is to be always prepared & ready to retire at a moments warning."[34]

There was never any realistic prospect that John Quincy would comply. Whether it was the severity of his early training and education as the eldest Adams son; or some biologically based proclivity inherited along with the color of his eyes and shape of his head; or, most likely, some seamless combination of nurture and nature, John Quincy derived his deepest emotional satisfaction from his work. He never felt the tension between public success and personal happiness that his father kept worrying about, because immersion in the hurly-burly of politics had become his life. He was like his father in so many respects—learned in the classics, fiercely combative whenever challenged, magisterial in his sense of where history was headed, suspicious of popularity, the epitome of the virtuous public servant. But he lacked altogether his father's human dimension, his capacity to love and be loved. "Of all the men whom it was my lot to accost and waste civilities upon," wrote one English diplomat, "he [John Quincy] was the most doggedly and systematically repulsive," adding that John Quincy sat in diplomatic assemblies "like a bull-dog among spaniels." This was a prejudiced view from one of the spaniels, but it accorded with most contemporary accounts and, most sadly, with John Quincy's own account of himself as "a cold, austere, and forboding character." He was his father's son in mind and will, but lacked altogether the redemptive qualities of the old man's personal warmth and heart. He was almost an intellectual caricature or clone of his father, but without his soul, without his irrepressible instinct for intimacy, for closing the distance with other people.[35]

One would like to believe that Adams kept trying, without success, to lure his son back home in order to complete his emotional education. More likely, and more in accord with the available evidence, he was motivated less by a sense of guilt or responsibility than by an elemental parental urge to help his son be happy.

JOHN QUINCY'S WIFE, Louisa Catherine, tended to concur with the judgment of the senior Adams: "If Mr. A [John Quincy] could bring his mind to it, I believe the best thing he could do would be to resign his place altogether." But Louisa Catherine cautioned her father-in-law not to be sanguine that his beloved son was capable of thinking clearly, especially after he became smitten with the prospect of the presidency. "A man who is ambitious to become President of the United States, must make his Wife visit the Ladies of the Members of Congress first," she complained caustically, "otherwise he is totally inefficient to fill so high an office." She did her best to turn John Quincy's preoccupation with political success into a humorous, all-in-the-family story of misguided dedication. "You would laugh could you see Mr. A," she explained to Adams, "every morning preparing a set of cards [i.e., calling cards] with as much formality as if he was drawing up some very important articles to negotiate in a commercial treaty. . . ."[36]

For his part, the senior Adams played along with the joke. The vision of his super-serious son trying to win political support from the members of Congress by staging elegant dinner parties, he observed, was "very interesting and entertaining to me, but I am afraid Mr. A is rather too profuse in replenishing his Decanters," which would have the unintended result of making "the grave Legislators unsteady" and thereby threatening the stability of the very republic that the next president must try to lead. In a more serious vein, he commiserated with Louisa Catherine's lot as wife of a highly visible public figure: "You will find in no department of public life any exemption from frequent twinges," he warned, concluding with the familiar plea that "You must retire to Montezillo or Mount Wollaston for perfect serenity."[37]

The reinvigorated correspondence with Louisa Catherine coincided with John Quincy's ascendancy toward the highest political office in the land. From her point of view, the need for a trusted outlet for her secret worries about her ambitious husband and her mounting insecurities about intensified public expectations explained her decision to reach out to the family patriarch at Quincy. "The old gentleman took a fancy to me," she recalled in her autobiography, "and was the only one [to whom] I was literally and without knowing it [more than] a fine Lady."[38]

From Adams's point of view, however, the closer relationship with Louisa Catherine helped to fill an emotional gap in his own life that, in the end, would never be completely closed until his death. "Now Sir, for my Griefs!" he had written to Jefferson in 1818: "The dear Partner of my Life for fifty four Years and for many Years more as a Lover, now lyes in extremis, forbidden to speak or be spoken to." Abigail had come down with typhoid fever. When she died the following week, Adams was the one member of the household to remain composed. He had simply stood alongside her bed and said: "I wish I could lay down beside her and die too."

She had been the emotional center of his mature life—his

friend, partner, lover, and accomplice in living a full life. Ironically, the record of their remarkable relationship is fullest for the
years when they were separated, since separation generated letters
that preserved an account of their closeness. During the retirement
years at Quincy, however, there was no need to correspond, so the
intimacies of their most prolonged time together are almost invisible. She remained without question his closest confidante, stoutest
defender, and most candid critic throughout this time, as well as
the supremely competent manager of the ever-buzzing brood of
relatives, visitors, and servants at the homestead. When she went,
Adams acknowledged that a part of himself died too, and that
"the grim spectre so terrible to human nature has no sting for me."
Nothing ever seemed quite the same again in the household or
in the deepest pockets of his personality. "My House is a Region
of Sorrow," he moaned to Vanderkemp almost a year after Abigail's death, "Inhabited by a sorrowful Widower . . . [who is] burdened with Multitudes of Letters from total Strangers, teazing me
with impertinent inquiries—and overloading me with newspapers
which I cannot read." He suddenly felt tired and old, complaining to a granddaughter that he had finally succumbed to "my dis-
temper, Old Age, which I will not say with Franklin is incurable,
because the ground will soon cure it."[39]

Louisa Catherine could never replace Abigail—no one could
ever do that—but Adams focused his affectionate energies on her
in the period after Abigail's death. If Louisa Catherine found him
to be a convenient outlet for her frustrations and fears as the wife
of John Quincy, Adams found her to be a helpful depository for
the ordinary effusions that would otherwise have been shared
with Abigail. He seemed to require—a lifetime with Abigail had

rendered the requirement a necessity—regular communication with a strong and intelligent woman. Louisa Catherine may have appeared frail; in fact, when Abigail first met her, she worried that "her frame is so slender and constitution so delicate that I have many fears that she will be of short duration." And Henry Adams, Louisa Catherine's grandson, remembered her as the epitome of charming delicacy, "like a Romney portrait . . . an exotic, like her Sèvres china, an object of deference. . . ." But after Abigail's death, Adams saw no reason to treat her daintily or delicately. Instead, he made her his most trusted and regular correspondent and confidante.[40]

"Wonderful woman," he exclaimed in a typical letter, "how is it possible for you . . . to go through such a hurry of visits, dinners and parties, converse with such a variety of Characters, Masculine and Feminine, and at the same time keep so particular a journal[?]" Louisa Catherine had been sending him long segments of her private record of political life among the powers-that-be in Washington. When she apologized for her prejudiced accounts of the debates over slavery in Missouri or John Quincy's dinner table conversation with Andrew Jackson, the patriarch of the Adams family told her not to worry: "I am myself too much under the influence of prejudices to have ever reproached you seriously with yours." Besides, she was positioned at the center of political life in the capital of the emerging world power, while he was imprisoned by old age in a "part of the World [where] nothing occurs but Morning, Noon and Night, New Moons and full moons, Spring, Summer and Winter." Without her regular reports he would be forced, as he put it, "to vegetate in solitude." The snatches from her journal had become "a kind of necessary life to me, I long for it the whole week." In short, he put the ever insecure Louisa Catherine at ease by assuming the posture of student to her teacher, provincial to her cosmopolitan, sensing instinctively that her impressive intelligence could flow fully only when nurtured and reassured.[41]

She proclaimed him to be the one member of the Adams family—and this pointedly included her husband in the list of the ignorant—who knew how to unlock her secret thoughts and feelings. She sent him her translations of Plato, copies of her poetry, worried motherly reactions to son George's poor grades at Harvard, extensive descriptions of the Senate debates over the Missouri question. Adams wondered admiringly how "amidst all the ceremonies, frivolities and gravities of a Court and of a Legislature [you] can find time to write so many and so excellent letters to me." And he speculated approvingly that "Two such Industrious honey Bees as John Quincy Adams and his Wife were never connected together before. . . ."[42]

When George was expelled from Harvard for flagrant misbehavior and loss of temper, Adams tried to intercede on the boy's behalf. He asked Louisa Catherine to "receive him tenderly, and forgive him." She was also to inform John Quincy that the senior Adams expected his son to treat his grandson kindly and listen with an open mind to George's side of the story. In effect, the patriarch was throwing his considerable weight behind his recalcitrant grandson, supporting Louisa Catherine's instinct for forgiveness against John Quincy's instinct for severity. It was a small but symbolic gesture that Louisa Catherine always cherished; the missing link in her husband's personality providentially provided, as it were, by the one man in the world John Quincy dared not defy, the one man in the world with the emotional range to match her moods with his own sturdier sentimentalism, the one man in the world temperamentally equipped to encompass her husband's moral standards and her own powers of forgiveness.[43]

WHATEVER CONTRIBUTION ADAMS made to Louisa Catherine's always perilous self-confidence, she helped—albeit from afar—to redress the imbalance created by Abigail's absence. Perhaps it was his congenital perversity, the life-long tendency to counter prevailing trends with his own surge of opposite-minded wisdom. Whatever the reason, he became more buoyant just when advancing age, physical decline, and outliving his generation ought to have made him a curmudgeon. It was all a matter of will, he declared, claiming that "there is in this world so much of dullness and dismals that it is a Moral virtue to . . . divert attention from gloomy contemplations, which might otherwise drive you Melancholy Mad."[44]

The one concern that could not be diverted was John Quincy. His son's inexorable advance toward the presidency caused friends and visitors to presume that the senior Adams felt unmitigated pride. The exact opposite was true. "He has a very hard, laborious and unhappy life," he confided concerning his son, "though he is envied by half the people in the United States for his talents and situation." When news of John Quincy's election reached him, as old friends offered congratulations, he remained restrained and apprehensive. "No man who ever held the office of President," he cautioned, "would congratulate a friend on obtaining it." John Quincy eventually fulfilled his fondest fears by staking out a principled position on federal power that envisioned planned economies and a national system of education and scientific research—notions that were over a century ahead of their time. He was, of course, hurled from office after one term in favor of a popular hero, like his father before him. In what turned out to be the last words of his last letter to Jefferson, Adams expressed his abiding parental worry that his son the president was suffering from "the usual perpetual chicanery and rather more personal abuse than there used to be. . . ." John Quincy was going to be chewed up and spit out by a political culture that treated principled probity of the Adams stripe in much the way the lions treated the early Christians. "Our American Chivalry is the worst in the World," he lamented to Jefferson. "It has no Laws, no bounds, no definitions; it seems to be all a Caprice." Here was the very theme that his great-grandson would make into an American literary classic: prepared by disposition and training to implement the values of the eighteenth century, John Quincy and then Henry after him were cast adrift into a nineteenth-century world that required a different kind of temperament, a more elastic code of morality, a more devious definition of duty. Adams had long since come to terms with the deuces-wild dynamism of democratic politics and his own alienation from its rhetorical requirements. What he fretted about in his last few years was not the larger pattern, but rather the personal fate of his own flesh and blood, who was caught up in it.[45]

In fact, he liked to say that the very act of worrying was itself evidence that he had not succumbed to senility. He told Josiah Quincy that "human society, like the ocean, needed commotion to keep it from putrefying." He wanted to worry; it was a sign of life. "For my own part," he insisted, "I should not like to live in the Millennium. It would be the most sickish life imaginable." Biblical descriptions of life in the hereafter seemed thoroughly boring to him. He preferred Cicero's description in *De Senectute,* where the next world was a reunion of old friends and antagonists: "That is just how I feel," he explained, "I agree with my old friend, Dr. Franklin, who used to say on this subject, 'We are all invited to a great entertainment. Your carriage comes first to the door; but we shall all meet there.' "[46]

Gala visits from Lafayette and the entire Corps of Cadets at West Point provided occasions for spirited displays of public oratory, which served to exhibit his persisting powers. But he was happiest and most himself in more informal and intimate gatherings of family, friends, and neighbors. "It is a surprise," wrote Josiah Quincy in his journal after one visit, "to find a great personage so simple, so perfectly natural, so thoroughly human."[47]

Thanks in large part to the young Quincy's journal accounts, we can catch glimpses of his conversation and flashes of the inimitable Adams style still flourishing at the end. At age eighty-nine, for example, he greeted an equally elderly woman whom he had known in his youth with the salutation: "What! Madam, shall we not go walk in Cupid's Grove together?" After an embarrassed pause, the woman, remembering the local lovers' lane of old, replied: "Ah, sir, it would not be the first time we walked together." Or there was the time he proceeded to demonstrate his innovative approach to statecraft, recalling that he had once confounded the Turkish ambassador by blowing smoke rings throughout their interview, delighting his audience with the same skill as he told the story. Then there was the time a group of young men gathered at the Adams homestead to debate the strengths and weaknesses of the several Christian sects; they were shocked to hear the old sage complain about the intolerance of all Christians, then advocate "the old Roman system of permitting every man to worship how and what he pleased." When one of the young men observed that this was paganism, Adams agreed that it was, and laughed heartily. Another young man reported hearing that, in the frontier settlements of Kentucky, "everybody was either a bigot or an atheist." To which Adams replied that "it was pretty much the same all the world over."[48]

The last description of his personality in full flight that survives dates from June of 1823. Despite a recent gash on his ankle, which Adams claimed would have healed nicely on its own if the local physicians had been prevented from prescribing "Bathes, Tents, and bandages and lotions," he walked over a mile to Josiah Quincy's house in order to share company and conversation. According to Quincy, he held forth for more than two hours, recalling local characters of old, speculating that John Jay was really the author of Washington's famous Farewell Address, and then explaining at great length why John Dickinson had worked so hard to prevent the passage of the Declaration of Independence. It seemed to him that Dickinson's real problem was a wife and mother who were devout Quakers; they tormented him with thoughts of pacifism. Poor Dickinson could not serve his country and his family simultaneously. Adams concluded the little story with the confession that, "If I had had such a mother and such a wife, I believe I should have shot myself."

Then he launched into a longer tale about old Judge Edmund Quincy, Josiah's grandfather, who was once accosted on the local road by a robber. As Adams reached the stirring climax of the story, he rose from his seat and lifted up his cane to demonstrate how the judge beat off the attacker, but the cane accidentally struck and demolished a picture hanging behind him. Adams began to laugh uncontrollably at his blunder, claiming he had not had such a good time in months. "If I was to come here once a day," he announced, "I should live half a year longer." When one of the guests countered that, if the spirited company had such a positive effect on the old man's health, he might consider coming "twice a day, and live a year longer," Adams noted the wisdom of the suggestion and declared that he planned to return again later in the day. And he did.[49]

In the annals of early American history there are several moments frozen in time by a memorable, if often romanticized, recounting of the illustrative events—Washington crossing the Delaware, Patrick Henry hurling his thunderous challenge at George III, Benjamin Franklin sauntering into Philadelphia as an aspiring youth with only the clothes on his back and two loaves of bread under his arm. Adams's choice for a tableau, which never materialized, was the early and impassioned defense of colonial rights by James Otis, a scene in which Adams himself appeared only in the background. But if Adams had possessed Franklin's genius for self-promotion, or if Josiah Quincy had chosen to dedicate his life to playing James Boswell to Adams's Samuel Johnson, they might plausibly have selected that afternoon at Quincy's house to memorialize.

The account would have depicted a very old, quite rumpled and wrinkled Adams, holding forth in his garrulous and animated style, telling all the old and slightly indiscreet anecdotes about his fellow members of the revolutionary generation, explaining why the true story of the American Revolution would never find its way into the history books, reviewing the litany of Adams lessons about balanced constitutions in state and self, the dangerous but unavoidable power of aristocracies, the seductive influence of political illusions. At the end, the account might have the patriarch murmuring to himself about paradoxes he had forgotten to mention as he trundled back to the Adams homestead or—a bit of fictional improvement here—rode home on his favorite donkey. Words and visual images would come together to convey the absence of pretense or self-delusion, the candor about himself and about his country, the reckless release of honest affection that could only find its fullest expression in the safety of an intimate circle of trusted friends.

CHAPTER SEVEN

Legacies

"Is it the Fourth?"

—Last words of Thomas Jefferson, July 3, 1826

"Thomas Jefferson survives."

—Last words of John Adams, July 4, 1826

A S THE FIFTIETH ANNIVERSARY of the Declaration of Independence approached, both Adams and Jefferson, along with Charles Carroll of Maryland, the only other surviving signer, were deluged with requests to attend official celebrations of the national birthday. Both men responded by pleading old age and ill-health, offering regrets, then providing self-consciously eloquent testimonials that they knew would be read out loud to the assembled guests. It was an ironic opportunity for Adams, who had spent much of his retirement criticizing the historical significance of the Declaration as anything more than an ornamental epilogue to the real story of the American Revolution. But the annual celebration on July 4 was now too well established to make his criticism sound like anything more than mindless carping. So for about a decade he had stopped complaining and accepted the fact that, misguided or not, this was the day when Americans remembered the great cause.

Although he received requests to participate in what was being called "the Jubilee of Independence" from as far away as Washington, Philadelphia, and New York, his most resonant reply went to the organizers of the Quincy celebration. After lamenting that his physical condition precluded attendance, Adams defied the customary sentiments and solemnities by declaring, in effect, that the ultimate meaning of the American Revolution was still problematic. He acknowledged that the revolutionary era had been "a memorable epoch in the annals of the human race," but the jury was still out on its significance. He warned that America was "destined in future history to form the brightest or the blackest page, according to the use or the abuse of those political institutions by which they shall in time to come be shaped by the *human mind*." Posterity, in short, would not only judge, it would play an active role in shaping the outcome. This was a disconcerting message for patriotic celebrants gathered to dispense praise rather than accept a challenge, but it was also vintage Adams irreverence. When a delegation from Quincy called on him a few days later to request a clarifying statement that might be presented as a toast in his behalf at the celebration, Adams uncharacteristically offered only an enigma: "I will give you INDEPENDENCE FOREVER," he replied. When prodded to enumerate, he refused. "Not a word," he insisted.[1]

Meanwhile, down at Monticello, the other great patriarch was receiving the same kind of requests. Jefferson was also too old and infirm to leave his mountaintop, but he, more than Adams, sensed that this might be the last occasion to register his personal stamp

on the public understanding of just what the American Revolution
had meant. His most eloquent response was sent to the committee
responsible for the Independence Day ceremonies in Washington.
Although his intestinal disorder had become nearly incapacitating,
Jefferson worked over the draft of his reply with great care, cor-
recting and revising with the same attention to detail that he had
brought to the original draft of the Declaration, producing one of
his most inspired and inspiring renditions of the Jeffersonian message. After gracefully excusing himself from the ceremonies at the
nation's capital, he regretted his absence from "the small band, the
remnant of that host of worthies who joined with us on that day,
in the bold and doubtful election . . . between submission and the
sword"; then he offered his distilled understanding of just what the
band of worthies had done:

> May it be to the world, what I believe it will be, (to some
> parts sooner, to others later, but finally to all,) the signal
> of arousing men to burst the chains under which monk-
> ish ignorance and superstition had persuaded them to bind
> themselves, and to assume the blessings and security of self-
> government. . . . All eyes are opened or opening to the rights
> of man. The general spread of the light of science has already
> laid open to every view the palpable truth, that the mass of
> mankind has not been born with saddles on their backs, nor
> a favored few, booted and spurred, ready to ride them legit-
> imately, by the grace of God. These are grounds of hope for
> others; for ourselves, let the annual return of this day forever
> refresh our recollections of these rights, and an undimin-
> ished devotion to them.[2]

Thomas Jefferson's "last letter," June 24, 1826, declining
the invitation to attend the Independence Day celebration in Washington, D.C.   *Collection of the Massachusetts
Historical Society*

Both the lyrical language and the uplifting theme were vintage Jefferson, and were immediately recognized as such when read
aloud before the distinguished gathering in Washington on the
Fourth. Some of the language, it turns out, had been borrowed,
either inadvertently or surreptitiously, from a famous seventeenth-
century speech by Richard Rumford, an old, one-eyed Cromwel-
lian soldier executed for treason by James II in 1685. The memorable
image of mankind being born without "saddles on their backs,"
and the passage about "a favored few, booted and spurred, ready

to ride them," came straight from Rumford's oration at the execution block. Jefferson owned copies of several English histories that reprinted the Rumford speech; certain telling phrases had obviously lodged themselves in his memory, then leapt into his mind as he wrote.[3]

But even if the felicity of the style was in part secondhand, the content provided a fresh and vigorous statement that contrasted nicely with Adams's more cautious message. For Jefferson, the American Revolution was the opening shot in what would eventually become a global struggle for liberation from all forms of oppression. Moreover, the final victory in that struggle was foreordained—"to some parts sooner, to others later, but finally to all"—and the end result toward which destiny was driving mankind, with America in the lead, was a freer individual and a more egalitarian as well as more prosperous social order. Adams, on the other hand, went out of his way to undercut intimations of American destiny, emphasizing the precarious and fragile character of the American experiment in republican government, challenging subsequent generations of Americans to meet the inevitable threats to national survival with the same realistic rationality that his and Jefferson's generation had managed to muster at the very beginning.

Adams's message, it is now abundantly clear, was much truer to and representative of the traditional values of the passing generation that he and Jefferson had come to symbolize, most especially in its unsentimental recognition that the corrosive forces that had undermined other nations and empires were a persistent threat to America as well. Jefferson, on the other hand, spoke a different, more unabashedly liberal, political rhetoric and idiom, one that emphasized the unprecedented impact of individual energies released into the world now that encrusted traditions and feudal privileges had been blown away. There was a providential, even fatalistic dimension to Jefferson's formulation, for it suggested that something wonderful and elemental had *already happened,* that it had occurred in America during the preceding fifty years, and that, like an explosion or natural force such as a river or lava flow, it was destined to run its course regardless of human foibles and intrusions. Perhaps the most beguiling feature of Jefferson's vision was its confident sense that, now that the American Revolution had propelled the country into a leadership role as the global model for what he called "self government," the fate of the American political experiment was no longer either in doubt or in human hands.

The Adams formulation suggested exactly the opposite: the destiny of the new nation was contingent upon wise and skillful leadership if it hoped to avoid the sad fate of all other republics and eventually all other empires. Whatever superiority the Adams version had as an accurate expression of his generation's best wisdom on the question of America's prospects, the rhetorical superiority of the Jefferson version was already obvious. Anyone poised to assess their relative appeal to posterity would have been forced to conclude that Adams's chances were just as problematic as his diagnosis of America's future.

But before the historic reputations of the two patriarchs could diverge, their lives were joined one final time in an episode that almost all the commentators described as an act of divine providence. On the evening of July 3, Jefferson, whose health had been declining since February, fell into unconsciousness. He awoke momentarily that night and uttered his last discernible words: "Is it the Fourth?" As midnight approached, his family, which had gathered around his bedside for the death watch, offered a prayer for "a few minutes of prolonged life." As if in response to their prayers, life lingered in him until the next morning and he died at twenty minutes past twelve noon on July 4.[4]

Meanwhile, Adams rose at his customarily early hour, wishing to keep his routine despite the special distinction of the day, and asked to be placed in his favorite reading chair in the study. Around midmorning, however, he began to falter and family members moved him back to his bedroom. Word went out to relatives attending the Independence Day celebration in Boston and to John Quincy in Washington to hurry home, that the founding father was dying. He lapsed into unconsciousness at almost the exact moment that Jefferson died. The end then came quickly, at about five-thirty in the late afternoon of July 4. He wakened for a brief moment, indicated his awareness that death was near and, with obvious effort, spoke his last words: "Thomas Jefferson survives."[5]

NEWS OF THE nearly simultaneous death of America's two most eminent elder statesmen seeped out to the world over the next few weeks. The prominent mathematician Nathaniel Bowditch calculated that "the chance that two of the signers of the Declaration of Independence in 1776 should survive half a century, and die on the 4th of July, was only one in twelve hundred millions." Richard Rush observed that most people were stunned at the coincidence. "We should pronounce it romantic," he declared, "did we not believe it providential." In what became a common image, Rush envisioned Adams and Jefferson "hand in hand ascending into heaven." Throughout the cities and states, and eventually in the nation's capital, plans for memorial services honoring the paired patriarchs proceeded apace. One of the few sour notes came from Horace Binney, the old Philadelphia Federalist, who despised Jefferson and recalled the long-standing political differences between the two men. "The most extraordinary feature of their history is that of a joint or consociated celebration," Binney noted. "Their tempers and dispositions toward one another would at one time have made a very tolerable salad . . . [and] it never entered into my conception . . . to admit one and the same apotheosis."[6]

Actually, the notion that Adams and Jefferson represented opposing impulses in the life of the early republic that blended together like the oil and vinegar of "a very tolerable salad" was one of the dominant themes in the eulogies. It was the old suggestion of Benjamin Rush; namely, that the two statesmen embodied "the North and South Poles of the American Revolution," but now orators from Maine to Tennessee developed the idea as a major reason for the success of the founding generation.

Adams was "the bold and eloquent debater . . . big with the fate of empires," while Jefferson was the skilled writer, who "embodied the principles of liberty in the language of inspiration. . . ." Adams represented the vigorous values of Rome; Jefferson the deep serenities of Greece. Adams drew upon the English political and constitutional tradition for his intellectual inspiration; Jefferson preferred the French *philosophes*. Adams was a noble descendant of the original Puritan settlers of New England; Jefferson could trace his ancestry back to the Cavalier dynasty of Virginia. Adams possessed an "ardent temperament . . . marked with great fervor and great strength . . . [and] characterized by active moral courage"; Jefferson was "calm, circumspective, reflective," and "kept at all times such a command over his temper, that no one could discover the workings of his soul." The correspondence between the "Sage of Quincy" and the "Sage of Monticello"—and these titles were now recognized as semi-official designations—even revealed compensating differences between the writing styles of the two patriarchs: Adams's prose was "plain, nervous and emphatic, and striking with a kind of epigrammatic force"; Jefferson's was "light and flowing with easy and careless melody." In short, Adams and Jefferson represented a kind of matched pair of minds and dispositions that allowed the infant republic to meet diverse challenges because "whatsoever quality appeared deficient in the one, was to be found in the character or talents of the other." Finally, an important emphasis for several of the eulogists was the claim that both the New Englander and the Virginian embraced a truly national vision and that "the two great chieftains of the North and South" thereby served as telling symbols of the need to defy sectional divisions.[7]

One could already detect the sectional bias that their lives allegedly warned against in some of the orations. John Tyler's address in Richmond, Virginia, focused almost exclusively on Jefferson, merely noting as an afterthought Adams's simultaneous demise. The eulogist in Charleston, South Carolina, ignored Adams altogether. On the other hand, New England orators tended to devote more space to Adams and to accord him primacy, claiming that "we owe our Independence more to John Adams than to any other created being, and that he was the GREAT LEADER of the American Revolution." Interestingly, neither man garnered much praise for his presidential policies. The Boston eulogist put the matter diplomatically: "Of him [Adams] as President we shall say nothing, for fear of bringing up, in the minds of some, an allusion to politics, which are banished from these consecrated walls on this day." Other speakers said much the same thing about Jefferson's presidency, studiously ignoring the disastrous embargo, preferring to avoid striking "a single chord that might not be attuned to harmony." The focus was on the great political collaborations of the 1770s and 1780s, then the great renewal of friendship in old age, with a studied avoidance of "that period of their lives when they were at the head of contending parties."[8]

Despite the sectional slightings and the evasiveness toward the political wars of the 1790s, most of the commentators concurred that both Adams and Jefferson deserved to be inducted into the same exclusive section of the American pantheon previously occupied only by George Washington. Both William Wirt, who delivered the eulogy in the nation's capital, and Daniel Webster, who spoke in Boston, made a point of ranking Adams and Jefferson right next to the great icon himself. "Washington is in the clear upper sky," said Webster, and now "these two new stars have joined the American constellation. . . ." Wirt even seemed relieved that America now could claim two heroes whose greatness did not depend at all on military or martial exploits, but rather on what he called "the triumph of the mind." This was a refrain running throughout several of the eulogies; namely, that Adams and Jefferson were distinctive American heroes whose fame rested on their intellectual leadership and their thoughtful statesmanship, unlike European heroes such as Caesar or Napoleon, who won renown with the sword.[9]

Taken together, the many testimonials delivered throughout the summer and fall of 1826 reflected a clear consensus that the two recently departed sages had made roughly equal contributions to the shaping of American history and deserved to be remembered as they had lived—even more remarkably as they had died—as equal partners in the grand, still unfolding saga of America's experiment with republicanism. There would be other heroes, of course, and Daniel Webster's bombastic testimonial before four thousand proper Bostonians at Faneuil Hall suggested that he had hopes of being one of them. But nothing quite like this brilliant pair of compatible opposites, so the eulogists concluded, was likely ever again to appear on the national scene.

Any detached assessment about the abiding reputation of John Adams made from the perspective of 1826, then, would have concluded that he was securely enshrined. Although his presidency was still too controversial to allow for an appreciation of his executive independence, the ghost of Hamilton's personal criticisms was apparently banished forever. His leading role in the making of the American Revolution was now acknowledged by all; a few of the eulogists had even endorsed his old insistence that the debates and decisions of May 1776 were more crucial than the approval of the Declaration in July; and many more quoted Jefferson himself on Adams's colossal role in the Continental Congress. Throughout New England, he was given credit for warning Americans against the excesses of the French Revolution. A few of the testimonials even managed to cite his youthful premonition of American destiny while teaching at Worcester, thereby enhancing his reputation as a prophet. Finally, he was linked historically with Jefferson as the supreme embodiment of the American dialogue: he was the words and Jefferson was the music of the ongoing pageant begun in 1776; he was the "is," Jefferson the "ought" of American politics. Not only were the respective reputations of Monticello and Quincy able to bask in the reflected glory of the other, their differences defined the proper limits of posterity's debate over the original intentions of the founding generation.[10]

OR SO IT seemed in the wake of their exquisitely timed exit. Within a few short years, however, a wholly different pattern began to become visible, a pattern that no one had predicted, one that would have surprised the eulogists of 1826 while confirming the most caustic prophecies of Adams himself.[11]

At the most elemental level, neither Adams nor Jefferson, nor any other member of the revolutionary generation for that matter, immediately ascended to the transcendent level of Washington. The notion that Adams and Jefferson were the rough equivalents of Washington and that they together "embodied the spirit of the revolution itself, in all its purity and force," died along with the echoes of the eulogists. There was Washington, to be sure, and then there was everyone else. And the latter group, which included Adams and Jefferson, also included Madison, Hamilton, Franklin, Jay, plus a host of others, membership depending on the political affiliation and regional loyalty of the person compiling the list. Most often, specific identities were subsumed under the collective label "the founders," or just as often, "the fathers," an aggregate of semi-sacred figures whose particular accomplishments and singular achievements were decidedly less important than their sheer presence as a powerful but faceless symbol of past greatness. For the generation of national leaders coming of age in the 1820s and 1830s—men like Andrew Jackson, Henry Clay, Daniel Webster, and John C. Calhoun—"the founders" represented a heroic but anonymous abstraction whose long shadow fell across all followers and whose legendary accomplishments defied comparison. "We can win no laurels in a war for independence," Webster acknowledged in 1825. "Earlier and worthier hands have gathered them all. Nor are there places for us . . . [as] the founders of states. Our fathers have filled them. But there remains to us a great duty of defence and preservation."[12]

If the major theme was reverence, the minor theme, barely suppressed, was resentment, the awkward sense of sons who would never be able to measure up. Ralph Waldo Emerson, who burst onto the cultural scene in the 1830s with a message designed to mobilize these suppressed resentments into a liberating philosophy, articulated most forcefully and most eloquently the frustrations of the rising generation: "Our age is retrospective," he observed in *Nature*. "It builds the sepulchres of the fathers. . . . The foregoing generations beheld God and nature face to face; we through their eyes. Why should not we also enjoy an original relation to the universe?" But while Emerson's formulation called for rebellion instead of reverence, it sustained the convention of "the fathers" as a noble but anonymous aggregate, a convention that allowed filiopiety and hostility to co-exist without apparent contradiction.[13]

The exception, of course, was Washington. The ultimate "father," Washington's achievements as the military leader in the war for independence and the precedent-setting first president of the new nation defied detached appraisal and catapulted his reputation beyond the reach of critics. But his actual achievements proved less important than his character, the stoical, classically inspired disposition emblematic of republican virtue. The best-selling and highly fictionalized biography by Mason Weems early in the century set the pattern for schoolbooks and patriotic orations throughout the antebellum era, making Washington the model of disciplined decorum and principled self-control, the man of unshakable morality and majestic magnanimity whose greatness, as Adams had predicted, flowed mysteriously out of his enigmatic silences and his sculpted serenity. If there was a Mount Olympus in the storybook version of American history in the middle third of the nineteenth century, Washington was the only occupant of the heights; and he was there less for what he had done than for what his alleged character symbolized. All the other members of the revolutionary generation, Adams and Jefferson included, were grouped together in a kind of generic cluster called "the founders," situated somewhere short of the pinnacle. And if an astute Adams advocate was perched in mid-air, attempting to gauge the pros-pects of the Sage of Quincy breaking free of the pack and dashing up the final ascent to join Washington at the top, the signs were discouraging. For if character was the key, and if coolness and dig-nified self-effacement were the hallmarks of character, then a man famous for his impetuous outbursts and indecorous candor was hardly a candidate for promotion.[14]

In fact, anyone committed to an Adams campaign for the votes of posterity soon encountered indirect but ominous evi-dence that it was Jefferson, not Adams, who had begun to ascend. Strictly speaking, Jefferson's reputation was soaring and diving at the same time, contingent upon one's location north or south of the Mason-Dixon Line. The clearest manifestation of the trend manifested itself in 1830 during the Webster-Hayne debate.

This dramatic confrontation on the floor of the Senate pitted Robert Hayne of South Carolina against Daniel Webster of Massachusetts in an oratorical duel over the relative powers of the state and federal governments. In a series of much-quoted speeches that offered a kind of dress rehearsal for the sectional conflict that would lead to civil war, Hayne cited Jefferson as the chief defender of states' rights and the sacred source for southern opposition to what he called "federal tyranny." Webster, on the other hand, whose ringing oration in behalf of the Union became a political catechism that northern schoolchildren were required to memorize for decades, mentioned Adams only in passing.[15]

Explaining an absence in history is usually a frustrating and ultimately futile exercise. Certainly Webster was aware of Adams's stature and political contribution; he had delivered one of the major eulogies in his behalf less than four years earlier. He was fully informed about Adams's lifelong insistence that national priorities must take precedence over sectional interests; he also knew that Adams was one of the most prominent New Englanders to condemn the Federalist threat of secession at the Hartford Convention in 1815. All of which made Adams the perfect and readily available foil for Webster to wield against Hayne's version of Jefferson. Whether he considered but rejected the idea, or whether it simply never occurred to him, the result was the same: in the first major national debate that focused on the political legacy of the founding generation, Adams was conspicuous only by his absence. The Webster-Hayne debate, it turned out, was as much a preview of what would happen to the relative reputations of Adams and

Jefferson as it was a preview of the sectional divisions that would produce the Civil War.[16]

THE MOST INADVERTENTLY prophetic words that Adams ever uttered were his last: "Thomas Jefferson survives." For it was the Jeffersonian image that broke free of the aggregated anonymity, "the founders" or "the fathers," and eventually ascended into heaven with Washington. During the course of the nineteenth and twentieth centuries, the Jeffersonian legacy became the most adaptable and all-purpose political touchstone in American political history. The story of the Jeffersonian legacy is so long and so astoundingly complex that the authoritative account by the leading Jeffersonian scholar of our time has required a book over five hundred pages in length, an account which necessarily touches on virtually every major political movement in modern American history. Jefferson has proved to be not just a man for all seasons, but also the patron saint of warring political camps: hero to the secessionist advocates in the antebellum South as well as to Abraham Lincoln and northern abolitionists, who drew inspiration from the Declaration of Independence; model for American intellectuals and educators as well as for religious fundamentalists like William Jennings Bryant, who made a pilgrimage to Monticello just before leading the assault on Darwin's theory of evolution in the Scopes Trial; Franklin Delano Roosevelt's favorite American, despite the fact that the New Deal represented a direct repudiation of Jeffersonian strictures against federal authority. The dedication of the Jeffersonian Memorial on the Tidal Basin in the nation's capital in 1943 culminated the story, in the sense that it represented the official enshrinement of Jefferson's memory as a national icon alongside Washington and Lincoln and beyond the reach of historical criticism or controversy.[17]

The search for the Adams political legacy, on the other hand, is more like the proverbial snipe hunt. Even before one begins, the futility of the quest is signalled by the awkward realization that there is no familiar and readily available word to characterize the Adams legacy. To speak of an "Adamite" or "Adamsian" tradition is to commit a verbal travesty, whereas "Jeffersonian," and even "Madisonian," roll off the tongue. But beyond the question of sonorous sounds, references to Adams's political wisdom simply do not show up in the historical locations where one might reasonably expect to find them.

A few examples must suffice to make the point, which is, after all, the kind of negative argument that could go on forever without exhausting the possibilities. Just as one might anticipate seeing Adams referred to at length in the Webster-Hayne debate, he also might be expected to turn up in the Lincoln-Douglas debates in 1858. The issue at stake in those famous exchanges was the future of slavery in the western territories. During the campaign for the Senate seat in Illinois, Stephen Douglas called for the repudiation of the geographical compromise reached over the Missouri question in 1820 and advocated the doctrine of popular sovereignty, whereby the settlers in each new territory would decide to admit or deny slavery by the time-tested practice of a democratic vote. Lincoln opposed popular sovereignty on the grounds that it had led only to violent confrontations and bloodshed in Kansas two years earlier and, more tellingly, that permitting the extension of slavery defied the wisdom of "the fathers," who had, in Lincoln's view, attempted to confine the institution to the South.[18]

Lincoln's attempt to enlist "the fathers" in the anti-slavery cause was more morally powerful than historically correct. Jefferson had indeed proposed the abolition of slavery in the original northwest territories in the 1780s, but by the end of his life had argued strongly for the extension of slavery into Missouri. The views of other members of the revolutionary generation were scattered across the spectrum. If there was a clear legacy passed down from the revolutionary generation, it was a legacy of compromise, a recognition that slavery was incompatible with the ideals espoused in the movement for American independence, but an equally strong commitment to gradualism and to a willful evasion of the moral issue in the hope that time would eventually eradicate the peculiar institution and make the matter mute.[19]

Adams, however, was one member of the revolutionary generation who fit Lincoln's prescription perfectly. In the Continental Congress he had opposed the attempt to place the abolition of slavery in the South on the agenda, fearing that it would subvert the national cooperation necessary for success in the Revolution, believing that slavery was an anachronism that would die out in good time because it was less productive than free labor. By 1820, however, when it became clear during the debate over Missouri that slavery was not going to die a natural death, Adams had vigorously opposed its extension on moral grounds, even claiming that such a policy was in accord with the best hopes of his fellow founders. And he had bequeathed that clear position to John Quincy, who spent the last years of his life opposing the extension of slavery on the floor of the House of Representatives.[20]

On the other side of the debate, Douglas could easily have cited Adams too, since the doctrine of popular sovereignty that he vainly espoused for the territories could be traced back to popularly elected conventions created to ratify the original state constitutions in 1776. Adams had been the leader within the Continental Congress on this constitutional issue, insisting that each new state constitution must be approved by representatives of the people-at-large. The very principle Douglas was advocating in the new territories drew upon the one political conviction that Adams embraced that was unabashedly and unequivocally democratic in spirit.

Of course, when it came to democracy, Jefferson was the hands-down champion. And so it would have been eminently plausible for Douglas to cite Jefferson as the founder who expressed the deepest faith in the capacity of ordinary citizens to decide their own fate; this would have then set up a mid-nineteenth-century version of the Adams-Jefferson dialogue, with Douglas wrapping his argument in the Jeffersonian rhetoric of majority rule and Lincoln countering with the Adams conviction that majorities have no magic pipeline to the truth, that crucial matters of principle—and slavery was certainly one such matter—were too important to be resolved at the ballot box.

Douglas, in fact, defended his case for popular sovereignty along just such Jeffersonian lines, claiming that the practicality of the solution was less compelling to him than its hallowed association with the Sage of Monticello. But Lincoln, instead of citing Adams, contested Douglas's appropriation of Jefferson. The key Jeffersonian document, as Lincoln saw it, was the Declaration of Independence, and he based his attack against Douglas on the immorality of slavery when judged by the Jeffersonian assertion of human equality in the Declaration. The Lincoln-Douglas debates, in short, drew on the wisdom of the founders all right, but both sides in the debate claimed to be speaking for Jefferson; or, to put it differently, the argument over the place of slavery in the republic became a dialogue between different sides of Jefferson's thought. Jefferson, it seemed, was everywhere; Adams was unmentioned, unnoticed, invisible.[21]

He was also conspicuously—and even more inexplicably— absent from the most influential critique of the Jeffersonian tradition ever written. The book was *The Promise of American Life* (1909), and the author was Herbert David Croly, a grotesque-looking wisp of a man, whose frail appearance belied his powerful ideas, ideas that shaped the terms of the national political debate from the Progressive era to the New Deal. Croly actually succeeded brilliantly in doing what so many journalists and aspiring intellectuals before and since have frustrated themselves in trying to do; namely, write a book steeped in scholarship and grounded in an understanding of American history that alters forever the way political leaders of the day think about government. Much of what Croly had to say about what was right and wrong with American politics was eerily reminiscent of Adams. But in what was a long and intricate book, Adams's name never appeared at all, either in the text or in the index. And to make matters worse, he had somehow been replaced in Croly's version of the great dialogue of American politics by the one person in the world Adams genuinely and thoroughly despised.[22]

Looking back from the vantagepoint of the early twentieth century, Croly discerned a dual tradition in the public discourse; as he put it, any thoughtful observer could detect "the existence from the very beginning of our national career of two different and, in some respects, antagonistic groups of political ideas. . . ." Clearly, one of the voices in the dialogue belonged to Jefferson, whose most effective and disarming quality was "a sincere, indiscriminate, and unlimited faith in the American people." No one was Jefferson's equal in articulating the democratic ideal, in dreaming the American dream, if you will, which envisioned a nation populated by free and enterprising individuals unburdened by government restrictions, and—thanks to the open-ended continent made available by God and then secured by the American Revolution for posterity— free to pursue the promise of American life with degrees of success and levels of serenity previously unknown in human history.[23]

If this sounded too good to be true, Croly observed in his dispassionately abstract prose, it was because Jeffersonian ideals were *not* true, except as seductive visions parcelled out to a gullible democratic audience that obviously appreciated being told that its judgment was infallible. The Jeffersonian sermon always took "the people" as its text and always closed with the comforting conclusion that, as Croly put it, "individual members needed merely to be protected against privileges and to be let alone, whereafter the native goodness of human nature would accomplish the perfect consummation."[24]

Croly had warned his readers early on that his analysis was not designed to be popular, that it would "meet with a far larger portion of instinctive opposition and distrust than it will of acquiescence." For over four hundred pages the hammer blows fell relentlessly and resoundingly on the unquestioned articles of faith underlying the Jeffersonian creed. Jefferson had misguidedly sought to achieve "an essentially equalitarian and even socialistic result by means of an essentially individualistic machinery." He had incorrectly presumed "a complete harmony both in logic and in effect between the idea of liberty and the idea of equality; and just in so far as there is any antagonism between those ideas, his whole political system becomes unsound and impracticable."

But by the early twentieth century, one did not need to be a brilliant logician or profound historian to recognize that Jeffersonian political beliefs had led directly, if inadvertently, to unprecedented levels of social and economic inequality, the enshrinement of private greed as a natural right by the American plutocracy— the so-called captains of industry—and the doctrinaire rejection of government's authority to do anything about it. Jefferson, in short, was an "amiable enthusiast" who had known how to turn phrases that appealed to popular illusions, but he and his followers had "perverted the American democratic idea" with a lullaby disguised as a set of political principles. Under any kind of honest scrutiny, the Jeffersonian side of the political dialogue must be judged, so said Croly, a baleful blend of "intellectual superficiality and insincerity."[25]

Croly's indictment of the Jeffersonian legacy was couched in a labyrinthian, intensely moralistic style—"Crolier than thou," as one angry critic put it—but stripped to its essentials, it recapitulated most of the criticisms that Adams had delivered in his personal correspondence with Jefferson and Jefferson's disciple, John Taylor. To be sure, Croly enjoyed the splendid advantage of hindsight, so his treatment of Jefferson's bucolic vision was informed by the experience of the Industrial Revolution, urban poverty, and the rationalizing nostrums of Social Darwinism, none of which either

Adams or Jefferson could have been expected to foresee clearly, if at all. On the other hand, even without the benefit of hindsight, Adams had warned Jefferson that individual freedom and social equality were incompatible ideas, that ignoring their conflict only assured the triumph of the privileged, as in fact happened. More tellingly, Adams had accused Jefferson of making a religion of "the people" that was just as fanciful as the old religion of "the king." And, again like Croly, Adams had insisted that government needed to play an active role in managing national priorities; that it was not, as Jefferson seemed to believe, only and always a source of oppression.

There were other similarities, but most of them only came clear in the context of the other side of Croly's argument, which must have sent the ghost of Adams into an apoplectic fit; for Croly claimed that Hamilton, not Adams, was the realistic counter to Jefferson's beguiling dreams, the sober and more far-sighted side of the American political dialogue. Croly's Hamilton was "the sound thinker, the constructive statesman, the candid and honorable, if erring, gentleman"; he was also admirable—Adams must have been flailing his arms at this—for his willingness to court unpopularity. Hamilton had his faults, Croly acknowledged, the chief one being that he "perverted the American nationalist idea almost as much as Jefferson perverted the American democratic idea." This was an indirect way of suggesting that Hamilton's commitment to a powerful executive and an energetic national government sometimes lurched over into a fondness for absolute monarchy or dictatorship and a total disregard for individual rights. Such autocratic dalliances did not overly disturb Croly, however, since he himself was prepared to admit that "the time may come when the fulfillment of a justifiable democratic purpose may demand the limitation of certain rights, to which the Constitution affords such absolute guarantees." It was Hamilton's unbridled nationalism that Croly most admired and that he saw as the historical precedent for a vigorous federal government and a proto-socialistic American state in the twentieth century.[26]

Croly's enshrinement of Hamilton would have seemed bizarre to most members of the revolutionary generation, who acknowledged him as a political genius of massive daring and vision, but too eccentric and dangerous to fit easily within the American ideological spectrum. If Adams and Jefferson were planets orbiting around the sun that was Washington, Hamilton was a comet that streaked through the late-eighteenth-century sky, blazing trails of glory, then disappeared. Until the Civil War, his name and reputation were largely ignored by historians and biographers as too exotic or Napoleonic to permit emulation. When he did appear, it was usually in the speeches of Jacksonian Democrats, who used his name as a combination curse and epithet, the symbol of the banking conspiracy and moneyed aristocracy.

After the Civil War, however, again like the proverbial comet, he reappeared, the beneficiary of several converging trends: the Union victory in the war generated a need for nationalistic heroes; American historians who studied in Germany or were influenced by the new German scholarship suddenly found charismatic leaders with despotic tendencies more necessary and alluring; Wall Street capitalists, who had always harbored a private affection for the one founder who appreciated the power of money, used the newfound status they enjoyed as cultural leaders in the Gilded Age to publicize a champion of wealth. By the time Croly sat down to

write *The Promise of American Life,* then, Hamilton's reputation
had surged nearly to the front rank; several of the standard histories had linked him symbolically with Jefferson as the opposing
presence, more relevant than Jefferson for a burgeoning nation-
state that was exploding onto the world stage as a commercial and
imperial power.[27]

Croly's elevation of Hamilton clinched and effectively sealed
his reputation for the twentieth century. *The Promise of American Life* proved to be one of the most influential books in modern American history, not just because it redefined the political
agenda of the liberal tradition, which it unquestionably did, but
also because it recast, in a way that proved both credible and
accessible, the political legacy of the founding generation. Croly
redefined the American dialogue so that it fit more neatly the
competing imperatives of the conservative and liberal mainstream
of the twentieth century, which usually translated into the competing platforms of the Republican and Democratic parties. It was
the few against the many, limited government against big government, capitalism against democracy, freedom against equality.
Croly's major theoretical contribution, of course, was to declare
the need for governmental power to offset and regulate corporate
power; the use of Hamiltonian means, as he put it, to achieve Jeffersonian ends. But his major historical contribution, if one can
call it that, was to adapt the legacy of the revolutionary generation
to the political needs of the twentieth century. And this necessarily entailed the suppression of the classical or republican mentality
that Adams epitomized.

Of course, all attempts at making the past relevant to the present inevitably require some measure of distortion. In Croly's case,

however, the distortion, though it proved functional and efficacious, achieved relevance at the expense of ignoring an entire way
of thinking about politics that predated the issues his version of
Hamilton and Jefferson symbolized. In Croly's formulation, the
American dialogue represented a disagreement over the proper
means to achieve agreed-upon ends, which ultimately boiled down
to a disagreement over the power and role of the federal government. By eliminating Adams from the dialogue, in short, more
fundamental questions about just what the promise of American
life was or ought to be became mute. For Jefferson, it was a birth-
right of personal contentment unencumbered by government. For
Adams, it was a legacy of public obligation rendered possible by
government. More on this major theme shortly. For now, it is sufficient to establish, not just another non-sighting of Adams in a
place where we might reasonably have expected to encounter him,
but also what proved to be the decisive episode in his permanent
deletion from the national discourse on the remembered meaning
of the American political tradition.

IF THE DIVERGENCE of the reputations of Adams and Jefferson would have surprised most of their contemporaries, hindsight
allows us to see that the historical forces responsible for Jefferson's
ascent and Adams's relative obscurity were in place and readily discernible at the time of their mutual departure. On July 7, 1826,
after the funeral ceremony for Adams at Quincy, a delegation of
officials and dignitaries were invited to inspect one of the earliest
railroad tracks in the new nation, which was being laid in order to
transport Quincy granite a few miles away to the site of the new

Bunker Hill Monument. This was exactly the kind of poignant and symbolic scene that Henry Adams, the great-grandson of the man just buried, would have found irresistibly evocative. For in the space of a few hours and within the compass of a few hundred yards, the dignitaries witnessed the death of the revolutionary generation and the birth of the major symbol of the Industrial Revolution, which was to transform the world of Adams and Jefferson more completely and more quickly than any force in modern history.[28]

Somehow, even the overly ripe and ever ironical intelligence of Henry Adams, the most brilliant of the Adams progeny, missed the significance of his ancestor's funeral. This was unfortunate, for the scene captured perfectly the central theme of his nine-volume *History* as well as his autobiographical masterpiece, *The Education of Henry Adams*. In both of those works, Henry Adams demonstrated a flair for marking the moment when emergent technology appeared on the American landscape and accelerated social change at dizzying rates of speed: Robert Fulton's steamboat paddling up the Hudson River, the original machine in the garden; the opening of the railroad between Boston and Albany, destined to carry commerce and people out of New England; Cunard steamers cutting through Massachusetts Bay like knives severing Boston's connection with the past. The funeral scene at Quincy was equally symbolic, showing the chasm that separated the world of the revolutionary generation from the world in which Henry Adams came of age. It evoked the sense in which anyone grounded in the eighteenth-century values of Adams and Jefferson had become irrelevant and anachronistic by the middle of the next century.[29]

When the eulogists of 1826 spoke of "the end of an era," they meant that the passing of the two patriarchs had ended any direct connection with the generation that had led the movement for American independence. Henry Adams meant something more than that. He meant that the social conditions and corresponding attitudes and values of the nation underwent a *deep* change during the very years that the Sage of Quincy was living out his retirement. In his formulation, the first truly "lost generation" in American history happened to be nothing less than the Founding Fathers themselves. For they, including both Adams and Jefferson, were rooted in the "lost world" that preceded the emergence of full-blown democracy, industrial capitalism, modern technology, and liberal ideology.

What Henry Adams offered as an inspired but wholly intuitive insight, one that he used in his *Education* to dramatize his own alleged irrelevance, has become a staple of historical scholarship over the past quarter century. The central feature of American history is no longer an event—the American Revolution or the Civil War—but a process. Whether it is called "industrialization" or "modernization," there is a scholarly consensus that this process altered the social structure and the mentality of America forever. If the Civil War has remained the Niagara Falls of American history, full of dramatic prowess and power, the first quarter of the nineteenth century has become the Grand Canyon, where a deep divide separates the way we were from the way we are, what is called "traditional" society or "classical" values from "modern" or "liberal" America.[30]

Merely to state the reigning scholarly interpretation in this bald and categorical fashion is to expose the verbal and conceptual limitations inherent in what might be called "the paradigmatic approach," which imposes a set of generically labelled categories on a stream of flowing events that, by their very nature, defy being fit into geometric shapes, resist being boxed and crated and shipped to our contemporary understanding with "Traditional" or "Modern" stencilled across their surfaces. The distinguishing feature of America's evolution toward modern democratic capitalism—Adams would say its most crucial feature—was its *gradual* character. Some historians have detected the seeds of modern or liberal values planted within the first settlers of Virginia or Massachusetts; other historians have insisted that the clinching supremacy of full-blooded capitalism did not establish itself until after the Civil War. What we have, in short, is a consensus that decisive social and economic changes produced a "before" and "after" effect in American history; an apparently unavoidable problem with clumsy language; and widespread disagreement about the precise moment when this great transformation actually occurred.[31]

While the language problem will continue to haunt us, the timing problem can be quickly resolved. The reason historians have such a difficult time locating the moment when American social conditions and corresponding attitudes changed is that such a moment does not exist. These changes, whatever we choose to call them, were not a discrete event; they were part of a process. Both Adams and Jefferson lived through a crucial phase of this process, which had begun before they were born and continued after their death. In that sense, they both stood astride the Great Divide in American history, a rather awkward posture in theory. But because they were mercifully unburdened with the verbal and paradigmatic baggage that subsequent historians would impose, they had little sense of living schizophrenic lives or harboring irreconcilable urges in their personalities. Strictly speaking, however, which is to say from a purely historicist perspective, both Adams and Jefferson internalized a mixture of old and new, traditional and modern, classical and liberal values. But the mix was somewhat different in the two men. And this difference became the major reason for the divergence of their respective reputations. For Jefferson's legacy was able to negotiate brilliantly the social and attitudinal shift in nineteenth-century America. The Adams legacy was not; it became one of the victims of the triumph of liberalism.

The dramatic difference between their respective reputations, then, was not exclusively or even primarily a function of the different personalities. To be sure, part of Jefferson's ability to translate across the ages was a result of his nearly infinite suppleness and pliability, the elusive and enigmatic quality that Adams had often criticized and sometimes admired. Henry Adams captured this quality more succinctly and deftly than any other commentator. "The contradictions in Jefferson's character have always rendered it a fascinating study," he wrote in his *History*. "A few broad strokes of the brush would paint the portraits of all the early Presidents with this exception . . . but Jefferson could be painted only touch by touch, with a fine pencil, and the perfection of the likeness depended upon the shifting and uncertain flicker of its semi-transparent shadows." Adams, on the other hand, was neither elusive nor enigmatic. And he tended to prefer standing in the full glare of sunlight, away from those flickering shadows. If Jefferson was the Mona Lisa of American heroes, Adams was one of those faces in a portrait by John Singleton Copley, close to the canvas, drawn with linear precision, looking squarely and directly back at the viewer.[32]

But Adams's lack of pliability or adaptability through the ages, while certainly a factor that helps explain his relative obscurity, cannot by itself account for his inability to translate. For, in the end, the underlying problem for the Adams legacy was *not* primarily the directness of his character so much as the character of his thought. In the search for a usable past, too much in Adams was simply not usable. And this brings us back to the transformation theme originally defined by Henry Adams and subsequently developed by recent scholars of early American history. Best to put the question squarely and unequivocally: what was it that grounded Adams in the eighteenth century so deeply and firmly that his reputation, unlike Jefferson's, could not fly across the ages and find a hospitable landing spot on this side of modernity?

To pose the question in this fashion is to suggest an answer that goes beyond surface considerations of imagery and malleability. Put simply, the deepest sources of Adams's thought and character were incompatible with the emergent values of nineteenth-century liberalism. In his political thinking, to be sure, Adams did embrace two of the central tenets of the liberal tradition: the doctrine of popular sovereignty, that is, the notion that political power ultimately derives from the people; and the principle of equality before the law, the view that justice is blind to the class, race, or gender of the accused. In these two areas, Adams was a liberal. Beyond these seminal commitments, however, he was unprepared to go. He was, in all other respects, the archetypal, unreconstructed republican, fundamentally resistant to an individualistic ethic, as well as to the belief in the benign effect of the marketplace, to the faith in the infallibility of popular majorities, to the conviction that America enjoyed providential protection from the corruptions of history, to celebrations of freedom undisciplined by government or, at the personal level, the release of passionate energies unmitigated by internal checks and balances.

The list, in fact, could go on almost endlessly, for it did not depend on books he had read or ideas he had acquired by formal education. The more encompassing meaning of "education" later used rather mischievously by Henry Adams—the entire scheme of premodern values and convictions in which the mind and heart of an eighteenth-century American was saturated—defined his character. Even those infamous Adams eccentricities—the perverse aversion to popularity, the punishing self-scrutiny and self-denial, the suspicion of success and corresponding comfort with hardship—were all intensified versions of mainstream republican tenets, which presupposed the easy if not inevitable corruptibility of all persons and nations, and the need to subsume selfish urges to larger public purposes. The Adams brand of republicanism was even more ascetic than the norm, born as it was out of his youthful decision to serve the public rather than God, but bringing the same moral fervor to the secular cause that he would have brought to the sacred.

And if American politics is conceived of as a religion with a set of creedal commitments, the catechism one learns early on makes Adams into a heretic. The catechism of liberal America was dominated by references to "freedom," "equality," "democracy," "individualism." The Adams catechism was dominated by references to "control," "balance," "aristocracy," and "public responsibility." Cultures and nations generally select the heroes they need. For a nation perched on the edge of an undeveloped continent, about ready to explode onto the world economically, full of energy and natural resources, as well as a youthful sense of immortality and destiny, just about the last thing needed was a voice counselling caution, social responsibility, and reconciliation to eventual decline.

The loss of that voice, however, meant the alteration of the American dialogue originally symbolized by Adams and Jefferson. The version that came to dominate public discourse in the nineteenth century, as we have seen, was initially a monologue between different sides of the Jeffersonian tradition; then, later in the century and beyond, it became a dialogue between Jefferson and Hamilton over the necessary means by which to reach agreed-upon ends, what Herbert Croly memorialized as "the promise of American life." What was different about the Adams-Jefferson dialogue was that it was not primarily a debate over means so much as over the ends themselves, not just a disagreement over how to fulfill the promise of the American Revolution so much as a conflict over what that promise had been.

For, at its nub or core, Adams's vision remained traditional and, as they say, pre-modern or pre-liberal. His whole way of thinking about politics and society resisted the assumption that the individual was the sovereign unit in the social equation. And, again unlike Jefferson but more typical of other members of the revolutionary generation, he did not conceive of personal or private happiness as the ultimate goal for government. His ideological orientation was inherently social and collectivistic, driven by the assumption that individual strivings—what Jefferson had immortalized in the phrase "the pursuit of happiness"—must naturally and necessarily be subordinated to public imperatives if the human potential unleashed by the American Revolution were to achieve its fullest realization. Ironically, it was precisely this kind of socialistic perspective that Herbert Croly called for at the end of his famous book; but by the time he wrote, the Adams legacy had been buried and forgotten for so long that it was beyond either memory or recovery. Indeed, given the nearly total triumph of Jeffersonian liberalism in nineteenth-century America, the traditional cast of Adams's thinking appeared not just irrelevant but even alien. Perhaps that fact provides the final piece of our puzzled explanation for Adams's mysterious obscurity: speaking from the far side of the Great Divide in our history, we can no longer hear his voice as recognizably American.[33]

AND THERE, WITH one important exception, is where the matter has remained throughout the twentieth century. The exception began to become visible in the 1950s, almost certainly as a consequence of the availability of those multiple boxes of letters and diaries that Adams had once threatened to inflict on posterity. Soon after the roughly 400,000 items that comprised *The Adams Papers* were put on microfilm and then, even more tellingly, after a modern letterpress edition began to issue forth from the archives of the Massachusetts Historical Society, the reputation of John Adams began to ascend within the community of professional historians.[34]

Starting in the 1950s, then continuing throughout the next two decades, Adams became the subject of several scholarly studies that praised his performance as president, refurbished his status as political thinker, and recovered the beguilingly human dimension of his personality. In addition, the discovery by Bernard Bailyn and Gordon Wood, and then a host of academic disciples, that the ideology of the revolutionary generation was heavily indebted to republicanism meant that Adams—one of the most forceful and articulate proponents of republican values—began to turn up in the many monographs and textbooks that revised our understanding of the meaning of the American Revolution. Indeed, by the time of the bicentennial of the American Revolution, Adams's reputation within the community of professional historians had recovered the lofty position it had occupied at the time of his death. When Robert Rutland reviewed the several modern editions of the papers of the Founding Fathers, he concluded that there was a fresh scholarly consensus: "Madison was the great intellectual . . . Jefferson the . . . unquenchable idealist, and Franklin the most charming and versatile genius, but Adams is the most captivating founding father on most counts." Rutland predicted that Adams's stock would continue to rise; for as new volumes of *The Adams Papers* rolled off the press, they would come to be regarded as one of the nation's most precious natural resources, "deserving as much public concern as the shale-oil deposits, and in the long run . . . more valuable."[35]

Although the new surge in Adams's reputation was almost entirely a scholarly affair, it did have some impact on the broader public appreciation of his place in American history. Certainly, the most visible manifestation of an enhanced public standing was the broadcast on public television of a thirteen-part series, *The Adams Chronicles*, in 1975. This massively funded and skillfully produced historical docudrama, which devoted six hour-long segments to Adams himself, exposed his accomplishments to the largest audience it had ever enjoyed. In one sense, it made Adams the supreme founding father of them all—in the literal sense of the term; that is, he became the patriarch of what was arguably the most prominent and intellectually distinguished family in American history.[36]

This proved both a blessing and a burden, for it revitalized his image as a major figure, but did so by conceiving his historical significance almost exclusively in terms of his biological legacy. For better and for worse, the public memory of the original Adams became inextricably imbedded in the fate of his remarkable family. This condition was surreptitiously reinforced by the intriguing fact that, of all the Founding Fathers judged worthy of a modern edition of their papers, only *The Adams Papers* made the entire family rather than the man himself its focus.

Despite his rising stock within the world of professional historians, and despite his enhanced visibility as the sire of a spectacular line of distinguished descendants, Adams's political legacy remains virtually invisible and his intellectual legacy remains a shadowy subject of exclusively academic interest. Even within the scholarly world, his chief contribution to political thought has been to serve as an articulate anachronism, the staunch advocate of a dying version of republicanism, a man who stubbornly resisted the inevitable democratization of American society. And even within the regional culture of his beloved New England—the local taverns, town halls, schools, and churches—he is commonly confused with Sam Adams, who has once again become "the famous Adams" because a popular regional brand of beer has adopted his name. Over two centuries after his French hosts made the same mistake, a distressingly large portion of native New Englanders still think of him as "the other Adams."[37]

Perhaps, when all is said and done, he is not the stuff out of which mythologies are made. Perhaps he is too idiosyncratic and iconoclastic ever to become a national icon, too damnably specific and disarmingly honest ever to win an election, even with posterity. Or perhaps we should not think of him as a mainstream figure at all, but should acknowledge that he belongs to that breed of American skeptics—Mark Twain, H. L. Mencken, and Thorstein Veblen come to mind—who patrol the margins of our political culture and whose wisdom derives from their alienation. Even though he has come to be regarded by historians as the most engagingly human member of America's founding generation, perhaps he was always miscast as a public figure entrusted with the exercise of political power. That, after all, was the ultimate verdict of Hamilton and the High Federalists. And it is also an explanation that makes more comprehensible the relative serenity and personal balance he was able to achieve only in his retirement years.

But there is also a distinct possibility that the problem is not primarily personal or psychological, but ideological. Which is to say that perhaps it is not so much that Adams's character steadfastly resists mythmaking, but rather that he represents a cluster of political principles that do not fit comfortably within the framework of our national political mythology. Memorials will only be erected to him, according to this train of thought, when the rhetoric of Jeffersonian liberalism ceases to dominate mainstream American culture; when the exaltation of "the people" is replaced by a quasi-sacred devotion to "the public"; when the cult of the liberated individual is superseded by the celebration of self-denial; when national development must vie for seductiveness with conservation; when the deepest sense of personal satisfaction comes not from consumption but production; when the acceptance of national and personal limitations seems less like defeatism than a symptom of maturity. In this sense, the time of John Adams has passed and not yet come again.

PROPHECIES

———•◆•———

An Epilogue

Where can we look but into the heart of man and the
history of his heart? In the heart were found those
appetites, passions, prejudices and selfish interests,
which ought always to be controlled by reason,
conscience and social affections; but which are never
so perfectly controlled, even by any individual, still less
by nations and large bodies of men. And less and less,
as communities grow larger and larger, more populous,
more commercial, more wealthy, and more luxurious.
—Adams to John Taylor, April 1814

From the year 1761, now more than Fifty years, I have
constantly lived in an enemies Country. And that without
having one Personal enemy in the World, that I know of.
—Adams to Benjamin Rush, January 8, 1812

WE ARE WHOLLY DESTITUTE of any direct evidence about the state of Adams's mind on the last morning of his life, as he sat alone in the upstairs study of the Adams homestead. It seems safe to presume that at least a portion of his mind was occupied with thoughts of Independence Day. Fifty years earlier, in what proved to be a prophetic letter to Abigail, he had predicted that the great day would be celebrated "by succeeding Generations, as the great anniversary Festival," and would be "solemnized with Pomp and Parade, with Shews, Games, Sports, Guns, Bells, Bonfires and Illuminations from one End of this Continent to the other from this Time forward forever more."[1]

Characteristically, his prophetic powers had gotten the story correct with almost eerie accuracy, right down to the fireworks, but still managed to put him out of step with his fellow Americans. For he had identified the date of Independence Day as "The Second Day of July 1776," which was the day he believed the clinching debate had occurred in the Continental Congress. His last words of tribute to Jefferson, muttered later that afternoon in 1826, suggest that he had finally reconciled himself to the Virginian's enshrinement as the author of independence. It is tempting to speculate that the last and most symbolic act of his life, which was to expire on July 4, represented an ultimate effort to bring his feisty and idiosyncratic personality into alignment with the official patriotic calendar, to reconcile the death if not the life of John Adams with the customs of his countrymen.

He had proven himself capable of similar gestures of accommodation with the emerging national ethos on several occasions during his quarter century of retirement. When aging Federalists bemoaned the decline of standards and the passing of the revolutionary generation, he loved to lecture them on the superiority of the rising generation of American statesmen. Pessimists who presumed that the Master of Montezillo would concur with their gruesome forecasts of an inevitable clash between erstwhile American aristocrats and democrats were surprised to hear him turn their fatalism into a joke: "That the first want of man is his dinner, and the second his girl," he observed, were truths "held in common by every democrat and aristocrat," and these primal urges would bind Americans together despite the apocalyptic predictions of factionalism by the faint of heart. "Our Country is or at least ought to be happy," he proclaimed to a downcast governor of New Hampshire, despite "gloomy forebodings into Futurity" by ignorant forecasters, who, he warned, tended to confuse their own personal despair with national decline. "If ever there existed upon this Globe a Nation of People who had so many causes and motives for Thanksgiving as our American Nation," he proclaimed, "it has never fallen under my observation or within my reading." In 1822 he reassured John Jay that, despite the Adams reputation for pessimism, in his old age he had "always endeavored to contemplate objects on the bright side." As proof of his sanguine temperament he apprised Jay that he was telling all visitors that "Our prospects at present are beyond example and beyond all comprehension." The only caveat he felt obliged to add—it was a paradox, Adams insisted, but not a contradiction—was that "this globe, and as far as we can see this Universe, is a theatre of vicissitudes."[2]

The caveat, of course, was the abiding Adams message. And the enduring Adams legacy, if such a thing can be said to exist at all, tends to take the form of a sober and realistic caveat to America's buoyant optimism and nationalistic pretensions. Adams was a pessimist by conviction and an optimist only when he felt the need to play contrarian. He rarely indulged in optimistic predictions except when presented with visitors or correspondents who, thinking he would agree, offered pessimistic estimates of the fate of the American republic. Then he would, as he put it, "jump upon the great See-Saw" and balance the political equation with reassuring observations that "the Federal Union . . . will last longer than we shall live," or that neither monarchy nor dictatorship will ever take root in America "unless Napoleon should make Aaron Burr a King . . . which I do not believe he is either willing or able to attempt." His optimistic forecasts, in short, were almost always expressions of his oppositional disposition, his instinct to serve as an alter ego to the dominant political wisdom of the moment, to make himself into the great American caveat.[3]

It would have been completely in character, then, for the old man sitting in his favorite chair that final morning to resist the swells of satisfaction he might be expected to feel on that special day. The whole country, after all, was celebrating an event that he, more than anyone else, had helped bring about. And the current occupant of the presidency, who officially presided over the nation's Independence Day festivities, was his own flesh and blood. The surges of pride and vanity generated by such historic triumphs must not be allowed to get out of hand, at least not in an Adams. Balance must be restored. Sagacity must prevail over passion.

If he remained true to his most prevailing version of political sagacity and sobriety, Adams would have encountered the prideful swells with healthy doses of apprehension. As for John

Quincy's glorious political achievements, for example, there was good reason to regard them as short-lived and, like his father before him, the son was destined for defeat in the next election. "Our government will be a game of leap-frog," Adams had observed throughout his retirement, predicting that the dominant political parties would "be leaping over one another's backs about once in twelve years, according to my computation." It was one of his favorite metaphors.[4]

The notion that American politics operated on a twelve-year cycle eventually became a special trademark of the Adams family's version of American history. Henry Adams provided the most precise description of the cyclical thesis in his *History*. "A period of about twelve years measured the beat of the pendulum," he wrote: "After the Declaration of Independence, twelve years had been needed to create an efficient Constitution; another twelve years of energy brought a reaction against the government then created; a third period of twelve years was ending in a sweep toward still greater energy; and already a child could calculate the result of a few more such returns." Wars and depressions could lengthen or shorten the cycle, but the great-grand-father of Henry Adams, who originated the theory, emphasized the regularity of the pattern. "It is always so," he had written to Rush in 1812: "When a party grows Strong and feels its power, it becomes intoxicated, grows presumptuous and extravagant and breaks to pieces. You may depend upon it. It is a Game of Leapfrog every twelve years." And it was the singular misfortune of the Adams family always to reach the presidency just when the cycle was ending. Or as Adams put it, Washington had inherited "a bowl of Punch, half brandy or Whiskey," but by the time Adams took office in 1796, the bowl had become "half Water with a large mixture of Sour Drops without a grain of Sugar." As for John Quincy's prospects, well, Andrew Jackson was already waiting in the wings, ready to play the role of Jefferson to John Quincy's version of his father in the next election and to catch the political cycle on its next lurch upward. As the nation prepared to set off firecrackers and lose itself in festivals and parades, the most comfortable and natural posture for the patriarch of the Adams clan was as the sober sentry, defiantly guarding the harsher truths that the family and the nation would need to remember once the parades ended.[5]

If John Quincy was fated to suffer the political defeat that seemed to stalk the Adams line—and he was—what about the nation itself? This was a question about the future that visitors and correspondents asked him almost as often as they asked about his recollections of crucial moments in the past, especially the revolutionary years. His characteristic response to both kinds of inquiries was to declare the questions absurd and the answers unknowable. One could no more foresee what was in store for the American people, he would lecture, than one could fathom what was in the minds of all the members of the Continental Congress fifty years ago. But invariably he would then contradict his own declaration of ignorance and revoke his vow of silence, recalling that about half the delegates who voted for American independence in 1776 did so with reluctance, or predicting that the sectional crisis would eventually lead to bloodshed if the slavery issue were not faced squarely by the rising generation.

The larger pattern, which he discerned in both the past and the future, was the cycle, the flow of empires and nations that rose and fell with the same regularity and for essentially the same reasons

that political parties came and went. The Adams version of the
cyclical pattern was less a formal theory than an instinctive way
of thinking. Since he regarded it as a matter of common sense—
indeed, Tom Paine's famous pamphlet of the same name depended
on the presumption that Britain and America were experiencing
different stages of the historical cycle—Adams never felt the need
to explain its major features. He regarded the cyclical pattern of
nations as a commonplace assumption shared by most members of
the revolutionary generation, one of those self-evident truths with
a darker side that Jefferson had neglected to mention in the Declaration. In fact, it was a way of thinking rapidly going out of style by
the time of his death. It then became nearly extinct in America for
most of the nineteenth and twentieth centuries, though it always
enjoyed great favor among subsequent generations of the Adams
family. In the late twentieth century it has made a modest but discernible comeback, largely as a consequence of America's relative
decline as a global economic power. For old man Adams, sitting in
his Quincy study that last morning, the historical cycle possessed
all the inevitability and undeniability of the biological imperatives
about to carry him to the hereafter.[6]

The essence of the theory was that all societies go through the
same developmental stages and the same aging process as human
beings. The Adams version of the cyclical perspective—this bears
repeating—represented a variation on a habit of mind shared by
most of his generation, who believed that all nation-states had limited lifespans. His view was distinctive primarily in the sense that
he gave special prominence to the influence that irrational forces
exerted on human motivations; the engines which drove nations
up and then down the cycle, as Adams conceived it, were fuelled

by the emotions he had spent a lifetime exploring inside himself. And perhaps it is also true that Adams seemed to derive perverse satisfaction from noting the exquisite charms of the cyclical pattern and its applicability to America as well as Europe.[7]

In the typical Adams formulation, every aspiring nation-state was like an enterprising young man. His ambition produces worldly success, which then corrupts his character until, sapped of his earlier energy and work habits, he descends into depravity. "Former ages have never discovered any remedy against the universal gangrene of avarice," he wrote in a characteristic version of the story, and "the steady advance of Wealth . . . has overturned every Republic from the beginning of time." The dramatic economic and geographic expansion the United States was experiencing throughout his retirement years, therefore, made him simultaneously proud and nervous. For while "our country is rising with astonishing rapidity in population and wealth," it was also "proportionally sinking in Luxury, Sloth and Vice." The idea of the historical cycle was such a fixture in Adams's mind that virtually every major event affecting America's social and economic development was made to fit into this developmental scheme, which functioned as a kind of plot outline that history had made available for all enlightened statesmen, who could presumably calculate where on the cycle their country was located and make policy accordingly. Indeed, Adams's ultimate definition of the natural aristocrat— utterly and obviously autobiographical—was the leader who had conquered his own internal demons, had thereby reached a fuller understanding of the emotional forces driving the cyclical dynamo and, therefore, could apply the appropriate social controls required at the current stage of national evolution.[8]

Given the cyclical mentality, however, and given his preoccupation with the irrational forces propelling the country through the cycle, Adams consistently preferred policies that *reduced* the pace of historical change. After all, if the ultimate destination was decline, the last thing the nation needed was leaders who accelerated social and economic development. "When clear prospects are opened before vanity, pride, avarice, or ambition," he had explained to John Taylor, "it is hard to resist the temptation." But that was what responsible American leaders should do—resist the temptations presented by an undeveloped continent and a land of unprecedented opportunity. They should monitor and manage demographic and economic growth in order to delay the day when America would become "more populous, more commercial, more wealthy, and more luxurious." For Jeffersonians and Jacksonians of the emerging liberal tradition, the primary task facing America's political leaders was to liberate individual energies, to destroy the institutional impediments to human progress. For Adams, the primary task was just the opposite—to make government a brake that slowed down the rate of change and thereby postponed America's inevitable encounter with history.[9]

It was axiomatic to Adams that the United States was destined to become a world power with a burgeoning population—he once estimated "more than two hundred millions"—and a flourishing capitalistic economy. Part of the reason for his certainty on this score was what he always called "our geographical advantages," meaning the isolation from Europe and the favorable soil and climate of North America. Another reason was the political institutions his generation had created, which he believed were the best instruments yet devised for balancing the dynamic interests of an expanding society. But perhaps the major reason was historical. The ubiquitous cycle on which America was travelling was actually a spiral: it simultaneously moved forward as well as revolving, so that each nation which repeated the age-old pattern of rise and fall also moved the human condition ahead a few notches in terms of the physical comfort, economic prosperity, and the social justice enjoyed by the overall population. Here was yet another instance when Adams and his old friend at Monticello shared a common vision of America's future but emphasized different features of the vision. Although Jefferson also harbored apprehensions about the long-term prospects for the country, after the continent was fully populated and the agrarian life he idealized gave way to cities and factories, he tended to focus attention on the robust years of the nation's lifespan and the progressive unfolding of America's destiny. He emphasized the forward movement of the American cycle, in short, while Adams emphasized its circularity. The glass was always half-full at Monticello and half-empty at Quincy, even though it was the same glass.

If Jefferson customarily described American progress over time in celebratory language, Adams almost always preferred the cautionary mode. Progress for Adams always seemed to come at a cost. "What Wars, foreign or civil, what forms of government or what divisions these changes may produce," he typically warned, no one could foresee clearly, except that history would exact a toll. Or when Jefferson speculated that the gradual unfolding of human rights might one day produce a condition of nearly idyllic personal freedom, Adams expressed only skeptical optimism: "When People talk of the Freedom of Writing Speaking or thinking, I cannot choose but laugh. No such thing ever existed. No such thing now exists. . . . I hope it will exist. But it must be hundreds of years after you and I shall write and speak no more." The only kind of progress Adams truly trusted came gradually, moving at an evolutionary pace that allowed institutions to adjust and expectations to remain under some modicum of control. The secret of the American Revolution's success, he believed, was that it was rooted in political values and constitutional ideas with longstanding acceptance throughout the colonial era. It therefore followed that the fulfillment of the Revolution's liberal promise, so elegantly articulated by Jefferson, should seep out slowly over the course of the next century, gradually and almost surreptitiously entrenching itself in the minds and hearts of subsequent generations. Adams clearly believed that two of the liberal promises—the abolition of slavery and the improved status for women—were certain of fulfillment. The promise of social and economic equality, on the other hand, struck him as unlikely, one of those ever-receding goals that Jefferson's spiritual descendants would pursue as the French *philosophes* had done before, and with equivalently futile results. Whatever gains and successes future Jeffersonians might enjoy would require future Adamses to nurture them slowly, to bring them along gradually, to integrate them into the social fabric, to consolidate them after each round of leapfrog.[10]

Meanwhile, however, the cycle would continue to turn. No one could say with certainty precisely how long it would take America to reach the apex of world power and then begin to slide down. One could only say that it would eventually happen, for, at least as Adams saw it, the story was as old as history and as predictable as the unquenchable appetite of the human passions. By disposition inclined to see America's ultimate fate lurking behind every political crisis or spurt of growth, Adams nonetheless gave himself plenty of latitude as a prophet. In a sour mood, he warned that the looming sectional crisis threatened to kill the republic "in about twenty years." On another more buoyant occasion, he predicted that the American cycle could last "more than one hundred and fifty years." Precise chronology was impossible to forecast accurately and Adams expressed his contentment to "leave that to others." Various members of the Adams family subsequently took him up on the offer and, true to the tradition of the patriarch, offered prematurely pessimistic estimates.[11]

AND SO IF we were to engage in one final, and admittedly fanciful, fling of the imagination, if we were to conjure up old man Adams, fidgeting about in his favorite chair that last morning, and if we were to grant him a glimpse into the future that is our present, we can be reasonably sure that he would lecture us on the grim lessons of history. He would probably express his surprise and pleasure that the republic he had helped to found had lasted this long. The size and density of our cities, along with our enormous industrial centers, would trouble him. (They would terrify Jefferson.) Most troubling, however, would be the malls, outlet stores, and visible trappings of consumer culture, along with the widespread presumption of unbridled individual freedom, unencumbered by any internalized sense of social responsibility and even justified as a fulfillment of the Revolution he had fought and wrought. We would certainly have to listen to one of his blistering jeremiads and a cascade of advice about how to strengthen government power in order to conserve our resources and manage our obvious decline.

He would also most surely want to know how his own reputation had fared. And he would probably derive a perverse sense of satisfaction in correctly predicting his own relative obscurity, noting for the record that no major mausoleums, monuments, or statues had yet been erected in his honor. In a final spasm of candor and irreverence, he might ask if his beloved republic, now in its third century of existence, had reached a sufficiently ripened stage of development to acknowledge his present relevance. Explaining in his defensive and over-animated way that he did not want to be famous so much as useful, he might propose the construction of an Adams monument on the Tidal Basin in the nation's capital, done in the classical style and situated sufficiently close to the Jefferson Memorial that, depending on the time of day and angle of the sun, he and Jefferson might take turns casting shadows across each other's facades.[12]

Notes

The notes below are both more and less than a conventional scholarly account of the sources used in writing this book. They are more, because I have tried to register my personal positions on the major arguments encountered in attempting to assess the meaning of Adams's life. Which is to say that the endnotes are also meant, on occasion, to serve as a bibliographic essay. They are less, because I have not tried to list all the secondary sources consulted, which would have burdened the book with more citations than any reasonable reader would find sensible. I have cited those major secondary works and those titles that had a decided impact on my thinking. And I have tried to cite all primary sources from which I quote in the text. As per scholarly custom, the full citation is provided when first encountered, then an abbreviated version is used thereafter.

MEMORIES: A PROLOGUE

1. For the most recent scholarly summary, see Ralph A. Brown, *The Presidency of John Adams* (Lawrence, 1975), 199–200.

2. James Sterling Young, *The Washington Community, 1800–1828* (New York, 1966), for the physical condition of the new capital; Abigail Adams to Mary Cranch, November 21, 1800, in Stewart Mitchell, ed., *New Letters of Abigail Adams, 1788–1801* (Boston, 1947), 259–60, for a description of the interior of the presidential mansion at the time.

3. Adams to Thomas Boylston Adams, December 17, 1800, *The Microfilm Edition of the Adams Papers* (608 reels, Boston, 1954–59), Reel 399. This microfilm collection, published by the Massachusetts Historical Society, which owns the originals, will hereafter be cited by date and reel number; Adams to Elias Boudinot, January 16, 1801, Reel 120.

4. Fisher Ames to Rufus King, September 24, 1800, Charles R. King, ed., *The Life and Correspondence of Rufus King* (6 vols., New York, 1895), III, 304; Fisher Ames

to Rufus King, August 26, 1800, *ibid.,* 295–97. See also Daniel Sisson, *The American Revolution of 1800* (New York, 1974), 379–80; Brown, *Presidency of John Adams,* 195–209; Stephen G. Kurtz, *The Presidency of John Adams: The Collapse of Federalism 1795–1800* (Philadelphia, 1957), 374–408. Throughout this book, italics in quotations appear in the original text, unless otherwise noted.

5. Harold Syrett, ed., *The Papers of Alexander Hamilton* (26 vols., New York, 1974–), XXV, 186, 190.

6. *Ibid.,* 222, 196, 208–09.

7. *Ibid.,* 187–88.

8. Adams to Uzal Ogden, December 3, 1800, quoted in *ibid.,* 183. The Syrett edition of the *Hamilton Papers* provides the fullest and fairest scholarly treatment of this entire episode in the notes to the text.

9. See *ibid.,* 178–81, for the Federalist correspondence in the wake of Hamilton's *Letter.* On the other side of the political spectrum, Madison rejoiced in a letter to Jefferson that "Hamilton's attack upon Mr. Adams . . . will be a Thunderbolt to both. I rejoice with you, that Republicanism is likely to be so *completely* triumphant. . . ." See James Madison to Thomas Jefferson, November 1–3, 1800, *ibid.,* 181.

10. For a full discussion of Adams's treatment of Hamilton in his autobiography and in the *Boston Patriot,* see below, chapter 2.

11. James Bayard to Alexander Hamilton, August 18, 1800, Syrett, ed., *Hamilton Papers,* XXV, 71, for the quotation on Adams's congenital irrationality. Much more on this theme will be coming up shortly.

CHAPTER ONE: THE EDUCATION OF JOHN ADAMS

1. The standard works on the Adams presidency are: Kurtz, *Presidency of John Adams;* Brown, *Presidency of John Adams;* Manning Dauer, *The Adams Federalists* (Baltimore, 1953). All tend to conclude with favorable assessments of Adams and critical assessments of the Hamiltonians or High Federalists. Eric McKitrick has graciously allowed me to read his chapters on the Adams presidency in *The Age of Federalism,* written with Stanley Elkins (to be published shortly, New York: Oxford University Press). Elkins and McKitrick adopt a more critical posture toward Adams and do so within the context of a truly magisterial narrative of the political history of the 1790s that promises to supplant all previous treatments of the decade. My own version differs from theirs in several respects, chiefly in absolving Adams of major blame for the collapse of the Federalist persuasion. But we concur that the personality of Adams was a crucial factor requiring extensive analysis. It will not do, in short, to dismiss Hamilton's charges as misguided, petty, or motivated solely by political jealousy.

2. Thomas Jefferson to James Madison, January 4, 1797, quoted in Kurtz, *Presidency of John Adams,* 209–10. For more on Jefferson's thinking at this time, see Sisson,

Revolution of 1800, 360–61; Joseph Charles, *The Origins of the American Party System* (Williamsburg, 1956), 73.

3. Adams to Abigail Adams, December 30, 1796, in Charles Francis Adams, ed., *Letters of John Adams, Addressed to His Wife* (2 vols., Boston, 1841), II, 233–35.

4. James Madison to Thomas Jefferson, December 5, 1796, quoted in Brown, *Presidency of John Adams,* 18; Thomas Jefferson to Adams, December 28, 1796, Andrew Lipscomb and Albert Bergh, eds, *The Writings of Thomas Jefferson* (20 vols., Washington, D.C., 1903), hereafter cited as *Writings of Jefferson,* IX, 356–57; Oliver Wolcott, Sr., to Oliver Wolcott, Jr., March 10, 1797, in George Gibbs, *Memoirs of the Administrations of Washington and John Adams* (2 vols., New York, 1846), I, 246. See also Kurtz, *Presidency of John Adams,* 222–24; Sisson, *Revolution of 1800,* 361–62; Syrett, ed., *Hamilton Papers,* 193–94. The scholarly literature on the emergence of political parties at this moment is both voluminous and spirited. In addition to the above-mentioned books by Charles and Sisson, see Noble Cunningham, *The Jeffersonian Republicans: The Formation of Party Organization, 1789–1801* (Chapel Hill, 1957); Richard Hofstadter, *The Idea of a Party System: The Rise of Legitimate Opposition in the United States, 1780–1840* (Berkeley, 1969); Richard Buel, *Securing the Revolution: Ideology in American Politics* (Ithaca, 1972).

5. The standard account of this elaborate episode is Alexander De Conde, *The Quasi-War: The Politics and Diplomacy of the Undeclared War with France* (New York, 1966). The best brief treatment is Jacob E. Cooke, "Country Above Party: John Adams and the 1799 Mission to France," in Edmund Willis, ed., *Fame and the Founding Fathers: Papers and Comments Presented at the Nineteenth Conference on Early American History* (Bethlehem, 1967), 53–79. Although all the accounts of the Adams presidency cover the story, the upcoming book by Elkins and McKitrick, *The Age of Federalism,* provides the fullest account by far and supports the interpretation offered here.

6. Thomas Jefferson to James Madison, January 20, 1797, and January 30, 1797, *Writings of Jefferson,* X, 367, 375; Adams to Elbridge Gerry, February 20, 1797, "Warren-Adams Letters," Massachusetts Historical Society Collections (Boston, 1925), 72–73.

7. George W. Comer, ed., *The Autobiography of Benjamin Rush* (Princeton, 1948); the Parker quotation is from Zoltán Haraszti, *John Adams and the Prophets of Progress* (Cambridge, Mass., 1953), 1; Charles Francis Adams, ed., *The Works of John Adams, Second President of the United States* (10 vols., Boston, 1850–56), IX, 194–221, hereafter cited as *Works,* for Adams's speeches on this subject.

8. Kurtz, *Presidency of John Adams,* 215–29, offers the most convenient account of this moment. I am not arguing that Jefferson ever gave serious consideration to Adams's offer of a bipartisan administration. Madison's intervention foreclosed the possibility, but Jefferson would almost certainly have reached the same conclusion on his own.

9. *Works*, X, 285–86.

10. Adams to Uriah Forrest, June 20, 1797, *Works*, VIII, 546–47, 320–22.

11. Adams to Elbridge Gerry, May 3, 1797, Reel 117; Adams to James McHenry, October 22, 1798, *Works*, VIII, 612–13; Adams to Harrison Gray Otis, May 9, 1823, Reel 124.

12. Adams to Oliver Wolcott, September 24, 1798, *Works*, VIII, 601–04; Minutes of a Conference with the President, March 26, 1799, Gerry Papers, Library of Congress; Syrett, ed., *Hamilton Papers*, XII, 388–94, 440–53, for Hamilton's correspondence concerning his plans for the military expedition; Fisher Ames to Rufus King, July 15, 1800, King, ed. *Life and Correspondence*, III, 275–76; Sisson, *Revolution of 1800*, 360.

13. The Sedgwick quotation is from Richard E. Welch, Jr., *Theodore Sedgwick, Federalist: A Political Portrait* (Middletown, 1965), 185–86. See Brown, *Presidency of John Adams*, 95–96, for the most incisive account of reaction in the Congress.

14. Syrett, ed., *Hamilton Papers*, XXII, 494–95, provides a full view of the Federalist reaction; Abigail Adams to Adams, March 3, 1799, Reel 393; Adams to Abigail Adams, February 22, 1799, *ibid.;* Elkins and McKitrick, *Age of Federalism*, chapter 12, part 5, offers the best scholarly account.

15. Robert Troup to Rufus King, November 6, 1799, King, ed., *Life and Correspondence*, III, 141–42; Alexander Hamilton to Theodore Sedgwick, May 10, 1800, Syrett, ed., *Hamilton Papers*, XXIV, 430–31; Uriah Forrest to Adams, April 28, 1799, *Works*, VIII, 637–37; Adams to Uriah Forrest, May 13, 1799, *ibid.*, 645–46; Adams to Benjamin Stoddert, September 21, 1799, *Works*, IX, 31–34.

16. [Anonymous], Adams to William Cunningham, November 7, 1808, *Correspondence Between the Hon. John Adams, Late President of the United States, and the Late William Cunningham, Esq. . . .* (Boston, 1823), 48. There is still a lively scholarly debate over whether an earlier resolution of the French question would have made any difference in the presidential election of 1800. The current consensus would seem to be that Federalist projections showed that the vote in New York was the key; and there Aaron Burr had already lobbied the delegates in the legislature on behalf of Jefferson, so that neither a favorable resolution of the quasi-war with France nor the suppression of Hamilton's *Letter* would have made a significant difference in the final tally.

17. See Doris Graber, *Public Opinion, the President, and Foreign Policy* (New York, 1968), 79; Brown, *Presidency of John Adams*, 77–78, 102, 193; and Elkins and McKitrick, *Age of Federalism*, chapter 12, part 5. For Adams's own first-hand version of his thinking at the time, see Adams to Timothy Pickering, August 6, 1799, and Adams to John Trumbull, September 10, 1800, Reel 120.

18. Theodore Sedgwick to Rufus King, September 26, 1800, King, ed., *Life and Correspondence*, III, 308; Fisher Ames to Rufus King, July 15, 1800, *ibid.*, 275–76. Several historians and biographers of Adams have suggested that our modern

perception of his long absence from the seat of government must be informed by the political values of the pre-modern era. Jefferson and Madison, for example, were absent as much or more than Adams. But it seems to me that the *timing* of Adams's absence was too crucial to be excused or explained as a function of more leisurely customs.

19. This is not the place to list the many major works on the coming of the American Revolution or the various books and articles that feature Adams as a key player. It is the place to note the enduring appeal of a semi-fictional account by Catherine Drinker Bowen, *John Adams and the American Revolution* (Boston, 1950), which still manages to recreate the atmosphere in the Continental Congress more imaginatively than any other historical account.

20. Adams to Abigail Adams, July 1, 1774, in Lyman Butterfield, ed., *Adams Family Correspondence* (3 vols., Cambridge, 1963), I, 118, hereafter cited as *Family Correspondence;* Adams to Abigail Adams, July 9, 1774, *ibid.,* 135.

21. Adams to James Warren, June 25, 1774 in Robert J. Taylor, ed., *Papers of John Adams* (6 vols., Cambridge, 1977–), II, 99, hereafter cited as *Papers;* Adams to James Warren, July 25, 1774, *ibid.,* 117; see also Adams to William Tudor, September 26, 1774, *ibid.,* 176.

22. Adams to Abigail Adams, September 25, 1774, *Family Correspondence,* I, 162–63; Adams to Abigail Adams, October 9, 1774, *ibid.,* 167.

23. Lyman Butterfield, ed., *The Diary and Autobiography of John Adams* (4 vols., Cambridge, 1961), II, 121, 182, 173, hereafter cited as *Diary and Autobiography.*

24. *Diary and Autobiography,* II, 150; see also Adams to William Tudor, October 7, 1774, *Papers,* II, 188.

25. *Ibid.,* III, 307, for the account of "Moody's Doctrine" in the autobiography; Adams to Abigail Adams, July 2, 1774, *Family Correspondence,* I, 121, for the contemporary version, which is slightly different; Adams to James Warren, April 9, 1774, *Papers,* II, 82–83; Adams to Moses Gill, June 10, 1774, *Papers,* III, 21.

26. Adams to Abigail Adams, April 15, 1776, *Family Correspondence,* I, 383; Adams to Horatio Gates, March 23, 1776, *Papers,* IV, 59; *Diary and Autobiography,* II, 181; Adams to Abigail Adams, October 1, 1775, *Family Correspondence,* I, 290, for the anecdote about the Reformation, which Adams first heard from John Zubly, the delegate from Georgia.

27. *Diary and Autobiography,* II, 131, 152–53, and *Papers,* II, 144–52, for his role in drafting the Declaration of Rights and Grievances; *Diary and Autobiography,* III, 309–14, for his somewhat haphazard recollection of the events of the fall and winter of 1774–75; *Papers,* II, 216–387, for the text of *Novanglus; Diary and Autobiography,* II, 161, for his thoughts at the time and an editorial note by Butterfield.

28. *Diary and Autobiography,* III, 327, 332–32, 358–59; Adams to William Tudor, April 12, 1776, *Papers,* IV, 118, 200–02, for the mistaken authorship of *Common Sense; ibid.,* 65–73, for *Thoughts on Government.*

29. *Diary and Autobiography*, III, 396–97, for his recollection of the speech, which several delegates confirmed was the dramatic and decisive event he described. The fullest account of the debate is in Julian Boyd, ed., *The Papers of Thomas Jefferson* (26 vols., Princeton, 1950–), I, 311–13; *Papers*, IV, 341–51, for the Declaration of Independence, and *ibid.*, 260–302, for the Plan of Treaties.

30. *Ibid.*, 252–59, for his service on the Board of War and Ordnance; Adams to Nathaneal Greene, April 13, 1777, *Papers*, V, 56; *Diary and Autobiography*, III, 447; Adams to William Tudor, March 27, 1777, *Papers*, V, 132, for his prediction about the war's duration; Adams to Abigail Adams, September 8, 1777, *Family Correspondence*, II, 337–39, for one of several examples of his strategic vision of the military campaign; William Gordon to Adams, March 27, 1777, *Papers*, V, 133, for the kudo.

31. *Diary and Autobiography*, III, 316, 383, 386–88.

32. *Diary and Autobiography*, II, 236; see also *ibid.*, 181 and Adams to Abigail Adams, May 12, 1776, *Family Correspondence*, I, 406, for his suspicion of conspiracy against him.

33. Adams to James Warren, July 24, 1775, *Papers*, III, 89–93, for the remarks about Dickinson in the letter that was intercepted by the British; *Diary and Autobiography*, II, 173–74, for his private reaction at the time of the incident; *Diary and Autobiography*, III, 318–19, for his version in his autobiography.

34. Adams to Samuel Chase, June 14, 1776, *Papers*, IV, 312; Adams to James Warren, August 21, 1776, *ibid.*, 482.

35. Adams to Abigail Adams, May 22 [1777], *Family Correspondence*, II, 245–46.

36. Adams to Abigail Adams, May 17, 1776, *Family Correspondence*, I, 410; Adams to Abigail Adams, June 2, 1776, *Family Correspondence*, II, 3.

37. See Edmund S. Morgan, "John Adams and the Puritan Tradition," *New England Quarterly*, XXXIV (1961), 518–29, for the earliest and still the best rumination on this theme; Mary McManus, "The Education of John Adams," senior thesis (1975), Mount Holyoke College, remains the best secondary account of the early Adams.

38. *Diary and Autobiography*, I, 1. See Norman Pettit, *The Heart Prepared: Grace and Conversion in Puritan Spiritual Life* (New Haven, 1966), for the best analysis of the morphology of conversion in seventeenth-century Puritanism.

39. Adams to Nathan Webb, October 12, 1755, *Papers*, I, 4–7. It seems likely that Adams had recently read, or talked to someone who read, the essay by Benjamin Franklin, *Observations on the Increase of Mankind* (1755), which forecast the demographic explosion in America and its implications for the relationship with England. Less scientific predictions of America's inevitable destiny were "in the air" about this time, often associated with Bishop Berkeley's poem, "Verses on the Prospect of Planting Arts and Learning in America" (1753). For a modern look at this optimistic tradition and what lay behind it, see the first two chapters of Joseph J. Ellis, *After the Revolution: Profiles of Early American Culture* (New York, 1979).

40. Adams to Richard Cranch, September 2, 1755, *Papers*, I, 3–4.

41. *Diary and Autobiography,* I, 25, 7–8, 37, 33–34, 13–14.

42. *Ibid.,* 6–8.

43. Adams to Charles Cushing, April 1, 1756, *Papers,* I, 13–14.

44. *Diary and Autobiography,* I, 42–43.

45. Adams to Abigail Adams, December 2, 1778, *Family Correspondence,* III, 125.

46. The classic statement of the relationship between the psychology of the reformed Christian pursuing God and grace and the modern capitalist is Max Weber, *The Protestant Ethic and the Spirit of Capitalism,* Talcott Parsons, ed. (New York, 1958). Strictly speaking, Franklin reversed the priorities of Puritan psychology, but even Franklin remained imbedded in Puritan values in ways that would have made him a stranger to nineteenth-century entrepreneurs.

47. Adams to Samuel Dexter, March 23, 1801, *Works,* X, 580–81; *Diary and Autobiography,* I, L; Adams to Benjamin Stoddert, March 31, 1801, *Works,* X, 582; Adams to Thomas Jefferson, March 24, 1801, Reel 118.

48. Adams to Elias Boudinot, January 26, 1801, *Works,* IX, 93–94; Adams to Joseph Ward, February 4, 1801, *ibid.,* 97.

49. Adams to Christopher Gadsen, April 16, 1801, Reel 118.

50. Abigail Adams to Thomas Boylston Adams, July 12, 1801, Reel 400.

CHAPTER TWO: HISTORY AND HEROES

1. Adams to Benjamin Rush, August 17, 1812, in Alexander Biddle, ed., *Old Family Letters Copied from the Originals for Alexander Biddle* (Philadelphia, 1892), 420, hereafter cited as *Old Family Letters.*

2. Adams to Francis Vanderkemp, November 24, 1814, Reel 122; also Adams to Elbridge Gerry, April 26, 1813, *ibid.* The quotation from the French visitor is in Haraszti, *Prophets of Progress,* 22–23.

3. Adams to Thomas Boylston Adams, September 15, 1801, Reel 118; Adams to Francis Vanderkemp, October 18, 1814, Reel 122.

4. Adams to Benjamin Waterhouse, August 16, 1812, Worthington Chauncey Ford, ed., *Statesman and Friend: Correspondence of John Adams and Benjamin Waterhouse, 1784–1822* (Boston, 1927), 81, hereafter cited as *Statesman and Friend.*

5. Adams to Benjamin Rush, May 14, 1812, Reel 118; Adams to John Quincy Adams, December 22, 1804, Reel 95.

6. *Diary and Autobiography,* I. LXIX, for the Adams quotation. *Ibid.,* I, XLIV— LXXIV, for the editorial history of the autobiography.

7. Adams to Benjamin Rush, August 31, 1809, *Old Family Letters,* 238.

8. The first use of what would become an Adams refrain that I can find is Adams to John Quincy Adams, January 8, 1808, Reel 118: "Shall I recommend to you the eternal Taciturnity of Franklin and Washington? I believe your nature is as incapable of it as mine."

9. *Diary and Autobiography,* III, 253. Adams began writing the autobiography on October 5, 1802.

10. Peter Shaw, *The Character of John Adams* (New York, 1976), 278–82, has a thoughtful comparison of the two autobiographies. Leonard Labaree, *et al.,* eds., *The Autobiography of Benjamin Franklin* (New Haven, 1964).

11. The quotation is from Adams to John Quincy Adams, November 12, 1818, Reel 123.

12. Adams to William Tudor, May 15, 1817, Reel 123. On Hutchinson's tragic role in the coming of the American Revolution, see Bernard Bailyn, *The Ordeal of Thomas Hutchinson* (Cambridge, 1974).

13. *Diary and Autobiography,* III, 434–35; Adams to Francis Vanderkemp, January 25, 1806, Reel 118; Adams to Benjamin Rush, August 7, 1809, *Old Family Letters,* 237.

14. *Diary and Autobiography,* IV, 5; *ibid.,* III, 330; Adams to Abigail Adams, March 19, 1776, *Family Correspondence,* I, 363; Adams to Benjamin Waterhouse, October 29, 1805, *Statesman and Friend,* 31.

15. *Diary and Autobiography,* III, 335–36.

16. Adams to Benjamin Rush, September 30, 1805, *Old Family Letters,* 86; Adams to Benjamin Rush, June 21, 1811, Reel 118; Adams to William Cunningham, September 27, 1809, *Correspondence Between Adams and Cunningham,* 167; Adams to Thomas Jefferson, November 12, 1813, Lester J. Cappon, ed., *The Adams-Jefferson Letters* (2 vols., Chapel Hill, 1959), II, 392–93, hereafter cited as *Adams-Jefferson Letters.*

17. Adams to Abigail Adams, May 17, 1776, *Family Correspondence,* I, 410–11; *Diary and Autobiography,* III, 335, 352.

18. *Diary and Autobiography,* III, 418–19. See also *ibid.,* IV, 118–19, for Adams's discussion of Franklin in Paris; Adams to William Temple Franklin, May 5, 1817, Reel 123; *Diary and Autobiography,* IV, 69; Adams to Rush, August 14, 1811, John A. Schutz and Douglass Adair, eds., *The Spur of Fame: Dialogues of John Adams and Benjamin Rush, 1805–1813* (San Marino, Calif., 1966), 185–86.

19. Adams to Benjamin Rush, March 14, 1809, *Spur of Fame,* 135.

20. Adams to Francis Vanderkemp, August 23, 1806, Reel 118.

21. Adams to Elkanck Watson, August 10, 1812, Reel 118; Adams to Thomas Jefferson, July [3], 1813, *Adams-Jefferson Letters,* II, 349; Adams to Harriet Welsh, March 22, 1822, Reel 124; Adams to James Perspignam, March 4, 1823, Reel 124. See also Adams to Richard Rush, August 24, 1815, Reel 122; Adams to Harriet Welsh, May 9, 1821, Reel 124; Adams to John Holmes, August 10, 1815, Reel 122.

22. Adams to Benjamin Rush, April 22, 1812, *Old Family Letters,* 375–81; *ibid.,* 161–73.

23. Adams to Nicholas Boylston, November 3, 1819, Reel 124.

24. Katherine Anthony, *First Lady of the Revolution: The Life of Mercy Otis Warren*

(New York, 1958). See also Lester Cohen, "Mercy Otis Warren: The Politics of Language and the Aesthetics of Self," *American Quarterly*, XXXV (1983), 481–98.

25. Adams to Mercy Otis Warren, January 29, 1783, in *Warren-Adams Letters*, Massachusetts Historical Society (2 vols., Boston, 1925), II, 188–89.

26. Adams to Mercy Otis Warren, July 11, 1807, in Charles Francis Adams, ed., *Correspondence Between John Adams and Mercy Warren*, reprinted in *Collections of Massachusetts Historical Society*, IV, 5th Series (1878), 21.

27. Adams to Mercy Otis Warren, July 27, 1807, *ibid.*, 354, 358.

28. Adams to Mercy Otis Warren, August 3, 1807, *ibid.*, 400–11.

29. Mercy Otis Warren to Adams, August 7, 1807, *ibid.*, 422–23; Mercy Otis Warren to Adams, August 15, 1807, *ibid.*, 449; Mercy Otis Warren to Adams, July 28, 1807, *ibid.*, 359, 364.

30. Mercy Otis Warren to Adams, July 28, 1807, *ibid.*, 360; Mercy Otis Warren to Adams, July 16, 1807, *ibid.*, 480; Mercy Otis Warren to Adams, August 15, 1807, *ibid.*, 456.

31. Mercy Otis Warren, *History of the American Revolution* (3 vols., Boston, 1805), III, 394–95; Mercy Otis Warren to Adams, July 28, 1807, *Adams-Warren Correspondence*, 363.

32. Adams to Mercy Otis Warren, July 20, 1807, *ibid.*, 335; Mercy Otis Warren to Adams, August 15, 1807, *ibid.*, 354.

33. A fuller discussion of Adams's political theory is offered below, in chapters 4 and 5. But particularly relevant for an understanding of the modern scholarly debate over "republicanism" as it related to Adams, the following have been helpful, even if they are not always in agreement about the meaning of that important term: Joyce Appleby, "The New Republican Synthesis and the Changing Political Ideas of John Adams," *American Quarterly*, XXV (1973), 578–95; Isaac Kramnick, "The Great National Discussion: The Discourse of Politics in 1787," *William and Mary Quarterly*, 3rd Series, XLV (1988), 3–32; Ralph Lerner, *The Thinking Revolutionary: Principle and Practice in the New Republic* (Ithaca and London, 1987); and Leslie Wharton, *Polity and the Public Good: Conflicting Theories of Republican Government in the New Nation* (Ann Arbor, 1980), especially 33–55.

34. Adams to Mercy Otis Warren, July 20, 1807, *Adams-Warren Correspondence*, 353; Adams to Mercy Otis Warren, August 8, 1807, *ibid.*, 432.

35. See Lester Cohen, "Explaining the Revolution: Ideology and Ethics in Mercy Otis Warren's Historical Theory," *William and Mary Quarterly*, 3rd Series, XXXVII (1980), 200–18. For a devastating and sprightly polemic against the efficacy of Warren's version of republicanism, see John P. Diggins, *The Lost Soul of American Politics: Virtue, Self-Interest, and the Foundations of Liberalism* (New York, 1985).

36. Adams to Mercy Otis Warren, August 19, 1807, *Adams-Warren Correspondence*, 477–78.

37. Adams to William Cunningham, February 22, July 31, and June 7, 1809, *Correspondence Between Adams and Cunningham*, 93, 151, 124.

38. Adams to James Lloyd, February 6, 1813, *Works*, X, 113.

39. Adams to James Davis, August 4, 1819, Reel 123.

40. See above, chapter 1, for treatment of the Adams presidency. The quotation is from Adams to James Lloyd, February 6, 1815, *Works*, X, 115.

41. Adams to Nicholas Boylston, November 3, 1819, Reel 124; *Works*, X, 310, which reprints the selection from the *Boston Patriot*.

42. *Ibid.*, IX, 281; Adams to William Cunningham, March 20, 1809, *Correspondence Between Adams and Cunningham*, 107; Adams to James Lloyd, February 11, 1815, *Works*, X, 119; Adams to Benjamin Waterhouse, March 6, 1813, *Statesman and Friend*, 92–93.

43. Adams to Mathew Carey, September 9, 1820, Reel 124.

44. Adams to George Washington Adams, February 3, 1823, Reel 124; Adams to John Quincy Adams, May 14, 1815, Reel 122.

45. Adams to Alexander Johnson, December 14, 1822, Reel 124; Adams to John Quincy Adams, March 13, 1819, Reel 123; Adams to James Davis, August 14, 1819, Reel 123; Adams to Harrison Gray Otis, March 21, 1823, Reel 124.

46. Adams to William Bentley, August 18, 1819, Reel 124.

47. Adams to Louisa Catherine Adams, May 3, 1821, Reel 124; Adams to Benjamin Rush, July 7, 1812, *Old Family Letters*, 401; Adams to Jedidiah Morse, March 4, 1815, *Works*, X, 133; Adams to Hezekiah Niles, January 3, 1817, Reel 123.

48. Adams to George Alexander Otis, July 2, 1820, Reel 124.

49. Adams to Louisa Catherine Adams, December 22, 1818, Reel 123; Adams to John Quincy Adams, December 24, 1818, Reel 123; Adams to Benjamin Rush, December 27, 1812, *Old Family Letters*, 432.

CHAPTER THREE: IRREVERENCIES AND OPPOSITIONS

1. *Diary and Autobiography*, I, x–xiv.

2. Adams to Benjamin Rush, February 27, 1805, *Spur of Fame*, 24; Adams to Benjamin Rush, December 22, 1806, *ibid.*, 72; Adams to Benjamin Rush, February 26, 1812, Reel 118.

3. Adams to Thomas Jefferson, June 11, 1813, *Adams-Jefferson Letters*, II, 328; Adams to Thomas Jefferson, July 16, 1814, *ibid*, 437; Adams to Francis Vanderkemp, December 27, 1816, *Works*, X, 235.

4. Adams to Thomas Jefferson, May 3, 1812, *Adams-Jefferson Letters*, II, 302; Adams to John Marshall, August 11, 1800, *Works*, IX, 73.

5. See the preface in Haraszti, *Prophets of Progress;* Thomas Jefferson to Adams, January 11, 1817, *Adams-Jefferson Letters*, 505.

6. Haraszti, *Prophets*, 21, for the quotations. I have browsed in the Adams collection

at the Boston Public Library to review the marginal comments for myself, but citations are to the Haraszti account, which is both readily accessible to readers and a model of spirited scholarship.

7. Isaac Kramnick, *Bolingbroke and His Circle: The Politics of Nostalgia in the Age of Walpole* (Cambridge, Mass., 1968), is the authoritative scholarly account of Bolingbroke's life and thought. See also H. T. Dickinson, *Bolingbroke* (London, 1970).

8. Haraszti, *Prophets*, 54–79.

9. *Ibid.*, 258.

10. *Ibid.*, 116–38.

11. *Ibid.*, 181–85, 187.

12. *Works*, VI, 279; Adams to Richard Price, April, 1790, quoted in Haraszti, *Prophets*, 81.

13. Adams to Thomas McKean, June 21, 1812, *Works*, X, 16; Adams to Jefferson, July 13, 1813, *Adams-Jefferson Letters*, II, 355.

14. Adams to Jefferson, July 15, 1813, *Adams-Jefferson Letters*, II, 357–58; Adams to Charles Holt, September 4, 1820, *Works*, X, 391; Adams to Benjamin Rush, February 27, 1805, *Spur of Fame*, 24. There are several other books in the Adams library that deal with the French Revolution and contain Adams's marginalia, but none with the volume or bite of his comments on Wollstonecraft. The secondary literature on the French Revolution is, of course, immense. The recent publication of Simon Schama's *Citizens: A Chronicle of the French Revolution* (New York, 1988) is a brilliant and colorful account guided by convictions that Adams would have found compatible with his own.

15. Haraszti, *Prophets*, 187, 203.

16. *Ibid.*, 187, 167. Adams's understanding of the new word "ideology" is itself a large subject, discussed at greater length in chapter 5.

17. *Ibid.*, 221–22.

18. *Ibid.*, 201.

19. *Ibid.*, 218–19, 214, 234.

20. Adams to Josiah Quincy, February 9, 1811, *Works*, IX, 630.

21. Adams to William Keteltas, November 25, 1812, *Works*, X, 23; Adams to Rush, June 12, 1812, Reel 118.

22. Adams to William Plumer, March 28, 1813, *Works*, X, 35; Thomas McKean to Adams, January, 1814, *ibid.*, 87–89; Adams to John Trumbull, March 18, 1817, Reel 123. For the best scholarly discussion of the signing confusion, see Gary Wills, *Inventing America: Jefferson's Declaration of Independence* (New York, 1979).

23. Adams to Alexander Everett, March 14, 1814, Reel 121; Adams to Thomas McKean, November 26, 1815, *Works*, X, 182.

24. Adams to William Tudor, April 5, 1818, Reel 123; Adams to John Quincy Adams, May 20, 1818, *ibid.* For a brilliant analysis of William Wirt's treatment of Patrick Henry, see William Taylor, *Cavalier and Yankee: The Old South and American National Character* (New York, 1961), 81–89.

25. Adams to Benjamin Waterhouse, January 20, 1818, *Works*, X, 279; Adams to William Tudor, June 5, 1817, *ibid.*, 262–63; Adams to William Tudor, June 1, 1817, *ibid.*, 259.

26. Adams to William Tudor, February 16, 1823, Reel 124; Adams to William Tudor, February 1, 1823, *ibid.*, Adams to Benjamin Waterhouse, March 19, 1817, *Statesman and Friend*, 126–28.

27. Adams to William Tudor, June 7, 1818, Reel 123. For a modern scholarly assessment of Otis's role in the Revolution, see John J. Waters, *The Otis Family in Provincial and Revolutionary Massachusetts* (Chapel Hill, 1968).

28. Adams to Hezekiah Niles, February 13, 1818, *Works*, X, 282.

29. Adams to Thomas Jefferson, August 14, 1815, *Adams-Jefferson Letters*, II, 455.

30. Adams to Hezekiah Niles, February 13, 1818, *Works*, X, 283.

31. Adams to Jefferson, May 29, 1818, *Adams-Jefferson Letters*, II, 525; Adams to William Tudor, September 18, 1818, *Works*, X, 359.

32. Adams to William Tudor, November 7, 1816, Reel 122; Adams to James Madison, July 25, 1818, Reel 123.

33. Adams to Benjamin Rush, December 8, 1812, *Old Family Letters*, 322; Adams to Benjamin Rush, September 30, 1805, *Spur of Fame*, 39. For more on Adams's notion of neutrality, see also Adams to Francis Vanderkemp, April 1, 1811, Reel 118; Adams to James Lloyd, March 29, 1815, *Works*, X, 146–49.

34. *Works*, IV, 401, for the quotation from the *Defence;* Adams to Benjamin Rush, October 22, 1812, Reel 118.

35. Adams to Francis Vanderkemp, April 1, 1811, Reel 118; Adams to Benjamin Rush, June 28, 1810, *Old Family Letters*, 258–59; Adams to Benjamin Rush, July 25, 1808, Reel 118.

36. Adams to Richard Cranch, August 11, 1813, Reel 121; Adams to Benjamin Waterhouse, September 17, 1813, *Statesman and Friend*, III.

37. Adams to William Cunningham, February 11, 1809, *Correspondence Between Adams and Cunningham,* 82; Adams to John Quincy Adams, February 5, 1806, Reel 118; Adams to John Adams Smith, October 10, 1819, Reel 124.

38. Adams to Thomas Truxton, November 30, 1802, *Works,* IX, 586; Adams to Joseph Varnum, December 26, 1808, Reel 118; *Diary and Autobiography*, III, 343–49.

39. Adams to Thomas Jefferson, May 1, 1812, *Adams-Jefferson Letters*, II, 301; Adams to Richard Rush, July 15, 1813, Reel 95.

40. Adams to Thomas Jefferson, June 28, 1812, *Adams-Jefferson Letters*, II, 311; Thomas Jefferson to Adams, May 27, 1813, *ibid.*, 325; Adams to Thomas Jefferson, June 11, 1813, *ibid.*, 329.

41. Adams to Richard Rush, October 8, 1813, Reel 95; Adams to Benjamin Rush, March 23, 1809, *Spur of Fame,* 137; Adams to Benjamin Rush, December 19, 1811, *ibid.*, 198–99. For the most recent study of the impact of the War of 1812 on American culture, see Steven Watts, *The Republic Reborn: War and the Making of Liberal*

America, 1790–1820 (Baltimore and London, 1987), especially 28–42, for a discussion of Adams. For a comprehensive review of the causes and consequences of the war, see J. C. A. Stagg, *Mr. Madison's War: Politics, Diplomacy, and Warfare in the Early American Republic, 1738–1830* (Princeton, 1983). The most recent scholarly monograph, which tends to endorse Adams's assessment of policy mismanagement, is Donald R. Hickey, *The War of 1812: A Forgotten Conflict* (Urbana, 1989). Finally, there is the classic account by Henry Adams, now conveniently available in the Library of America edition, *History of the United States of America During the Administrations of Thomas Jefferson and James Madison* (2 vols., New York, 1988).

42. Adams to John Quincy Adams, December 23, 1813, Reel 95; Adams to Benjamin Rush, August 17, 1812, *Spur of Fame;* Adams to Benjamin Rush, February 23, 1813, *ibid.,* 276; Adams to Richard Rush, January 7, 1814, Reel 95.

43. Adams to Mathew Cary, July 7, 1813, Reel 95; Adams to Richard Rush, December 12, 1813, *ibid.;* Adams to William Smith, November 20, 1814, Reel 122; Adams to Governor Plummer, December 4, *ibid.*

44. Adams to James Madison, November 28, 1814, *Works,* X, 106; Adams to John Quincy Adams, February 25, 1815, Reel 122; Adams to John Quincy Adams, March 11, 1815, *ibid.;* Adams to Richard Rush, October 12, 1814, *ibid.;* Adams to Horatio Gates Stafford, June 4, 1815, *ibid.*

CHAPTER FOUR: THE AMERICAN DIALOGUE

1. Adams to Thomas McKean, June 21, 1812, *Works,* X, 16; Adams to Robert Fulton, June 23, 1813, Reel 95; Adams to Benjamin Rush, November 29, 1812, Reel 118.

2. *Adams-Jefferson Letters,* preface, for the statistical evidence on the correspondence; Adams to Benjamin Rush, February 3, 1813, *Old Family Letters,* 338.

3. For the most convenient summary of the history of the correspondence and public reaction to it, see *Adams-Jefferson Letters,* I, introduction.

4. Adams to Benjamin Rush, February 11, 1810, *Spur of Fame,* 44; Adams to John Quincy Adams, July 15, 1813, Reel 95; Adams to Benjamin Rush, March 4, 1809, Reel 118; Adams to William Cranch, May 23, 1801, Reel 118. Adams's critique of Jefferson's leadership as president has found a modern voice in Robert W. Tucker and David C. Hendrickson, *Empire of Liberty: The Statecraft of Thomas Jefferson* (New York, 1990).

5. Adams to Colonel Ward, January 8, 1810, Reel 118. For the most psychologically sensitive account of the Sally Hemings accusation by modern historians, see Winthrop Jordan, *White Over Black: American Attitudes Toward the Negro, 1550–1812* (Chapel Hill, 1968), 461–69.

6. The best secondary account is Merrill D. Peterson, *Adams and Jefferson: A Revolutionary Dialogue* (Oxford, 1978); Abigail Adams to Thomas Jefferson, June 6, 1785, *Adams-Jefferson Letters,* I, 28; see also Joyce Appleby, "The Jefferson-Adams

Rupture and the First French Translation of John Adams' Defence," *American Historical Review*, LXXIII (1968), 1084–91; on the fear of the Hamilton wing of the Federalists that Adams and Jefferson might form a political alliance in 1796, see Charles, *Origins of the American Party System*, 54–74; Fisher Ames to Rufus King, September 24, 1800, *Life and Correspondence of King*, III, 304.

7. Adams to William Cunningham, January 16, 1804, *Correspondence Between Adams and Cunningham*, 7–9; Adams to Benjamin Rush, April 18, 1808, *Spur of Fame*, 107–08.

8. Adams to Benjamin Rush, December 21, 1809, *Old Family Letters*, 249. Jefferson had already made an indirect and unsuccessful attempt to resume the friendship in 1804. He wrote to Abigail in response to her letter consoling him on the recent death of his younger daughter. Jefferson conceded that Adams's "midnight appointments . . . gave hurt," but claimed he was willing to forgive. But the gesture went unanswered by Adams, who was still too raw and resentful in 1804. See Thomas Jefferson to Abigail Adams, June 13, 1804, *Adams-Jefferson Letters*, II, 270.

9. Adams to Benjamin Rush, August 31, 1809, *Old Family Letters*, 246; Adams to Benjamin Rush, July 3, 1812, *ibid.*, 297–98.

10. Thomas Jefferson to Benjamin Rush, December 5, 1811, Paul Leicester Ford, ed., *The Writings of Thomas Jefferson* (New York, 1892–99), IX, 300. See also Lyman H. Butterfield, "The Dream of Benjamin Rush: The Reconciliation of John Adams and Thomas Jefferson," *Yale Review*, 40 (1950–51), 297–319.

11. Adams to Jefferson, January 1, 1812, *Adams-Jefferson Letters*, II, 290; Adams to Benjamin Rush, February 10, 1812, Reel 118; Donald Stewart and George Clark, "Misanthrope or Humanitarian? John Adams in Retirement," *New England Quarterly*, XXVIII (1955), 232, for the Adams remark about "a brother sailor."

12. Thomas Jefferson to Adams, January 21, 1812, *Adams-Jefferson Letters*, II, 291–92.

13. Adams to Thomas Jefferson, February 3, 1812, *ibid.*, 295; Thomas Jefferson to Adams, April 8, 1816, *ibid.*, 467; Adams to Thomas Jefferson, May 3, 1816, *ibid.*, 471.

14. Thomas Jefferson to Adams, January 21, 1812, *ibid.*, 291–92; Adams to Thomas Jefferson, February 3, 1812, *ibid.*, 295; Adams to Thomas Jefferson, September 24, 1821, *ibid.*, 576.

15. Adams to Thomas Jefferson, May 21, 1812, *ibid.*, 304, and note by Cappon.

16. Adams to Thomas Jefferson, June 11, 1819, *ibid.*, 542; Thomas Jefferson to Adams, July 9, 1819, *ibid.*, 543–44; Adams to Thomas Jefferson, July 21, 1819, *ibid.*, 545; Adams to Francis Vanderkemp, August 21, 1819, Reel 124.

17. Thomas Jefferson to Adams, August 10, 1815, *ibid.*, 452–53; Adams to Thomas Jefferson, July 3, 1813, *ibid.*, 349.

18. Adams to Thomas Jefferson, July 9, 1813, *ibid.*, 350.
19. Adams to Thomas Jefferson, June 14, 1813, *ibid.*, 330; Adams to Thomas Jefferson, June 30, 1814, *ibid.*, 346–47.
20. Adams to Thomas Jefferson, May 18, 1817, *ibid.*, 515; Adams to Thomas Jefferson, July 18, 1813, *ibid.*, 361–62; Adams to Thomas Jefferson, February 2, 1816, *ibid.*, 461.
21. Peterson, *Adams and Jefferson*, 8–9; Thomas Jefferson to Adams, April 8, 1816, *Adams-Jefferson Letters*, II, 467.
22. Adams to Thomas Jefferson, May 6, 1816, *ibid.*, 472–73.
23. Thomas Jefferson to Adams, August 1, 1816, *ibid.*, 483; Adams to Thomas Jefferson, September 3, 1816, *ibid.*, 487–88; Thomas Jefferson to Adams, October 14, 1816, *ibid.*, 490.
24. Adams to Thomas Jefferson, December 25, 1813, *ibid.*, 409; Adams to Thomas Jefferson, June 20, 1815, *ibid.*, 446; Adams to Thomas Jefferson, September 30, 1816, *ibid.*, 489; Adams to Thomas Jefferson, July 15, 1813, *ibid.*, 358.
25. Adams to Thomas Jefferson, August 20, 1821, *ibid.*, 574; Thomas Jefferson to Adams, September 12, 1821, *ibid.*, 576.
26. Merrill D. Peterson, *Thomas Jefferson and the New Nation* (New York and Oxford, 1970), 952; Thomas Jefferson to Adams, August 15, 1820, *Adams-Jefferson Letters*, II, 566–67.
27. Thomas Jefferson to Adams, June 27, 1813, *ibid.*, 335–37.
28. Adams to Thomas Jefferson, June 30, 1813, *ibid.*, 347; Adams to Thomas Jefferson, July 9, 1813, *ibid.*, 351.
29. The quotation is from Thomas Jefferson to Samuel Kerchevel, July 12, 1816, Ford, ed., *Writings*, X, 37. This is not the place to attempt an exhaustive account of the many valuable works on Jefferson's political philosophy, which, like Jefferson the man, has attracted countless interpreters. Adrienne Koch's *The Philosophy of Thomas Jefferson* (New York, 1943) is still a helpful guide. Richard K. Matthews, *The Radical Politics of Thomas Jefferson: A Revisionist View* (Lawrence, 1984), and Harold Hellenbrand, *The Unfinished Revolution: Education and Politics in the Thought of Thomas Jefferson* (London and Toronto, 1990), are the newest books on the topic. My own interpretation is closest to Joyce Appleby, "What Is Still Living in the Political Philosophy of Thomas Jefferson," *William and Mary Quarterly*, 3rd Series, XXXIX (April 1982), 287–309. On the history of popular sovereignty as an idea or, if you will, a fiction, see Edmund S. Morgan, *Inventing the People: The Rise of Popular Sovereignty in England and America* (New York, 1988).
30. Adams to Thomas Jefferson, July 13, 1813, *Adams-Jefferson Letters*, II, 355–56.
31. Adams to Thomas Jefferson, November 13, 1815, *ibid.*, 456.
32. Adams to Thomas Jefferson, December 16, 1816, *ibid.*, 500–01; on Tracy's book, see Adams to Jefferson, February 1, 1817, *ibid.*, 506–07.
33. Adams to Thomas Jefferson, July 9, 1813, *ibid.*, 351.

34. Modern-day historians and political scientists have been less interested in Adams's psychological reflexes than the intellectual implications of his political vocabulary. His obsession with aristocracy, in this view, was merely part of a larger commitment to classical categories of analysis that had become anachronistic in the emerging democratic culture of post-revolutionary America. The seminal account of Adams as an attractive anachronism, rooted in the classical politics of pre-modern America, is Gordon Wood's *The Creation of the American Republic, 1776–1787* (Chapel Hill, 1969), 567–92. I am trying to argue that Adams had several piercing insights into the forces shaping American politics and society *precisely because* he refused to accept the modern vocabulary of Jeffersonian democracy. Wood implicitly acknowledges this in his treatment of Adams, and explicitly does so at the end of the chapter cited above: "For too long and with too much candor he had tried to tell his fellow Americans some truths about themselves that American values and American ideology would not admit." Precisely. More on this important theme follows in chapter 5 below.

35. Adams to Thomas Jefferson, July 9, 1813, *Adams-Jefferson Letters*, II, 351–52; Adams to Thomas Jefferson, Aug [14?], 1813, *ibid.*, 365; Adams to Thomas Jefferson, December 19, 1813, *ibid.*, 409.

36. In the margins of his copy of Harrington's *Oceana*, Adams wrote: "The controversy between the rich and the poor, the laborious and the idle, the learned and the ignorant, distinctions as old as the creation and . . . grounded on unalterable nature . . . will continue, and rivalries will spring out of them." See Haraszti, *Prophets of Progress*, 34–35.

37. Adams to Thomas Jefferson, July 13, 1813, *Adams-Jefferson Letters*, II, 355.

38. Thomas Jefferson to Adams, October 28, 1813, *ibid.*, 387–92.

39. Adams to Thomas Jefferson, November 15, 1813, *ibid.*, 400; Adams to Thomas Jefferson, July 16, 1814, *ibid.*, 437–38.

40. Adams to Thomas Jefferson, September 15, 1813, *ibid.*, 376; Adams to Thomas Jefferson, September 2, 1813, *ibid.*, 371–72; Adams to Thomas Jefferson, November 15, 1813, *ibid.*, 398.

41. Adams to Joseph Mulligan, November 20, 1818, Reel 123.

42. Benjamin Rush to Adams, February 17, 1812, *Spur of Fame*, 211. Professional historians have been engaged in a furious debate about the evolution of republicanism as an ideology after the Revolution. In that debate, which has at times taken on a superheated character reminiscent of the scatalogical rhetoric of the radical Whigs in the 1760s and both political parties in the 1790s, Adams is generally cast as the prototype of the classical mentality, fundamentally at odds with the emerging liberal mentality represented by Jefferson. While this formulation accurately conveys Adams's disenchantment with most of the values associated with Jeffersonian liberalism—its embrace of an individualistic ethic, its contempt for the past, its faith in the workings of the marketplace, its repudiation of activist government—too

often the formulation makes Adams into a notorious anachronism, out of touch with the triumphant impulses of democratic capitalism. If we are to embrace a strict historicism, both Adams and Jefferson, as well as all their colleagues in the revolutionary generation, were time-bound creatures whose political values were shaped in a world that is lost forever to us. If we step back from strict historicism, however, and ask what enduring ideas underlay Adams's vision and his classical vocabulary or idiom, it seems clear that he is best understood as a critic of liberalism whose reverence for the past and for gradual change links him with latter-day conservatives, whose diagnosis of inherent social inequality links him with latter-day radicals, and whose belief in the active role of government links him with what in twentieth-century politics is, ironically, referred to as the liberal tradition. For an appreciation of Adams's role as critic of the Jeffersonian camp, see the often brilliant book by Watts, *The Republic Reborn*. For a critical assessment of the Jeffersonian legacy, see Drew McCoy, *The Elusive Republic: Political Economy in Jeffersonian America* (Chapel Hill, 1980). For the most incisive introduction to the terms of the debate among professional historians, see the matched pair of scholarly articles: Joyce Appleby, "Republicanism in Old and New Contexts," and Lance Banning, "Jeffersonian Ideology Revisited: Liberal and Classical Ideas in the New American Republic," both in *William and Mary Quarterly*, 3rd Series, XLIII (1986), 3–34.

43. Adams to Thomas Jefferson, January 29, 1819, *Adams-Jefferson Letters*, II, 532; also Adams to Jefferson, February 24, 1819, *ibid.*, 534–35.

44. Adams to Thomas Jefferson, February 1, 1817, *ibid.*, 507; Thomas Jefferson to Adams, May 5, 1817, *ibid.*, 513.

45. Adams to Thomas Jefferson, January 22, 1825, *ibid.*, 606; Thomas Jefferson to Adams, February 15, 1825, *ibid.*, 609.

46. Adams to Thomas Jefferson, December 16, 1816, *ibid.*, 501; Adams to Thomas Jefferson, February 21, 1820, *ibid.*, 561; Thomas Jefferson to Adams, January 22, 1825, *ibid.*, 607.

47. Adams to Thomas Jefferson, May 21, 1819, *ibid.*, 540.

48. Thomas Jefferson to Adams, October 12, 1823, *ibid.*, 601.

49. Adams to Thomas Jefferson, November 10, 1823, *ibid.*, 601–02.

50. Adams to Thomas Jefferson, December 21, 1819, *ibid.*, 551; Adams to Thomas Jefferson, February 3, 1821, *ibid.*, 571.

51. Thomas Jefferson to George Logan, May 11, 1805, Ford, ed., *Works*, X, 141; the quotation from Coles and Jefferson's response are conveniently available in Peterson, *Thomas Jefferson and the New Nation*, 999. See also McCoy, *The Last of the Fathers*, for a splendid discussion of the inadequacy of Jefferson's legacy as it faced the persistence of slavery.

52. Thomas Jefferson to Samuel Kercheval, July 12, 1816, Ford, ed., *Works*, XII, ii; Thomas Jefferson to Adams, August 1, 1816, *Adams-Jefferson Letters*, II, 484; Jefferson's autobiography in Ford, ed., *Works*, I, 77.

53. Adams to Reverend Coleman, January 13, 1817, Reel 123; see also the letter to Peter Ludlow and James Sheys, February 21, 1819, Reel 123, where Adams acknowledges there was a rough equivalency to the problem presented by slavery and by the proper conduct toward the Indians.

54. Adams to William Tudor, November 20, 1819, Reel 124; Adams to Joshua Cushman, March 16, 1820, Reel 124; Adams to Louisa Catherine Adams, January 29, 1820, Reel 124; see also the same views expressed in Adams to Robert J. Evans, June 8, 1819, *Works*, 379–80; Adams to Robert Walsh, January 19, 1820, Reel 124; Adams to Louisa Catherine Adams, December 23, 1819, Reel 124.

55. Thomas Jefferson to Hugh Nelson, February 7, 1820, Ford, ed., *Works*, X, 156; Thomas Jefferson to John Holmes, April 22, 1820, *ibid.*, 157–58; Thomas Jefferson to Joseph Cabell, November 28, 1820, *ibid.*, 165–68. The best secondary account is Peterson, *Thomas Jefferson and the New Nation*, 981–95.

56. Adams to Thomas Jefferson, February 25, 1825, *Adams-Jefferson Letters*, II, 610.

57. This view of Jefferson's decline at the end is in keeping with Merrill Peterson's treatment in *Thomas Jefferson and the New Nation*, 980–1009. See also Peterson's *Adams and Jefferson*, 126–28, where even Peterson, one of Jefferson's ablest defenders, concludes that by the 1820s "the two men seemed to change places. Adams was serene, Jefferson morbid. The New Englander found the path of tranquility . . . while . . . the Virginian lost it in the gloom that invaded a declining [southern] society. . . ."

CHAPTER FIVE: ERUDITE EFFUSIONS

1. Adams to Thomas Jefferson, September 15, 1813, *Adams-Jefferson Letters*, II, 376; Thomas Jefferson to Adams, October 28, 1813, *ibid.*, 392; Adams to Thomas Jefferson, November 12, 1813, *ibid.*, 394; Adams to Richard Rush, November 5, 1813, Reel 122.

2. Adams to John Langdon, February 21, 1812, Reel 118; Adams to Thomas Jefferson, November 12, 1813, *Adams-Jefferson Letters*, II, 394; the Adams correspondence with John Taylor is published in *Works*, VI, 443–521, without dates for the individual letters.

3. John Taylor, *An Inquiry into the Principles and Policy of the Government of the United States* (New Haven, 1950; first published 1814); *A Defence of the Constitutions of Government of the United States of America* and *Discourses on Davila* are available in *Works*, IV, 270–588, V, VI, 3–399; Adams to Benjamin Rush, December 27, 1810, *Old Family Letters*, 270.

4. Adams to Mathew Carey, June 21, 1815, Reel 122; Adams to Francis Vanderkemp, July 5, 1814, *ibid.* The claim of influence on Burke is at best an exaggeration and at worst a total fabrication.

5. The marginal comment of 1812 is reproduced in *Works*, VI, 227; the comment on

the likelihood of civil war, dating from 1813, is in Haraszti, *Prophets of Progress*, 173.

6. Adams to Benjamin Franklin, January 17, 1787, John Bigelow, ed., *The Works of Benjamin Franklin* (New York, 1904), XI, 298–99; Adams to James Warren, January 9, 1787, Ford, ed., *Warren-Adams Letters*, II, 281.

7. *Works*, IV, 274; Adams to Nicholas Boylston, July 24, 1819, Reel 123.

8. See Haraszti, *Prophets of Progress*, 46–48, 167–68, for the most reliable assessment of both works in terms of originality.

9. The chief books on Adams as a political theorist are: Correa M. Walsh, *The Political Science of John Adams* (New York, 1915); Edward Handler, *America and Europe in the Political Thought of John Adams* (Cambridge, Mass., 1964); and John R. Howe, Jr., *The Changing Political Thought of John Adams* (Princeton, 1966), which remains the best full-length treatment, even though the interpretation of Adams as changing dramatically in the 1780s strikes me as misguided. The wisest book on Adams as a political thinker remains Haraszti, *Prophets of Progress*. The most insightful treatment of Adams's political theory within the context of the republican ideology, and therefore the starting point for any modern reinterpretation, is Wood, *Creation of the American Republic*, 567–92. Leslie Wharton's *Polity and the Public Good* links Adams's political theory to the social conditions of New England in intriguing ways. Ralph Lerner's *The Thinking Revolutionary* is critical of Wood for "overcontextualizing" Adams's ideas, and distinguishes between "thought" and "ideology" in ways that suggest Adams's continuing relevance. Among the scores of scholarly articles, two strike me as most helpful: Stephen Kurtz, "The Political Science of John Adams: A Guide to His Statecraft," *William and Mary Quarterly*, 3rd Series, XXV (October 1968), 605–13, and Joyce Appleby, "The New Republican Synthesis and the Changing Political Ideas of John Adams," *American Quarterly*, XXV (1973), 578–95.

10. *Works*, IV, 287, 371.

11. *Ibid.*, 219, 287, 290, 292; Adams to James Madison, April 22, 1817, *Works*, X, 257. See also Howe, *Changing Political Thought*, 133–55; McCoy, *Elusive Republic*, 96–100; and Wood, *Creation of the American Republic*, 567–79, for the best secondary accounts.

12. James Madison to Thomas Jefferson, June 6, 1787, Boyd, ed., *Papers of Thomas Jefferson*, XI, 401–02.

13. *Works*, IV, 398; Haraszti, *Prophets of Progress*, 223; Adams to Josiah Quincy, February 18, 1811, *Works*, IX, 634.

14. Adams to Benjamin Rush, March 26, 1806, *Old Family Letters*, 96; Adams to John Quincy Adams, November 22, 1815, Reel 122; Haraszti, *Prophets*, 178; Adams to Thomas Jefferson, August 15, 1823, *Adams-Jefferson Letters*, II, 595–96.

15. *Works*, IV, 290.

16. *Ibid.*, 380–81.

17. *Works*, III, 447–64, for the *Dissertation; Works*, IV, 396–97, and Adams to Benjamin Rush, April 18, 1808; *Spur of Fame*, 108, for typical Adams formulations on housing the aristocracy in the upper house. DeLolme's work was originally published in London in 1771. The influence of DeLolme is the main point of Appleby's interpretation, cited above. Despite his insistence throughout his retirement that he never sanctioned anything but election to the Senate, in *Davila* Adams suggested at one point that "hereditary descent would be better." See *Works*, VI, 249.

18. Taylor, *An Inquiry*, 34; Wood, *Creation*, 587–92, which was the first account to recognize the implications of Taylor's argument for Adams's "irrelevancy." Indeed, it is Taylor's critical perspective that Wood adopts as his own throughout his treatment of Adams's *Defence*, even though it is clear from his tone and concluding paragraph that Wood admires Adams's analysis and thinks it more profound than the liberal ideology that displaced it.

19. *Works*, VI, 482.

20. Taylor, *Inquiry*, 31–34, 37, 158–59, 372.

21. *Ibid*, 54, 101, 171, 372, 374.

22. *Works*, VI, 483, 476–77, 511.

23. *Ibid*, 467.

24. *Ibid*, 453–54, 457.

25. *Ibid*, 452.

26. *Ibid*, 469, 457.

27. *Ibid*, 461–62.

28. *Ibid*, 458; Adams to William Cunningham, March 15, 1804, *Correspondence with Cunningham*, 18–19.

29. Adams to Benjamin Rush, December 27, 1810, *Spur of Fame*, 174; *Works*, VI, 456–57, 460.

30. Adams to Benjamin Waterhouse, August 7, 1805, *Statesman and Friend*, 28–29.

31. Adams to Benjamin Rush, December 27, 1810, *Spur of Fame*, 175; Adams to Benjamin Rush, August 1, 1812, *ibid.*, 235; Adams to Benjamin Rush, February 25, 1808, *ibid.*, 104; Adams to Franklin Vanderkemp, February 16, 1809, *Works*, IX, 610. These citations represent only a small fraction of the Adams correspondence devoted to the evils of banking.

32. Taylor, *An Inquiry*, 41, 244–45; the fifth chapter of the *Inquiry* was entitled and devoted to "Banking." Adams to Thomas Jefferson, September 15, 1813, *Adams-Jefferson Letters*, II, 376; Adams to Benjamin Rush, August 28, 1811, *Spur of Fame*, 193; Adams to Benjamin Rush, July 3, 1812, *ibid.*, 228.

33. Adams to Benjamin Rush, February 13, 1811, *Old Family Letters*, 281; Taylor, *Inquiry*, 48–49, 289.

34. Robert Shalhope, *John Taylor of Caroline: Pastoral Republican* (Columbia, S.C., 1980), offers the best overview of Taylor's life and his views on the banking industry. See Jacob E. Cooke, *Tench Coxe and the Early Republic* (Chapel Hill, 1978),

for a good look at the republican arguments in support of banks. The standard overview of the banking industry is Bray Hammond, *Banks and Politics in America from the Revolution to the Civil War* (New York, 1957).

35. Adams to John Pope, April 4, 1818, Reel 118; Adams to John Taylor, March 12, 1819, *Works*, X, 375; Adams to Benjamin Rush, August 28, 1811, *Spur of Fame*, 193.

36. *Works*, VI, 277. See also Haraszti, *Prophets of Progress*, 167, for the best discussion of the composition of *Davila*.

37. *Works*, VI, 239, 258–62; Adams to Francis Vanderkemp, August 9, 1813, Reel 95.

38. *Works*, VI, 232–34.

39. *Ibid.*, 237. My point here about Veblen and Puritanism is not to suggest any direct causal connection either forward toward Veblen's theory of the leisure class or backward toward Jonathan Edwards or John Cotton. There is no evidence that Veblen ever read *Davila,* or that Adams studied the sermons of Edwards or Cotton. But then important attitudes and perspectives seldom get conveyed in such a simplistic and straightforward fashion. It would be more accurate and sensible to note that Adams grew up listening to New England sermons and to the constant talk about the complex relationship between works and grace. Likewise, the affinity between Adams's and Veblen's common recognition that non-material considerations underlay the scramble for wealth probably has something to do with each man's lifelong preference for paradoxical insights that verged on the perverse. Both men were also struck by the fact that the material necessities were more readily available in America, so that explanations of human motivation based primarily on basic material needs did not suffice.

40. *Ibid.*, 247–48; Adams to George Washington Adams, December 27, 1821, Reel 124; Adams to Josiah Quincy, February 18, 1811, *Works*, IX, 633–34.

41. *Works*, VI, 245.

42. *Ibid.*, 240.

43. *Ibid.*, 241–43.

44. *Ibid.*, 245, 397.

45. *Ibid.*, 248; Adams to J. A. Smith, January 7, 1817, Reel 123.

46. *Ibid.*, 248, 262, 254.

47. *Ibid.*, 254–56.

48. *Ibid.*, 266.

49. The matter of Adams's legacy receives extended treatment in chapter 7. For now, it might be noted that his reputation as a political thinker or theorist has oscillated wildly: he has been "discovered" by scholars who were not otherwise inclined to appreciate his brand of wisdom; and he has been "dismissed" by scholars who otherwise claimed to admire his intellectual integrity. The standard work remains John R. Howe, Jr., *The Changing Political Thought of John Adams* (Princeton, 1966). One of his unlikely champions is Vernon L. Parrington, a stalwart defender of

Jeffersonian values and "democratic liberalism," who nonetheless concluded that Adams's political insights "merit a larger recognition than has been accorded them by a grudging posterity," and that Adams "remains the most notable political thinker—with the possible exception of John C. Calhoun—among American statesmen." See Vernon Parrington, *Main Currents in American Thought* (2 vols., New York, 1927), I, 325. The strongest Adams advocate among contemporary scholars of American political thought is John Diggins, *The Lost Soul of American Politics*, 66–99, who sees Adams as the most astute student of political power within the founding generation. My own understanding of Adams as a political thinker has been greatly enriched by a spirited correspondence with Diggins, who sees Adams as an early-day deconstructionist and a precursor of Neitzsche, Derrida, and Foucault, a group that I suspect Adams would regard as an unholy trinity of "ideologians."

CHAPTER SIX: INTIMACIES

1. Bernard Bailyn, *Faces of Revolution: Personalities and Themes in the Struggle for American Independence* (New York, 1990), 3–21.

2. Adams to Shelton Jones, March 11, 1809, Reel 118.

3. *Diary and Autobiography*, II, 362–63, for the comparison to a lion; Josiah Quincy, *Figures of the Past* (Boston, 1883), 61.

4. Quincy quoted in Richard McLanathan, *Gilbert Stuart* (New York, 1986), 147.

5. Adams to Elihu Marshall, March 7, 1820, *Works*, X, 388–89.

6. Adams to John Jay, March 6, 1821, Reel 124; Adams to Vine Alttey [?], September 10, 1819, Reel 124; Theodore Parker, *Historic Americans* (Boston, 1871), 210, for the quotation about the Adams talkativeness.

7. Adams to Daniel Cory, January 23, 1820, Reel 124; Adams to Charles Francis Adams, November 17, 1815, Reel 122.

8. John Taylor to Adams, April 8, 1824, *Works*, X, 411–12.

9. Adams to Louisa Catherine Adams, June 17, 1820, Reel 124. Robert Dawidoff, *The Education of John Randolph* (New York, 1979), is the best biography, and William Taylor, *Cavalier and Yankee: The Old South and American National Character*, offers the most illuminating study of the Cavalier as type.

10. Adams to Louisa Catherine Adams, April 27, 1820, Reel 124; Adams to David Sewall, January 18, 1816, Reel 122; Adams to David Sewall, May 22, 1821, Reel 124; Adams to David Sewall, May 13, 1811, Reel 118.

11. Adams to Benjamin Rush, February 26, 1812, Reel 118.

12. Adams to Thomas Jefferson, September 14, 1813, *Adams Jefferson Letters*, II, 372–73; *Diary and Autobiography*, I, 57.

13. Adams to Richard Rush, November 13, 1816, Reel 123. See also Adams to William Tudor, August 12, 1813, *ibid*.

14. Adams to William Cunningham, June 16, 1810, *Correspondence Between Adams and Cunningham*, 216–17; see also *ibid.*, v–vii, for the critical assessment of Adams as president.
15. Adams to Mercy Otis Warren, August 17, 1814, Reel 122. See above, chapter 2, for a fuller discussion of the argument over Warren's *History*.
16. The standard work on gender relations in the post-revolutionary era remains Nancy F. Cott's *The Bonds of Womanhood: "Woman's Sphere" in New England, 1780–1835* (New Haven, 1977); Barbara Welter's *Dimity Convictions: The American Woman in the Nineteenth Century* contains the seminal essays on the shifting roles of middle-class women during the first third of the nineteenth century; the crucial work on the intersection of republicanism and gender is by Linda K. Kerber, *Women of the Republic: Intellect and Ideology in Revolutionary America* (Chapel Hill, 1980). Mercy Otis Warren still awaits a biographer who can integrate her life into the scholarship on ideology and gender generated over the past two decades.
17. Adams to Francis Vanderkemp, April 8, 1815, Reel 122.
18. Adams to John Quincy Adams, May 30, 1815, *ibid.*
19. Adams to Emma Willard, December 8, 1819, Reel 124; Adams to John Adams Smith, May 12, 1821, *ibid.;* Adams to Caroline de Wint, July 8, 1822, *ibid.*
20. Thomas Jefferson to Nathaniel Burwell, March 14, 1818, Ford, ed., *Writings*, X, 104. The most comprehensive study of Jefferson's educational thought is Harold Hellenbrand, *The Unfinished Revolution: Education and Politics in the Thought of Thomas Jefferson;* Adams to Caroline de Wint, February 11, 1820, Reel 124, for the reading list.
21. Adams to Francis Vanderkemp, July 13, 1815, *Works*, X, 169. Paul C. Nagel's *Descent from Glory: Four Generations of the John Adams Family* (New York, 1983) is a brilliant exploration of the emotional life of the entire Adams family that, in its early chapters, offers the fullest account of domestic life at Quincy. While I do not agree completely with Nagel's interpretation of Abigail, which strikes me as somewhat hostile, his familiarity with the sources is unsurpassed by any other scholar, save perhaps the editors of *The Adams Papers*.
22. Adams to John Quincy Adams, August 27, 1815, Reel 122.
23. Adams to Alexander Johnson, January 2, 1814, *ibid.;* Adams to John Adams Smith, June 15, 1812, Reel 118.
24. Adams to George Adams, December 15, 1815, Reel 122; Adams to John Quincy Adams, May 20, 1816, *ibid.;* Adams to John Quincy Adams, June 8, 1815, *ibid.;* Adams to George and John Adams, May 3, 1815, *ibid.*
25. Adams to George Adams, January 27, 1822, Reel 124; Adams to Richard Peters, March 31, 1822, *Works*, X, 402; Adams to Thomas Jefferson, February 10, 1823, *Adams-Jefferson Letters*, II, 587; Adams to Benjamin Waterhouse, May 30, 1815, *Statesman and Friend*, 117; Adams to George and John Adams, May 6, 1815, Reel 122; Adams to John Quincy Adams, March 14, 1815, *ibid.*

26. Adams to Louisa Catherine Adams, January 14, 1823, Reel 124.

27. Adams to John Quincy Adams, October 17, 1815, Reel 122; Adams to John Quincy Adams, March 11, 1815, *ibid.;* Adams to John Quincy Adams, February 28, 1815, *ibid.;* Adams to John Quincy Adams, June 30, 1815, *ibid.;* Adams to John Quincy Adams, August 26, 1816, *ibid.*

28. John Quincy Adams to Adams, July 7, 1814, Worthington C. Ford, ed., *The Writings of John Quincy Adams* (7 vols., Boston, 1913–17), V, 57. The magisterial account by Samuel F. Bemis, *John Quincy Adams and the Foundations of American Foreign Policy* (New York, 1949), remains the authoritative version of John Quincy's public career. But his private life, and the connection between that life and his statesmanship, still await a biographer. There is a brilliant sketch of his character in George Dangerfield's *The Era of Good Feelings* (New York, 1952), 7–10, which has yet to be surpassed.

29. Adams to John Quincy Adams, February 8, 1819, Reel 123; Adams to John Quincy Adams, November 13, 1816, *ibid.*

30. John Quincy Adams to Adams, January 3, 1817, Adrienne Koch and William Peden, eds., *The Selected Writings of John and John Quincy Adams* (New York, 1946), 289–91.

31. Adams to John Quincy Adams, April 23, 1813, Reel 95; Adams to John Quincy Adams, November 28, 1813, *ibid.*

32. Adams to Louisa Catherine Adams, December 17, 1822, Reel 124; Adams to John Quincy Adams, March 14, 1815, Reel 122; Adams to John Quincy Adams, November 26, 1815, Reel 123.

33. Quoted in David F. Musto, "The Youth of John Quincy Adams," American Philosophical Society, *Proceedings,* CXIII (1969), 269–82; see also Musto's "The Adams Family," Massachusetts Historical Society, *Proceedings,* XCIII (1981), 40–58. Musto is a psychiatrist who attributes John Quincy's neurotic behavior to excessive parental pressure during childhood and adolescence, and singles out Abigail, more than John, as the chief culprit. Edith B. Gelles, "The Abigail Industry," *William and Mary Quarterly,* 3rd Series, XLV (October 1988), 656–83, concurs with the notion that John Quincy experienced excessive pressure in his youth, but defends Abigail against the charge of being the most relentlessly demanding parent. My own instinct, as a historian and parent, is to recognize the plausibility of such psychologizing, but to embrace agnosticism; there are some things we will never know.

34. Adams to John Quincy Adams, October 28, 1817, Reel 123; Adams to John Quincy Adams, May 24, 1815, Reel 122; Adams to Alexander Johnson, January 4, 1823, Reel 124.

35. The "bulldog among spaniels" observation is by the British diplomat W. H. Lyttleton in a letter to Sir Charles Bagot, January 22, 1827, quoted in Dangerfield, *Era of Good Feelings,* 7.

36. Louisa Catherine Adams to Adams, March 12, 1820, Reel 264; Louisa Catherine Adams to Adams, December 22, 1819, *ibid.*

37. Adams to Louisa Catherine Adams, February 20, 1820, Reel 124; Adams to Louisa Catherine Adams, January 29, 1820, *ibid.*

38. Louisa Catherine Adams, *The Adventures of a Nobody*, Reel 269, 122.

39. Adams to Thomas Jefferson, October 20, 1815 [1818], *Adams-Jefferson Letters*, II, 529; see Nagel, *Descent from Glory*, 129–30, for a description of the deathbed scene; Adams to Francis Vanderkemp, September 25, 1819, Reel 124; Adams to Caroline de Wint, March 15, 1820, *ibid.* There is, of course, an enormous secondary literature on Abigail, though the focus tends to be on the earlier years. Edith B. Gelles, "The Abigail Industry," is the best review of the many biographies; see also her insightful "Abigail Adams," *New England Quarterly*, LII (1979), 500–21. Finally, Paul C. Nagel's *The Adams Women* (New York, 1983) offers a more critical assessment of Abigail and a highly laudatory interpretation of Louisa Catherine.

40. The Abigail quotation is from Nagel, *Descent from Glory*, 174; Henry Adams, *The Education of Henry Adams: An Autobiography* (Boston, 1961), 17–18.

41. Adams to Louisa Catherine Adams, January 14, 1823, Reel 124; Adams to Louisa Catherine Adams, November 11, 1821, *ibid.;* Adams to Louisa Catherine Adams, February 20, 1820, *ibid.;* Adams to Louisa Catherine Adams, December 17, 1822, *ibid.*

42. Adams to Louisa Catherine Adams, June 25, 1819, Reel 123.

43. Adams to Louisa Catherine Adams, January 29, 1820, *ibid.;* Adams to Louisa Catherine Adams, May 10, 1823, Reel 124; Adams to Louisa Catherine Adams, April 22, 1823, *ibid.*

44. Adams to Nicholas Boylston, August 24, 1822, *ibid.*

45. Quincy, *Figures of the Past*, 61, 73–74; Adams to Thomas Jefferson, April 17, 1826, *Adams-Jefferson Letters*, II, 614.

46. Quincy, *Figures of the Past*, 77, 74–75.

47. *Ibid.*, 65.

48. *Ibid.*, 69, 71.

49. Adams to Jefferson, December 2, 1822, *Adams-Jefferson Letters*, II, 586; Quincy, *Figures of the Past*, 80–82.

CHAPTER SEVEN: LEGACIES

1. Lyman H. Butterfield, "The Jubilee of Independence, July 4, 1826," *The Virginia Magazine of History and Biography*, 61 (1953), 119–40, for the best account of the celebration. Adams to John Whitney, June 7, 1826, *Works*, X, 416–17, for the letter to the Quincy committee.

2. Thomas Jefferson to Mayor Roger Weightman, June 24, 1826, which is available in

several editions of Jefferson's papers, but the handwritten original is in the Massachusetts Historical Society.

3. Douglass Adair, "Rumford's Dying Speech, 1685, and Jefferson's Last Words on Democracy, 1826," in Trevor Colbourn, ed., *Fame and the Founding Fathers: Essays by Douglass Adair* (New York, 1974), 192–202.

4. Henry S. Randall, *The Life of Thomas Jefferson* (New York, 1858), III, 544–48, which reprints the first-person recollections of the family gathered at the bedside.

5. Eliza Quincy, *Memoirs of the Life of Eliza S. M. Quincy* (Boston, 1861), 205–09; *Niles' Weekly Register*, July 22, 1826; Butterfield, "Jubilee of Independence," 134–35, summarizes the scenes at both bedsides.

6. *Niles' Weekly Register*, July 22, 1826, for the Rush quote; Merrill Peterson, *The Jefferson Image in the American Mind* (New York, 1960), 2–10, for the Binney quote and for an excellent account of the national response to the simultaneous departure of the two patriarchs.

7. *A Selection of Eulogies, Pronounced in the Several States, in Honor of Those Illustrious Patriots and Statesmen, John Adams and Thomas Jefferson* (Harford, 1826), 98, 94, 121–22, 128, 422, 282.

8. *Ibid.,* 3–17, 336, 149–50, 180.

9. *Ibid.,* 380, 256, 233.

10. *Ibid.,* 336, 178–79, 185–86, 94, 160.

11. My discussion of the image of "the founders" in the following paragraphs is indebted to Wesley Frank Craven, *The Legend of the Founding Fathers* (New York, 1956); George Forgie, *Patricide in the House Divided: A Psychological Interpretation of Lincoln and His Age* (New York, 1979), 13–53, which raises the analysis of the psychological role of "the fathers" to new levels of sophistication; and to McCoy, *The Last of the Fathers,* 9–38, which offers fresh insight into the characteristics being held up for emulation.

12. Daniel Webster, *The Writings and Speeches of Daniel Webster* (18 vols., Boston, 1903), I, 252–53.

13. Robert E. Spiller and Alfred R. Ferguson, eds., *The Collected Works of Ralph Waldo Emerson* (Cambridge, Mass., 1971), I, 7. The quotation is from Emerson's *Nature*.

14. Marcus Cunliffe, ed., *The Life of Washington* (Cambridge, Mass., 1962), which is a modern edition of the Mason Weems biography. See also John Marshall, *The Life of George Washington . . . First President of the United States* (5 vols., Philadelphia, 1804–07), which is the biography Adams joked about as a verbal mausoleum. The best books on Washington's popular image in the nineteenth century are: Marcus Cunliffe, *George Washington: Man and Monument* (Boston, 1958); Paul Longmore, *The Invention of George Washington* (Berkeley, 1988); and Barry Schwartz, *George Washington: The Making of an American Symbol* (New York, 1987).

15. Peterson, *Jefferson Image,* 36–37, offers the best succinct version of Jefferson's role in the Webster-Hayne debate. Richard E. Ellis, *The Union at Risk: Jacksonian*

Democracy, States Rights, and the Nullification Crisis (New York, 1987), provides the best of the recent secondary accounts.

16. Charles M. Wiltse, ed., *The Papers of Daniel Webster* (Hanover, NH, 1986), I, 285–348, for the famous Webster reply to Hayne.

17. Peterson, *Jefferson Image*, which is the most comprehensive and probing study of any prominent American's reputation as it moves from generation to generation and adapts to different contexts.

18. Forgie, *Patricide in the House Divided*, 123–58, offers the fullest review of the role of "the founders" in the slavery debates of the 1850s. For the speeches themselves, see Henry V. Jaffa and Robert W. Johannsen, eds., *In the Name of the People: Speeches and Writings of Lincoln and Douglas in the Illinois Campaign of 1859* (Columbus, Ohio, 1959).

19. For Jefferson's tortured and inconsistent position on slavery, see William Cohen, "Thomas Jefferson and the Problem of Slavery," *Journal of American History,* 56 (1969), 503–26; also, a more pro-Jefferson view that plays down his views on the Missouri question, William Freehling, "The Founding Fathers and Slavery," *American Historical Review, 77* (1972), 81–93.

20. Interestingly, there is no scholarly study of Adams's views on slavery. The starting place for such a study is the 1770s, especially Adams's correspondence in the Continental Congress. See, for example, the anonymous requests sent him, pleading for an immediate end to slavery, in *Papers,* III, 18–20, 411–12. The clearest statement of his own view, which tended to warn against insisting on emancipation because of the divisions it would create in the shaky confederation against England, can be found in *Papers,* IV, 208–12, 469, and V, 242. For his position on the Missouri question, the correspondence with Louisa Catherine in 1819–20 is the best source, discussed above in chapter 4. The interpretation offered here is too abbreviated to do full justice to the nuances of Adams's response to what proved to be the most glaring failure of the revolutionary generation. The subject deserves a full-length treatment.

21. See Peterson, *Jefferson Image*, 220–22, for an elegant summary.

22. For the background to Croly's book, see Eric F. Goldman, *Rendezvous with Destiny: A History of Modern American Reform* (New York, 1956), 146–61.

23. Herbert D. Croly, *The Promise of American Life* (New York, 1909), 28, 45–46.

24. *Ibid.,* 42–43.

25. *Ibid.,* 30, 33, 41, 46.

26. *Ibid.,* 29, 36.

27. There is no scholarly study of Hamilton's legacy akin to Peterson's book on Jefferson. My interpretation here relies primarily on Peterson, *Jefferson Image,* 221–26. See also Henry Cabot Lodge, *Life and Letters of Alexander Hamilton* (Boston, 1882).

28. See Butterfield, "Jubilee of Independence," 128, for the description of the Quincy

railroad track. For the most insightful study of Henry Adams as historian, see William H. Jordy, *Henry Adams: Scientific Historian* (New Haven, 1952).

29. Henry Adams, *History of the United States of America During the Administrations of Thomas Jefferson and James Madison* (2 vols., 1988); Henry Adams, *The Education of Henry Adams: An Autobiography* (New York, 1961), which is the most convenient and accessible version of the classic originally published by the Massachusetts Historical Society in 1918. See also Jordy, *Henry Adams*, 43–120, 256–88.

30. The secondary literature here is almost as boundless as the America allegedly coming into existence in the 1830s. Two recent books strike me as seminal: John Higham, *From Boundlessness to Consolidation: The Transformation of American Culture, 1848–1860* (Ann Arbor, 1969), and Robert Wiebe, *The Opening of American Society: From the Adoption of the Constitution to the Eve of Disunion* (New York, 1984). Older but still standard accounts include Curtis Nettles, *The Emergence of a National Economy, 1775–1815* (New York, 1962), and Douglass C. North, *The Economic Growth of the United States, 1790–1860* (New York, 1961). For a nice summary of current historical wisdom on the shift from republicanism to liberalism, see the symposiums on Gordon Wood's *Creation of the American Republic* in *William and Mary Quarterly*, 3rd Series, XLIV (July 1987), 549–640. Finally, I find John Murrin's version of the ideological issues at stake most cogent in his "The Great Inversion, or Court Versus Country: A Comparison of the Revolutionary Settlements in England (1688–1721) and America (1776–1816)," in J. G. A. Pocock, ed., *Three British Revolutions* (Princeton, 1980), 368–453.

31. Two of the best examples of "the paradigmatic approach"—and I mean that they are excellent histories caught up in the category/language problem—are John L. Brooke, *The Heart of the Commonwealth: Society and Political Culture in Worcester County, Massachusetts, 1713–1861* (Cambridge, England, 1989), and Isaac Kramnick, *Republicanism and Bourgeois Radicalism in Late Eighteenth-Century England and America* (Ithaca, 1990). For a noble but failed attempt to resolve the language problem, see James T. Kloppenberg, "The Virtues of Liberalism: Christianity, Republicanism, and Ethics in Early American Discourse," *Journal of American History*, 74 (1987), 9–33.

32. Henry Adams, *History*, I, 187. As always seems to be the case with Henry Adams, there are layers of irony in his treatment of Jefferson. On the one hand, one could argue that his decision to make Jefferson the tragic hero of his *History* represented the ultimate slap in the face for John Adams, who could also lay claim to the mantle. On the other hand, the characterization of Jefferson in the *History* is double-edged and cuts deeply into the mythology of Jefferson, making him a somewhat naive victim of events and a prisoner of his own anachronistic ideals. Which is to say that Henry Adams makes Jefferson suffer the cruelest fate, as a victim of "progress," rather than his great-grandfather.

33. Croly, *Promise of American Life*, 399–454, for Croly's preferred, semi-socialistic vision.

34. For the publication history of *The Adams Papers*, see Lyman H. Butterfield, "The Papers of the Adams Family: Some Account of Their History," *Massachusetts Historical Society, Proceedings*, 71 (1953–57), 328–56.

35. Robert Rutland, "Recycling Early National History Through the Papers of the Founding Fathers," *American Quarterly*, XXVIII (1976), 250–62. The references to scholarly reappraisals of Adams in the decades after publication of his papers in a modern edition are cited in the acknowledgments section above and are sprinkled throughout the notes to chapter 1. It also bears mentioning that the two leading historians of early America, Edmund Morgan and Bernard Bailyn, were commissioned to write review essays on the first volumes of the Butterfield edition as they emerged in the early 1960s: see Morgan, "John Adams and the Puritan Tradition," *New England Quarterly*, XXXIV (1961), 518–29, and Bailyn, "Butterfield's Adams: Notes for a Sketch," *William and Mary Quarterly*, 3rd Series, XIX (1962), 140–61. Virtually every major newspaper and magazine in the nation also ran advertisements and reviews; the Massachusetts Historical Society staged the largest reception in its history to mark the publication; and the *American Historical Review* published a review by an amateur historian named John F. Kennedy.

36. The interpretation of Adams offered in the PBS series was sophisticated and historically accurate. In fact, much of the dialogue was taken directly from his letters and diaries. The text accompanying the series was by Jack Shepherd, *The Adams Chronicles: Four Generations of Greatness* (Boston, 1975).

37. One of the ironies of the scholarly literature on Adams is that no one has done more to recover both our appreciation and dismissal of Adams as the prototypical republican than Gordon Wood. See above, chapter 4, note 34, for Wood's treatment of Adams as a political thinker. On the other hand, Wood's respect for Adams's abiding political realism is also coupled with a sad but strong verdict on his "irrelevance." In his most recent book, which appeared as this account was going to press, the underlying reasons for Wood's verdict are made clearer, for he describes republicanism as a transitional ideology that helped to stabilize post-revolutionary American politics, but then was swept away and superseded by democratic values that were latent in the movement for American independence. See Wood, *The Radicalism of the American Revolution* (New York, 1992). The other seminal account by a modern scholar of Adams's intellectual legacy is by John Diggins, *The Lost Soul of American Politics*, 69–99, which recognizes Adams as a critic of the emerging liberal ideology in a way that acknowledges his political relevance for our own time. My own view is that Wood provides the best analysis of Adams's republican values, while Diggins provides the best analysis of Adams's prominent role as a political thinker who still has something to say to post-liberal America. The persistent popular confusion of John with Sam Adams—largely a consequence

of a regional New England beer that trades on Sam's name—was the object of an utterly unscientific study by yours truly in several local bars and watering holes in western Massachusetts.

PROPHECIES: AN EPILOGUE

1. Adams to Abigail Adams, July 3, 1776, *Family Correspondence,* II, 30.
2. *Works,* VI, 516; Adams to John Langdon, December 12, 1810, Reel 118; Adams to John Jay, March 10, 1822, Reel 124.
3. Adams to Thomas Foxcroft, February 13, 1807, Reel 118.
4. Adams to Benjamin Rush, June 20, 1808, *Spur of Fame,* 110; Adams to Benjamin Rush, May 14, 1812, Reel 118; Adams to Francis Vanderkemp, February 5, 1805, *Works,* IX, 589–90.
5. Henry Adams, *History,* I, 636; Adams to Benjamin Rush, May 14, 1812, Reel 118; Adams to Theodore Foster, October 6, 1811, *ibid.*
6. See Arthur M. Schlesinger, Jr., *The Cycles of American History* (Boston, 1986), 22–48, for a modern review of the cyclical approach; and Paul Kennedy, *The Rise and Fall of the Great Powers* (New York, 1987), for the most influential argument on behalf of the cyclical pattern as an explanation for the fate of nation-states over the past five centuries.
7. Much of the vast secondary literature on republican ideology makes at least glancing reference to the habit of mind discussed here. It is the central focus of Drew R. McCoy's *The Elusive Republic* and of McCoy's more recent book, *The Last of the Fathers,* 39–84, 171–216. For the most recent and comprehensive claim that the "declension model" was losing its hold on most Americans even before the Revolution, see Jack P. Greene, *Pursuits of Happiness: The Social Development of Early Modern British Colonies and the Formation of American Culture* (Chapel Hill, 1988). I tend to agree with McCoy, whose version of Madison is quite similar to my version of Adams. The liberal mentality that Greene discovers emerging in the mid-eighteenth century only becomes dominant, so I would argue, about the time Adams and Jefferson died.
8. Adams to Benjamin Rush, June 20, 1818, Reel 118; *Works,* VI, 484.
9. *Works,* VI, 484, 487–88.
10. Adams to Thomas Jefferson, July 15, 1817, *Adams-Jefferson Letters,* II, 519.
11. Adams tended to avoid specific forecasts, preferring to focus on the psychological forces that needed managing rather than chronology. In his low moods he sometimes declared that decline had already begun and in more buoyant moods he referred to postponing America's judgment day for several centuries. The quoted phrases cited here are both from the same letter to Thomas Foxcroft, February 13, 1807, Reel 118. For the pessimistic predictions of Henry Adams, see his "The Rule of Phase Applied to History," in *The Tendency of History* (New York, 1919).

12. Three recent books which focus attention on the intellectual tradition that Adams represents in ways that celebrate rather than denigrate its significance are: Diggins, *Lost Soul of American Politics;* Albert O. Hirschman, *The Rhetoric of Reaction: Perversity, Futility, Jeopardy* (Cambridge, Mass., 1990); and Christopher Lasch, *The True and Only Heaven: Progress and Its Critics* (New York, 1990).

Index